Solo

Solo

The Everything Guide to Writing, Performing, and Producing Your One-Person Show

Arlene Malinowski
and
Julie Ganey

NORTHWESTERN UNIVERSITY PRESS
EVANSTON, ILLINOIS

Northwestern University Press
www.nupress.northwestern.edu

Printed in the United States of America

10 9 8 7 6 5 4 3 2 1

ISBN 978-0-8101-4971-7 (paper)
ISBN 978-0-8101-4972-4 (ebook)

Cataloging-in-Publication Data are available from the Library of Congress.

Contents

People Your Play

Making a Good Show Better

Putting It Together Bit by Bit

Construction and Deconstruction

Rehearsing and Performing

Sellin' Yourself

Introduction

Congratulations! You're here. Welcome.

Writing and performing a solo play is exhilarating, daunting, demanding, sometimes terrifying, and fantastically rewarding. You'll need tools and a whole lot of faith, and this book is here to support you. We've done it, lots of people have done it, and you can too.

Storytelling has always been a vital part of human expression, and in recent decades, solo performance has emerged as one of its most powerful and accessible forms. With rising production costs and an appetite for bold, personal narratives, theaters are increasingly turning to solo plays. Solo shows like *Kristina Wong, Sweatshop Overlord* and Heidi Schreck's *What the Constitution Means to Me* were finalists for the Pulitzer Prize for Drama, and the solo adaptation of *The Picture of Dorian Gray*—in which Sarah Snook portrayed twenty-six characters—garnered six Tony nominations. The genre continues to grow, increasingly recognized as an essential part of the theatrical landscape. Many solo plays have been adapted for film, television, and streaming platforms, extending their reach far beyond the stage—such as in the work of Mike Birbiglia and Ruben Santiago-Hudson. *Fleabag* and *Baby Reindeer*, both of which began as solo performances, were later developed into successful series. All of these solo works began with a single performer onstage telling a story. That's the beauty of solo work—it starts with one voice, one moment of truth, and it can go anywhere. You don't need permission. You just need to begin.

People decide to write a solo show for many different reasons. Some have a longtime dream of bringing a certain story to life. Others are active in the live lit storytelling scene and ready for a new challenge. We also work with actors who are tired of waiting for casting directors and want to create work that feels meaningful. Though we work with many artists who are veterans in the solo genre, we are especially excited to work with those who are brand new to the form.

This book will help move your work forward no matter where you are in the process. You'll find many tools for developing narrative structure, creating an arc, writing strong characters, and using theatrical elements to build your show. You'll find performance tips and a blueprint for rehearsals and working with a director, as well as a guide for producing and touring your work. In addition, this book contains advice from successful solo artists, directors, and storytellers who are working in the field.

Why We Wrote This Book

Over our many years of teaching, students would sometimes ask us what books we could recommend to support them outside of class on their solo projects. Though there are plenty of books out there on writing and acting in general, we found only a handful that address the specifics of solo play writing, performance, and production. Those that do exist are not necessarily written by professionals with deep knowledge and personal experience in the form. Most address just one or two aspects of solo work. So, we decided to write our own book—one that attempts to address the unique challenges of creating solo work.

This book is the toolkit we wish we'd had when we first started dreaming about our own solo shows. We've developed this material over a combined fifty years of teaching. Between us, we've written and performed eight original solo plays, along with countless short pieces. We've spent decades coaching, directing, producing, and helping others create their own shows. Much of what we share here was born in our classrooms, developed in performance, and shaped by feedback. It's built on experience—ours and that of the hundreds of solo artists we've worked with whose creativity inspired and influenced our work.

The first rule of solo show creation is that there is no one right way to do it. We come to the work with our own experiences, points of view, preferences, and methods. You may find gaps, assumptions, and biases in this book. We offer you what we know in the hopes that it will become a springboard for you to go out and discover what is good and true for yourself. Because ultimately, creating solo work is as much about discovering who you are as an artist as it is about sharing your story with an audience.

How We Got Here

Arlene's Story

I was working as an actor in Los Angeles, doing theater and scrapping for guest-star spots on TV (some of it good, most of it eh). I was lucky to be a member of West Coast Ensemble, a theater company located just two blocks from the famous corners of Hollywood and Vine. We were convinced that with such proximity to greatness, we, too, were destined for it. The theater was a ramshackle, three-story building that had once been a funeral home, rumored to have embalmed Hollywood luminaries like Bela Lugosi.

We did everything—building sets, running the board, doing PR, and working box office. Before company meetings, I would get onstage and tell stories about growing up as a CODA (a hearing child of Deaf adults). I told tales of lights strobing when the doorbell rang, having to explain to my incredulous father that farts had a sound, and how I knew I was a Deaf girl in a hearing body.

During one of these meetings, Anne Etue, with her glorious head of wild hair, leaned over and whispered, "You have a story," and took me to see a play she directed at the HBO Workspace. It was Amy Hill's *Tokyo Bound: Growing Up Not Asian in America*, an autobiographical solo show about a young Japanese-Finnish American's journey to Japan, her mother's homeland.

Sitting in the audience, I watched Amy tell a story—her story—breaking the fourth wall, playing characters, creating scenes. I felt a strong stirring of familiarity. I knew this kind of storytelling! She was using the techniques of the Deaf storytellers of my youth. After I stopped sobbing, I turned to my husband, pointed to the stage, and said, "That. I can do that."

The wonderful Mark Travis was known for cultivating this kind of work, and in his class I wrote, struggled to learn craft, cried, tried to find my voice, and wrote some more—a lot more. As I was developing the work, I was lucky to find other excited solo artists, and we performed wherever we could—bookstores, fringe festivals, church basements, and dumpy theaters.

West Coast Ensemble produced *What Does the Sun Sound Like* on the existing set of a play about the Middle East, on nights when the theater was dark. I'm sure audiences were confused about all of the sand in a one-person show about growing up in a Deaf family—but there I was. The play was nominated for a couple of awards. I didn't win, but I had found my voice as an artist.

Then luck came again when the magnificent Nobuko Miyamoto hired me to tour with Great Leap, a multicultural organization that uses art to deepen relations among diverse cultures. It was there that I realized how my work about Deafness and disability could become a powerful tool for social justice.

My solo shows have taken me around the world, connected me to strangers in profound ways, and taught me to listen with compassion. My teaching feeds my writing, which feeds my performing, which feeds my soul. For me, solo has become one big creative circle. It is my wish that you find a feeding circle in your artistic life through your own writing and performance.

Julie's Story

I'd been working as a professional actor for two decades when I went to my first live lit storytelling show in 2008. This was back when the scene was just beginning to bloom in Chicago—the form felt very fresh and new. I loved the personal stories, and though I didn't consider myself a writer, on a whim I submitted an original piece to a storytelling series called 2nd Story. I was asked to perform the ten-minute story in one of their shows a few weeks later. That night, as I sat on a barstool and told my story in front of a small crowd, it felt electric to perform words I had written, and somehow very *right*. After that, I began making space in my life to write. I felt like I had something to say, though I wasn't sure what. I wanted to find out. I didn't abandon theater, but I started channeling a lot of my passion into writing and storytelling.

A few years later, when I had several stories under my belt, friends started saying, "You know, you should put those pieces together into a one-woman show." At that point in my life, I'd only seen a handful of full-length solo plays, mostly what fellow students had created at college: self-indulgent confessional pieces that, as an audience member, left me with a feeling of being held hostage. But as I sought out professional solo plays, I found that the best of the form had little in common with those pieces. One of the shows I saw in this period was Arlene's *Aiming for Sainthood.* I remember sitting in the audience at Chicago Dramatists, watching Arlene perform, and having a feeling that I have only felt a few times in my life. It was similar to the feeling I had when I met my husband, or the first time I was onstage, or the first time I was in front of a classroom of students. It was something like *This is for me.* I knew that I didn't know how to do what Arlene was doing onstage *yet,* and that I didn't really know how to construct a solo play *yet,* but I had the feeling that, with some work, I could figure it out and be pretty good at it.

Since then, I've written and performed four full-length solo shows, which were developed while I was also teaching, working as an actor, running an education program for a nonprofit theater, touring with an improv group, facilitating corporate workshops, and raising a daughter. Through it all, solo is the art form that has allowed me to feel the most like me, the form that has asked the most of my abilities, and the form that brings me the most joy. I've had the honor of teaching solo classes and doing private coaching with students all over the country—artists whose work you will become acquainted with throughout this book. Artists just like you.

How to Use This Book

We invite you to read this book cover-to-cover, use it as a step-by-step workbook, or consult it as a reference guide. You can dog-ear, underline, and bring it to rehearsal. The book is organized sequentially, in the order that you would generally address the topics in the creation of a solo show. Many chapters include an exercise that will give you a chance to apply a tool or strategy to your play. We suggest you don't just read or think about them, do them! These are tried and true assignments we have used in our classes for years, and they are a concrete way to build your skills, move forward, and improve your show bit by bit. The book is full of illustrative examples from a variety of sources: solo plays, multicharacter plays, movies, and excerpts from our students' writing. (Thank you, students! We love you!)

There's no wrong way to create a solo show. We approach it from a writing standpoint, meaning we start by crafting the text, but we recognize that you may be developing your solo show through other methods, such as improvising, devising, or building an avant-garde performance piece. If that's your process, you'll still find sections of this book useful, such as the seven keys that make a solo show work, developing dialogue, tools for bringing characters to life, and marketing your play.

Our Best Advice

It takes a lot of courage to write and perform a one-person show. Start from where you are. Trust that tiny inner voice that draws you to this form. As artists, that voice is our most powerful tool. It propels us, guides us, and keeps us company when we feel overwhelmed and want to throw in the towel.

See as much solo work as you can, good and not so good, in large and small theaters, and on streaming platforms. Start considering yourself part of the community of solo playwrights while you are on the way there. They are your people.

Solo

Take the Plunge!

What the Heck Do I Write About?

If you are holding this book in your hot little hands, chances are you already have an idea of what you want your solo show to be about. You have a story you're itching to tell, or an idea you want to explore. This is usually the case with our students—they come to us because they have a story that has been chasing them for years, and they're finally ready to devote the time to fleshing it out. Or they're galvanized by an idea or a cause that they want to share with an audience, and they've come to us to help them make it into an actual play with characters and events.

Other times, however, our students come to us not sure what they want to write about. They may be actors or writers who feel drawn to solo or know they would like the challenge of developing and performing a solo play, but they don't know what it would be about or where to begin. If that's you, then you're in the right place.

We believe that everyone has a solo show inside them. This chapter consists of various ways to get at the answer to this question: *What story are you uniquely positioned to tell?*

This question can help you home in on a subject, whether you're imagining an autobiographical solo play, or even a protagonist who is a historical or fictional character.

The prompts and exercises we offer are some of our favorite ways to explore themes and subjects with our students. We invite you to dig in and see what emerges. If these aren't tickling your fancy, there's this thing called the internet, and you'll find lots of story and play prompts there, too.

What's the Story That Won't Leave You Alone?

What's the thing that has kept you up at night? What's the tale you should have told a long time ago and now have the courage to tell? It could be an idea that preoccupies you, something you dream about, or something that you've been avoiding. Often, these stories make for wonderful shows. One of our students was deeply civically engaged and found herself concerned about the politics in our country. She started writing from those worries. The result was her beautiful, unique solo show—an amalgamation of memoir, a rousing civics class, and a call to action.

Or consider what you know that no one else does. What story are you solely positioned to tell—YOU, lovely *you*, with your unique combination of experiences and what you have learned over and over the hard way, and your strange fascinations and charming mistakes and the quest that you have never let go of?

Your Life Story in One Hundred Words

In September 1999, *The Washington Post* asked readers to submit autobiographical sketches of one hundred words or less. There were no other requirements, except that the stories be true. They printed stories from old and young, famous and not famous, by people of different races, socioeconomic statuses, and genders, and each was fascinating. We like to use this exercise in our classes because it encourages students to synthesize the major moments and influences in their life or their protagonist's life. We often have students read their pieces out loud and then ask the class which moments made them say, "Oh, I want to hear more about that."

Generally, we don't encourage people to write a solo show that covers their entire life story. Think more along the lines of a memoir, which is typically thematic in nature or focuses on a specific career path, series of events, or time period, rather than a full autobiography. Please *don't* start your solo play with your birth and end it at the present moment. There would be far too many events to cover, and you wouldn't have time to go deeply into anything. Frankly, we're a little overwhelmed just thinking about it, aren't you? Choosing moments from your life or your character's life to put into context for an audience allows you to create a focused and compelling narrative.

Previously Written Stories

You might start by looking at what you've already written. Are you a storyteller or writer who has files full of shorter pieces you've written over the years? Maybe you've squirreled away notes and ideas in your phone. If so, how might some of them fit together into a longer show? Can you see how five or six of the pieces might form an arc for an audience?

One of our students discovered that she had several short stories about her parents' time in a Japanese internment camp during World War II and the way their experiences impacted her life. Using those shorter pieces as anchors, she began adding, cutting, and rearranging material until she found an arc that felt right. Alternatively, other students of ours have started with one short story and expanded and deepened it into a longer piece that ultimately became their show.

Follow Your Passions and Obsessions

Do you have a passion for historical or cultural moments? Maybe you're like Anna Deavere Smith, who's known for her documentary plays and her focus on social justice. Her show *Fires in the Mirror* is about the Crown Heights riot in Brooklyn in 1991 and its aftermath. Another of her plays, *Notes from the Field*, investigates the US justice system through the voices of some of the young people caught up in it. Perhaps you have a person or character who fascinates you. Students in our classes have written beautiful solo shows about the humorist Mark Twain; the author of *The Wonderful Wizard of Oz*, L. Frank Baum; and Margaret Sanger, who fought to legalize birth control in the 1800s.

Natalie Goldberg, author of *Writing Down the Bones*, explains, "Writers end up writing about their obsessions—things that haunt them, things they can't forget, stories they carry in their bodies waiting to be released." We've worked with people who have written solo shows about skateboarding, yoga, online dating, and struggling to have a child. Consider how you can parlay what you most love or the things that occupy real estate in your head into a solo play with a satisfying arc and your strong point of view.

Thirty-Six Questions

Many years ago, Arlene read an article in *The New York Times* by Daniel Jones based on a research study by Arthur Aron. The article, "36 Questions That Can Lead to Love," outlined questions that could help people form a quick and deep emotional connection on a date. Despite being married to a spectacular man, Arlene is a romantic, so she studied the list with the kind of concentration reserved for teenagers playing Call of Duty. Now she uses the list in class. The questions always provide interesting and provocative stories.

Here are some of her favorites:

- If a crystal ball could tell you the truth about yourself, your life, the future, or anything else, what would you want to know?
- Is there something that you've dreamed of doing for a long time? Why haven't you done it?
- What is the greatest accomplishment of your life?
- When did you last cry in front of another person? By yourself?
- If you were to die this evening with no opportunity to communicate with anyone, what would you most regret not having told someone? Why haven't you told them yet?

Can you see how these questions can be used as a jumping off point for material and stories for your solo show? (Just in case you're interested in falling in love, there is a downloadable PDF online of the thirty-six questions used in Arthur Aron's experiment.)

Common Themes

Here are some common themes for solo shows (and also movies, books, epic poems, etc.). Circle the themes for which you think you have a corresponding story: coming of age, resilience and transformation, identity or origin story, redemption and forgiveness, David and Goliath, social injustice and inequality, illusion and reality, meaning and purpose, and slaying the dragon. Remember, you'll want a story or series of events to ensure you are not just lecturing the audience about your favorite ideas and important opinions. We're sure they're great! But they might not make a great solo show.

Make Some Lists

Lists are a wonderful way to begin generating material because they're written fast, off the top of your head. Look and respond to any of the prompts below that capture your attention:

- moments or life experiences that had the biggest impact on you
- adventures or journeys that changed you
- things you want to remember and things you want to forget
- jobs that made you, broke you, or formed who you are today
- lessons that brought you hard-earned insight or wisdom
- people and places that have shaped you
- things that you've won and things that you've lost
- significant historical or cultural movements that interest you
- personal challenges and obstacles, past or present
- societal issues or injustices that you feel passionately about
- books, music, theater, films, famous speeches, paintings, or artworks that have influenced you
- family stories, traditions, and cultural heritage that formed you
- important milestones in your life, such as weddings, deaths, graduations, and births
- traumas, big or small
- successes and failures in your work life and career choices
- decisions that changed the course of your life or someone else's
- relationships, friends, family members, and strangers you have encountered that have affected your sense of self
- lovers, sexual experiences, dating and matings that shaped you

Ask Other People

Sometimes our friends and family members can see us more clearly than we see ourselves. Try sitting down with someone who knows you and asking, "If I told you today that I was going to write a solo show, what would you guess it would be about?" Or you could ask, "What is the story you think I could tell the world that no one else could tell?" Listen and see if anything resonates!

Trust that your show will find you. It can be a little like attracting a hummingbird: a combination of putting out the sugar water, waiting, and a little luck.

EXPERT ADVICE

Often, in solo work, we are the entire vessel and the entire vehicle, so we have to be very aware of what we contain. For instance, will I be the most effective storyteller to retell the story of George Washington? Probably not, right? But if I were to take the narrative of Eartha Kitt in her early years, that would make more sense. We have to be aware of our own vessel, especially when we talk about decolonized storytelling. For solo artists, it's really bringing those specific experiences of culture and identity from the margins into a main-stage performance that can be theatricalized and canonized. We need to make sure that we have more people of color coming from different experiences to expand our breadth of work. This is something that a lot of solo artists of color have been doing over a span of decades, Sarah Jones being one of the most prolific. She does that beautifully through autobiographical and ethnographically specific work.

Melissa DuPrey
Actor, Writer, Storyteller

Getting Words on The Page (or Fingers on the Keys!)

When Arlene decided to start the third solo show of her solo quartet, *A Little Bit Not Normal*, it felt daunting. She had been noodling around with it for over a year and had a deadline floating around in her limbic system—the part of the brain responsible for firing up motivation. She joked that she wasn't sure hers was even working.

It took her forever to get in front of the computer to start. Her plan was to begin writing on a specific date in June. That morning, as she sat down, she realized she might be a little peckish, so she made a snack of granola and Greek yogurt. She looked at the orchid on the counter and wondered if you could actually keep them alive by feeding them one ice cube a week. This one looked perfectly healthy, but who doesn't want to know? (Turns out the ice cube trick does work, but you need to use three, in case you were wondering.) After that, she checked her email and . . . and . . . and . . . Fast-forward a few weeks, and there she was, feeling stressed, disappointed, and guilty. Guilty! GUILTY!

In a nutshell, that's Arlene's default writing mode, and she hates it. It's the option she ends up using unless she intentionally sets out to do something different. Through trial and error, she's learned that she likes soft and early deadlines, as well as being surrounded by other artists for good company and accountability. How does she do that? For the past ten years, she's been a part of a writing group of terrific, compassionate women who keep her on track and give feedback.

Each person in her group has a different working style. Veronica wakes up and happily floats to her desk, turns on bird sounds, and writes for a few gentle hours. Michele and Teresa manage their personal writing amid their all-day schedules of meetings, seminars, university classes, mentoring, work-related articles, and prepping for presentations. And Pam? Well, she doesn't always love writing. When asked, she said, "Writing is hard and painful and sometimes I really hate it, but I keep coming back."

Moving forward with your solo show can be exciting and overwhelming, often at the same time. The big question to ask yourself is "Does my default mode serve or hinder me as an artist and as a person?" Are you happy with working like this? Does it make you feel productive and motivated? Is it time to try something different?

The following suggestions may sound familiar or trite to you, but make a conscious decision to try one. We've seen too many people let their dream of a solo show fall by the wayside because they couldn't get started or lost their mojo along the way.

1. Write When You're Inspired

Ah, the allure of the Muse. It's such a romantic notion—a mystical force guiding you toward glorious, transcendent work. However, based on our experience with artists of all types, we must be honest and say that only a small percentage of people can successfully complete a large-scale project, such as writing a one-person show, just by waiting for the elusive Muse to show up.

If you're one of those individuals who can count on a visit from the Muse, make the most of it when she arrives and don't assume she'll stick around.

2. On Your Mark, Get Set, Plan!

Many folks in our classes find that having a regular writing routine is helpful and can train the brain to create a habit. Yeah, yeah, everyone knows that the prevailing wisdom from big-shot writers like Stephen King is that you should sit down every day at the same time and write, and we say, if you can, do it. Please. However, for many of us, it may not be feasible because of work, family, and life commitments.

Some people like writing at a particular time of day, maybe at 8:30 P.M. after you've put on comfy clothes. Others find it easier to write during their lunchtime three times a week. If you're a morning person (we're so jealous), you might choose to write before work on Tuesdays and Thursdays. Put it in your calendar like you would schedule a haircut or a meeting with your boss or a dinner reservation at Red Lobster.

3. Tick Tock, It's a Clock

It's easier to trick yourself into working for fifteen minutes than for three hours. Fifteen minutes is less time than it takes to boil a pot of water and throw in some pasta. Several of our students swear by the Pomodoro Technique, which includes twenty-five-minute periods of "focused bursts followed by five-minute breaks." Each segment is known as a "pomodoro," the Italian word for tomato. Who doesn't love a cute tomato chiming to tell you that you've been a rock star? We've always been amazed at how many students mew like a sick cat about not being able to get their writing started but then produce great work when given a prompt and a time limit.

4. Make It a Numbers Game

Write your target number of words and then you're done for the day? Yes, please! Just for fun, we searched on Google for "What are the daily word counts for famous writers?" It turns out there's a plethora of lists with the daily word counts of famous writers. Stephen King aims for two thousand words, Margaret Atwood 1,000–2,000 words, Ernest Hemingway targeted 500 words, Tom Wolfe 135 words. The marvelous rebel Dorothy Parker claimed she set her sights on just five words per day. Our takeaway: It's OK to go slow. It's not OK to stop.

5. A Place to Call Your Own

Figure out specific locations where you can do your best work. We all know people who escape to a crowded Starbucks, put on their headphones, and get into the zone. There are writers who prefer a secluded corner or closet to work. Meanwhile, others need to disconnect the Wi-Fi to avoid temptation. Julie chooses to put on big headphones that play brown noise to signal to her family: "I'm busy. Buzz off, fly face."

Stuck in a rut and can't write at home? Consider renting one of those coworking office spaces available by the hour. These venues usually offer various work configurations and a shared common area with snacks. Some apartment complexes provide lobbies, office space, and rec rooms for free or for a nominal fee.

6. Rituals and Totems

Many artists, athletes, and even grandmothers attest to their unique rituals that help them achieve the right mindset. One abuela we know tapped her pot twice with whatever utensil she had at hand before she started cooking. This sweet little ritual was her way of signaling "It's time."

Maya Angelou's process involved renting a hotel room for a few months, taking down all the art, and asking housekeeping not to enter the room to ensure they wouldn't throw away anything important. Basketball icon Michael Jordan used to wear his lucky shorts from college underneath his Chicago Bulls uniform in every NBA game of his career. It's said that Isabel Allende likes to set up flowers, light candles, and meditate before she starts writing. And Stephen Colbert's pre-show ritual was to eat one Altoid, shake hands with every crew member, and slap himself in the face twice—indeed, twice!

Many artists are superstitious and like to keep a personal totem near them while they work. Here are some of the totems that people we know keep by their desks for inspiration: a lucky penny, a picture of their child, shells from Puerto Vallarta, an altar of goddesses, an old-fashioned spindle from a childhood job, an Oscar (he's fancy like that), and a Rubik's Cube (she's nerdy like that). One writer we know has two crystals to amplify good energy and provide clarity. Do they work? Who knows, but she likes to think they might have some mystical power. If a ritual or totem helps you center, focus, and get into a creative space, we say go for it.

7. Break It Down

Break down your solo show into smaller, bite-sized chunks so it doesn't feel so overwhelming. Decide to write one small scene or the next bit of dialogue.

One of our students had a full, busy life and often felt angry and ashamed for not producing work. When she registered for our class again, we sat down with her to find a way to avoid another bad experience. She admitted she only had time to write just before class. We encouraged her to do exactly that—write right before class, no apologies. Sometimes she brought in six sentences, other times more, and we all cheered her on. We also agreed that, instead of participating in the fifteen-minute writing prompt with the rest of the class, she would spend that time editing her material. After eight weeks, she had crafted a beautiful fifteen-minute story for the stage, complete with a solid beginning, middle, and end, along with a couple of really good laughs.

8. A Little Carrot to Nibble On?

Who doesn't like the pot of gold at the end of a rainbow? The reward concept is simple: when you're finished, you get to have a candy bar, go to a yoga class, lay down, look on VRBO for your next "maybe" trip, or watch twenty TikToks in a row. But first, you write.

9. Talk It Out

Not everybody learns or creates in the same way. Maybe using a computer isn't the best way for you to work. One of our students writes everything longhand as their first draft and then types it into the computer as the second draft. Another simply uses the dictation feature on their computer, which transcribes as they talk and think out loud. Some like a hybrid and speak the material out loud as they write.

We've also worked with individuals who have benefited from getting up on their feet and improvising their material or who devised material with others. We've had musicians sing in class. Others have pitched ideas so we can ask questions or steer them in a direction. In an interview with Seattle Repertory Theatre, playwright Charlene

Woodard discussed her solo play *The Night Watcher*, which was based on her personal experiences as an aunt, godmother, and friend to numerous children. Woodard revealed that she didn't adhere to a writing schedule. Instead, her creative process involved telling stories aloud to family and friends for an entire year. She refined and edited these narratives through continuous retelling before finally sitting down at her computer to commit them to paper.

It's a brave thing to want to write a solo show, but it's often a solitary sport. (That's why they call it solo!) Abraham Lincoln was quoted as saying, "Discipline is choosing between what you want now and what you want most." Keep moving forward. Push through the obstacles and remember that they are temporary, but they're only temporary if you keep writing. Know that on the other side of those challenges is a stage waiting for you.

EXPERT ADVICE

How did you write your show?

The biggest learning curve was figuring out how to actually get my stories on paper. I started typing, and it didn't feel right. It didn't sound like the way I talk. But I know I'm a good storyteller, and I got the idea that maybe I could dictate the stories on my phone. So, in my car on the drive to work, I would tell a single story, maybe three times out loud, to my own damn self. And then when I came home that night, I'd hit record, and I'd tell it again. It worked. The big thing I learned was that when I was typing, I wasn't quite getting my voice—and that was something I'd heard from stand-up comedians, too. I needed to capture my rhythm and my weird sense of humor, and then transcribe it on the page.

Kurt Naebig
Solo Performer, Actor, Director

EXPERT ADVICE

Do you have a regular writing practice?

I will try any bit of process advice from any book, any writer—I've tried it all. Most of it hasn't really worked for me, with the exception of the idea that even if you only have five minutes, write for five minutes. I try to do that. And it's never at the same time of day, and sometimes it's only four minutes, and sometimes it turns out to be an hour, but I just write something every day. And I always carry a notebook with me. I have tried to journal all my life and I cannot do it, but I always have a notebook with me to write things down.

Willa Taylor
Storyteller, Dramaturg, Teacher, Activist

Be Accountable for Your Actions

That's what teachers, parents, and college RAs have always chided us to do. When it comes to writing your solo show, it means surrounding yourself with optimistic and supportive cheerleaders. Figure out how you can stay accountable to yourself and them. Here are some different ways to do that.

Take a Class or Workshop

Look for a writing workshop or class, online or at a local theater. We both teach classes in person and online, and we've seen how motivating and inspiring it is for our students to be part of a class that requires them to deeply listen and support others' work while showing up each week with their own. The trust and camaraderie that forms over time can last well beyond the class.

Of course, the teacher plays an important role, but much of their value lies in the environment they create. Learning in a class goes beyond craft—it's about discovering what works and what doesn't work by listening to others. It's not essential that every student be a top-notch writer, but it is crucial that they show up with a spirit of collaboration.

Julie has worked with a group of writers at the Goodman Theatre for more than a decade. Students joined the class years ago at all levels of proficiency—some were published novelists and poets, and others hadn't written anything since high school. Julie provides assignments and prompts, and the deadlines encourage everyone to produce writing and come to class with work. Week after week, year after year, students show up and make art together, and everyone has become a better writer, regardless of where they started.

We understand that most classes cost money and that finances can be a very real barrier. However, many organizations offer a sliding scale or scholarships for their classes. Do some digging and find out. Julie works for two highly reputable organizations that offer workshops at no cost to all students.

And please, once you find a class, go to each session even if you don't have work to share or don't feel like it—*especially* when you don't feel like it. You can still learn something valuable and leave feeling inspired. We promise you.

Work with a Coach

Another way to stay accountable is to work one-on-one with a solo coach for more intensive guidance. A good coach will be your biggest fan, challenge you as an artist, keep you on track, and hold you to your highest self. You can book one session or a series. With a coach, you'll get more individualized attention focused specifically on your work than you will in a class. If you plan to submit your work to theaters for production consideration, working one-on-one can be great for getting your play looking professional and in the best possible shape before sending it off.

Both of us have used a coach at some point in our writing process for every full-length play we have ever written. When Julie was working on her first solo show, she ended up with a big, messy, overflowing first draft that read at two and a half hours in length. She set up a coaching session with a very patient coach here in Chicago who gave her guidance on shaping the piece, primarily places to cut. Years later, she offers this same kind of help to other writers but still seeks out coaches to help her with her own writing.

You can consult a coach at any stage. You may have an idea that is gestating, a partial script, or a nearly completed project. Be clear about what you need for the next stage of development and chat with the coach ahead of time to see how they prefer to work.

When working as coaches, we try to be as flexible as possible. We've had people improvise dialogue and story on Zoom, pitch ideas, talk about the rudiments of putting the work together, or bring in concepts to bounce around. We ask questions and provide ideas and direction. Usually, we ask clients to send us pages of writing or a script in advance and request that they have a hard copy of the script available during the session for specific references and notes. Another approach we use is having the writer/performer read the script aloud so we can listen as an audience member.

Know that feedback from a coach is typically direct and focused, so if you have specific questions you'd like addressed, let the coach know before the session or their pre-read. When offering feedback on an autobiographical piece, we stress that our feedback pertains to the character in the play and is not a judgment about you or your life choices. If you feel that a coach doesn't respect this boundary, move on fast.

Finally, in addition to helping you write your script, many coaches can help you work on related issues. Some direct solo pieces themselves or have a fantastic network of directors to refer you to.

Coaches may have ideas for lighting, music, sound, props, and media. Some can give you information on producing that includes developing a press kit, navigating the festival circuit, and advice on marketing and promotion. They can even help you coordinate a reading or facilitate a curated feedback session.

A word of caution: there are more and more organizations, theaters, and instructors offering workshops for solo shows. Do your research and check the background of the instructors. Many are good, which is wonderful for our genre. However, there are some out there who don't have much writing experience or teaching ability. Make sure your instructors have experience with solo writing and performing and a real understanding of the craft. You'd be surprised how many don't. You wouldn't take golf lessons from someone who has only played casually on weekends, nor would you get your hair cut by someone who learned from a YouTube tutorial last month. Similarly, you want your solo show coach to have more than just basic or amateur-level experience.

There are many theater artists or writing instructors who can tell you if a script isn't working. The key is finding someone who can not only pinpoint problem areas, but also explain *why* they aren't working, while offering recommendations for improving the work. Don't be afraid to talk to other solo artists, interview instructors and writing coaches, or sit in on a class. In our coaching practice, we always offer potential clients an opportunity to chat about goals and see if we're a good fit. Vet your teachers. It's worth it!

Join a Writers Group

A writers group is a great way to keep your work moving forward. How can you find one? Reach out to theaters in your area to see if they have a playwrights group. Google "playwright groups in [your city]" to find local options. Social media platforms also have their own groups for writers—make inquiries that way. Don't limit yourself to only playwriting groups. A more general writing group might serve you as well. After all, these are folks who understand story, plot, arc, and character. Try local bookstores and see if they host a writing group or know of some in the community. Librarians may also have a list.

Can't Find a Group? Create Your Own

If you can't find an existing group, consider creating one yourself. Gather a group of like-minded folks who can commit to meeting regularly and sharing ideas. These could be friends or people you've met through theater, workshops, or classes. We've had all kinds of groups spring out of our classes and workshops. Or you can advertise online. Decide on days, times, purpose, and structure before you send out invites so people know what they are getting themselves into.

We suggest no more than eight writers for a group. Each session should have a specific time limit, no more than two and a half hours. Otherwise, you will get sprawling all-night sessions that no one will want to come back to. Your group can meet weekly, biweekly, or monthly, but meetings should be scheduled in advance so members can block off time on their calendars ahead of time. For some writers, an ongoing commitment may be too much. Try every week for six weeks or every other week for three months and see how it goes.

One way to structure this type of group is to have designated writers bring in a scene, ten pages, or a chunk of work. Determine a time limit for each playwright that includes feedback. Designate a facilitator to keep track of time and to gently quash the ramblers. A quick check-in with each playwright is always nice: "How did your writing go this week?" Sharing goals and progress can provide an extra layer of motivation and support. Snacks are fantastic, though we've found that it's important to ensure that food and chatting don't become the main focus.

If possible, set guidelines for the group. Writers can ask for specific feedback when it is their turn, such as:

- What worked for you in this piece?
- What did the greedy listener want more of?
- What could be clearer? Where did you get confused or drop out?
- What is the story about?
- What is the story really about? (The Big Story? The Universal Truth?)
- Talk to me about the dialogue or narration in this section.

Finally, we like to share the concept of a "brave space" in all of our classes and coaching sessions. There are many formats out there. Here's one that Arlene's adapted from the teaching curriculum at Chicago Dramatists: "We strive to create a brave space where everyone's experiences, perspectives, stories, and lived experiences are valued. We recognize that certain topics may bring up concerns, fear, or discomfort, and when that happens, we commit to listening deeply and responding with our best selves."

Someone to Watch Over Me

Being accountable to a specific person can be a great way to stay motivated. Sometimes when we see a student struggling with their writing, we ask them to email us a rough draft three days before our session. We assure them that we won't read it but will be waiting for it.

Try planning an informal "playdate" with another writer. For example, we have two writer/performer friends who live in different cities. They set up Zoom sessions where they show up and quietly work on their material independently, but together, cameras on. It's sweet. Like listening to your cat sleep.

You can also plan an informal reading of your work-in-progress at a theater or in your living room. Better yet, have a friend host it and invite people well in advance. It's harder to back out that way.

Last, in a category all her own, one solo artist we know famously takes accountability to the next level. She books and pays for a theater upfront and then works backward to write, rehearse and market her shows. While this makes us gasp, it's worked beautifully for her.

EXPERT ADVICE

How do you hold yourself accountable as a writer?

I'm extremely motivated by a deadline. I heard Ira Glass on NPR the other day saying that he wouldn't write a thing if it wasn't for his show every week, and I'm like that too. I try to say yes when people ask me to perform somewhere, even if it scares me. Because then I know, "OK, I'm gonna have to be there and do that." Taking classes and being with other people who write really helps me too. I have a Monday class where we have a different writing prompt every week, so that at the end of eight weeks I have eight stories. Maybe not eight *great* stories, but I have eight different stories to work on and develop if I want to. That keeps me rolling.

Connie Shirakawa
Solo Performer, Writer

There's More Than One Way to Get Where You're Goin'

We'd like to highlight two ways to craft a solo show: "destination playwriting" and "adventure playwriting." Neither is better than the other; each method has its own advantages and disadvantages. Their effectiveness depends on your personal writing style, the way your brain is wired, and the specifics of your particular project.

Think of it like a road trip from Los Angeles to New York. There are some people who like to travel using the destination approach. They have a schedule to stick to, a mapped-out route, chosen sights, booked tickets, and reserved hotel rooms. They know where they are going and when they will arrive. This travel method might mean that they miss out on spontaneous detours and surprises, like stumbling upon Hadley's Fruit Orchard in the middle of the desert and discovering the world's best banana date shakes (Trust us on this one), but they're not scrambling for a hotel room at midnight.

On the other hand, some travelers embrace the adventure approach. They know they're heading from the West Coast to the East, but they're OK with not knowing the exact route or arrival time. They go with the flow and let curiosity guide them. They might stop at a restaurant, not because they're hungry but because it looks fun and funky. While they might miss some things due to lack of research, they might also stumble upon the world's only museum of ventriloquism. With no set arrival time in New York, getting lost along the way becomes part of the adventure.

Both trips take you to the same place. It's the same with writing solo.

Destination playwriting often starts with creating an outline that maps out the entire solo show, from the beginning to the conclusion. The outline functions as a guide that assures a cohesive narrative. One of the benefits of this method is its efficiency. Although it requires more time for planning and organizing before the actual writing begins, many writers find the process faster and less stressful because they know where the play is headed.

However, we've worked with clients for whom the outline limited their ability to explore new directions or make unexpected discoveries along the way. We've seen writers become frustrated when the story felt too structured or predictable or when they've written themselves into a corner. The playwright can miss the point of the entire solo show because they're imposing their preconceived notions onto the story. In our coaching, we've insisted that our destination playwrights be willing to take breaks along the way. We encourage them to step back, analyze and reflect on the direction of the play, and be willing to change course and incorporate new insights as they pop up.

Adventure playwriting refers to creating a solo show without a preconceived outline and with a willingness to discover along the way. Many of our solo artists have a general idea of the topic they want to develop but may not have in mind a specific style or format, a progression of events, or even the exact content of the show.

Adventure playwriting leads to a more free-form and exploratory approach where the play unfolds organically through the creative process itself. Often, writers using this method are more inclined to trust their instincts, allowing unexpected stories and characters to emerge. We've coached many writers who, through this method, have discovered untapped stories and insights or unlocked the essential question. Yes, the results can be unpredictable, but that's part of the excitement and magic of the creative process.

However, this more organic approach comes with challenges. Without a structured plan, the writing and editing process can take longer. Without a clear direction, some writers may find themselves lost or stuck, which can lead them to throw their hands up in frustration and, in the worst case, to abandon their solo show altogether. In our coaching, we've encouraged adventure playwrights to pause, take a deep breath, and list the smaller stories or events they've written so far. We then ask them to assess what the story is revealing to them in its current form. That simple act often provides clarity.

Many writers, ourselves included, work with a hybrid approach that combines structure with flexibility. This method uses a loosey-goosey outline to maintain some type of structure and direction while also allowing for intuitive exploration. It blends elements of both adventure playwriting and destination playwriting. Our students who use this method find that it allows them to plan, figure out the big picture, and create a loose framework, while still embracing a creative, intuitive flow.

No matter which technique you choose or which chooses you, be willing to change it up if it's not working or serving your show. Stay flexible and trust that your unconscious will support your writing process. Your unconscious mind can generate ideas and solutions that you might not have considered, making connections between seemingly unrelated concepts. The best piece of advice Arlene ever heard about the writing process came from the beloved American radio host, actress, screenwriter, and producer Kelly Carlin, who confidently declared to a room full of solo writers, "I am the master of my own process."

And so is everyone.

EXPERT ADVICE

The very best storytellers I know are people who are willing to lay down narrative long enough to behold and engage with real life. They walk slow, pocket their devices, and meet a day with open eyes. They notice smells and colors and sounds while they move through the world, enough to remember those details later; they notice new graffiti and seasonal changes and tiny urban rabbits, the way that a river in their town looks different now, and when birdsongs go away. They see the tenderness and trying in other people's faces, and they notice strangers who need help or seem kind. They listen to others' points of view—not to argue, but because they're interested. Paying attention in this way, they find surprising beauty, have unexpected adventures, make unlikely friends, fall in love, rise to the moment, confront injustice, and become their own heroes. And they have really frickin' great stories to tell.

Janna Sobel
Storyteller and Teacher

The Fourteen Types of Solo Shows

Humans have been telling stories for thousands of years. Before we had spoken language, early humans probably used gestures and pantomime to share their experiences—acting out the excitement of the hunt or the drama of giving birth to the baby with an unusually large head. Once spoken language came along, these stories evolved into myths, legends, and cultural traditions that shaped the identities of entire communities.

Our solo ancestors were storytellers, shamans, bards, and minstrels. Solo work as we know it can be traced to the griots of West Africa and the bards of classical Greece, who passed down stories, traditions, and cultural values. In medieval Europe, jesters and troubadours used humor, song, and storytelling for entertainment as well as social commentary.

Charles Dickens and Mark Twain brought literary solo performance to the stage in the 1800s—prolific writers and natural performers embodying their own characters live. Vaudeville expanded solo performance with a wide variety of acts, from monologists and comedians to a single actor portraying multiple characters. One of the earliest performers to build a career with solo work was Ruth Draper, an American actress who, with just a chair, shawl, and a side table as her only props, performed internationally in multiple languages for decades. In the mid–1980s, Spalding Gray helped bring autobiographical solo work into the mainstream. Since then, solo work has been honored with major awards like the Tony, Emmy, and Drama Desk Awards, as well as Pulitzer recognition for Anna Deavere Smith's *Fires in the Mirror* and Doug Wright's *I Am My Own Wife*.

"Solo performance" is the broad term that encompasses one person performing for an audience. Throughout this book, we will use the phrases "solo show," "solo play," and "one-person play" interchangeably to refer to this theatrical genre, which contains clear plotlines and takes an audience on a journey from beginning to end.

The Fourteen Types

The following styles demonstrate the depth and breadth of the solo show genre. Being familiar with them can help you figure out how you might best tell your story onstage. The type of solo show you are writing may reveal itself to you over time, so don't feel you must figure out what kind of show you're writing before you start. For some, though, understanding these categories early on can introduce possibilities and provide direction. You may also find that being able to delineate types and styles can provide you with a framework and vocabulary with which to analyze other solo works.

Three questions will help you determine the style or styles that may work for you:

- What will best serve the story?
- What will serve you as a writer?
- What will serve you as a performer?

Perhaps you are an artist/performer who is adept at doing characters, taking on their physical or vocal personalities. If so, you may want to incorporate the use of characters into your show. Maybe your solo show revolves around a specific event. Knowing this will allow you to focus on building smaller supporting events that contribute and build to the primary event. While some solo shows use only one style, many incorporate several styles in the crafting of the work. Understanding the scope of what is possible may allow you to see a different way into the story. We've included three examples for each type of solo style to allow you to go to the source and investigate.

1. **The Narrative One-Person Show.** This form uses narration and exposition to tell the story—the way we tell a story in our daily lives. The concept is "Let me tell you about . . ." The primary vehicle for this style is a narrator telling the story in their own voice, breaking the fourth wall, and addressing the audience directly. A narrative one-person show demands clean writing and a strong point of view.

   Grounded by George Brandt
   - This show's narrator is a grounded female drone pilot struggling with raising a baby and engaging in remote-controlled warfare.

   Other examples
   - *Fleabag* by Phoebe Waller-Bridge
   - *The Year of Magical Thinking,* adapted from the book by Joan Didion

2. **The Dialogue-Driven Play.** The primary vehicle for telling the story is lines of dialogue spoken between two or more characters. Each character has their own voice, language, and point of view. No narrator is guiding the audience through the story. The characters address each other within the context of the play.

   I Am My Own Wife by Doug Wright
   - This show is a conversation between John Marks, a bureau chief for *U.S. News & World Report,* reporter Doug Wright, and Charlotte von Mahlsdorf, an East German transgender woman. The play recounts how her life was impacted by World War II and the Nazis.

   Other examples
   - *The Search for Signs of Intelligent Life in the Universe* by Jane Wagner
   - *Krapp's Last Tape* by Samuel Beckett

3. **The Character-Driven Play.** The major vehicle for the storytelling is the use of characters. Usually, these characters break the fourth wall and directly address the audience rather than each other.

Unveiled by Rohina Malik

- This solo show is told through the viewpoints of five Muslim women who serve tea and uncover what lies beneath the veil in a post-9/11 world. The play explores racism, hate crimes, love, Islam, culture, and language. Each character—a Pakistani immigrant and dressmaker, a Moroccan American lawyer, and a young hip-hop artist among them—tells their story directly to the audience.

Other examples

- *Back to Broadway* by Whoopi Goldberg
- *Bridge and Tunnel* by Sarah Jones

4. **The Theme-Driven Play.** This type of solo show examines a specific theme, topic, or central idea, often using narratives and reflections to delve into the complexities and nuances.

The Vagina Monologue by V (the writer formerly known as Eve Ensler)

- *The Vagina Monologues* explores women's experiences with sex, relationships, and their bodies.

Other examples

- *Beyond Glory* by Stephen Lang
- *Prima Facie* by Suzie Miller

5. **The Event-Driven Play.** This style of one-person show explores a specific event or happening.

Twilight: Los Angeles, 1992 by Anna Deavere Smith

- This play explores the three days of rioting in Los Angeles in the wake of the Rodney King verdict, issued April 29, 1992, when four white Los Angeles police officers were acquitted of charges of assault and police brutality.

Other examples

- *The Testament of Mary* by Colm Tóibín
- *Remember This: The Lesson of Jan Karski* by Clark Young and Derek Goldman

6. **The Autobiographical Play.** This type of one-person play focuses on the life story, or some aspect of the life story, of the person who wrote and performed it.

   Every Brilliant Thing by Duncan Macmillan with Jonny Donahoe

   › This show recounts Duncan Macmillan's attempts, as a young boy, to fix his mother's depression by creating a list of "the best things" in the world. This list grows as he grows from child to adult.

   Other examples

   › *Swimming to Cambodia* by Spalding Gray
   › *The Night Watcher* by Charlayne Woodard

7. **The Biographical Play.** This style of show recounts the life story or some aspect of the life story of a character who is not the writer/performer.

   The Belle of Amherst by William Luce

   › This solo show is a portrait of nineteenth-century American poet Emily Dickinson and is based on her poems, letters, and notes.

   Other examples

   › *Ann's First Campaign* by Taylor Holland
   › *Lillian* by David Cale

8. **The Cultural Autobiography.** This type of play tells one's own story within the context of a cultural group. It revolves around the writer's experience of belonging to a particular race, gender, sexual orientation, religious group, et cetera.

   What the Constitution Means to Me by Heidi Schreck

   › This Tony-nominated one-person show speaks to gender and is an examination of the US Constitution and its effects on generations of women, including the solo artist herself.

   Other examples

   › *Lackawanna Blues* by Ruben Santiago-Hudson
   › *What? No Ping Pong Balls?* by Dan Kwong

9. **The Cultural Biography.** This type of solo show is written about a person who is not the playwright within the context of a specific group—for example, a particular culture, faith, gender, sexual orientation, race, or disability.

   Primo by Antony Sher

   › This play tells the story of Primo Levi and his life in Auschwitz. It is based on the book *If This Is a Man*.

   Other examples

   › *Golda's Balcony* by William Gibson

   › *Frida . . . A Self Portrait* by Vanessa Severo

10. **Cabaret.** These solo shows combine songs with narrative elements to convey a larger story.

    Bruce Springsteen on Broadway by Bruce Springsteen

    › Springsteen shares personal stories and acoustic versions of songs connected to them.

    Other examples

    › *The Lion* by Benjamin Scheuer

    › *Tell Me on a Sunday* by Andrew Lloyd Webber and Don Black

11. **Stand-up.** This style of solo show consists of long-form comedy and usually includes the format of setup and punchline. However, this type of solo piece takes the audience on a journey and reflects a change in the main character.

    Just For Us by Alex Edelman

    › This Emmy-winning solo show follows Alex as he covertly attends a meeting of white nationalists. It's a thoughtful, wired meditation on the place of Jewish people in an anti-Semitic society.

    Other examples

    › *The Old Man and The Pool* by Mike Birbiglia

    › *Baby J* by John Mulaney

12. **The Anecdotal Show.** This type of one-person show is usually a series of anecdotal stories that may not have a discernible throughline or contain a character who has an arc or transformation.

Wishful Drinking by Carrie Fisher

› The actor Carrie Fisher's one-person show recounts stories about her famous parents and stepparents, Hollywood, her days on a movie set, and her dysfunctions.

Other examples

› *Laughter and Reflections* by Carol Burnett
› *Elaine Stritch at Liberty* by Elaine Stritch

13. **Performance Art.** These types of works are a nontraditional art form that often explores political or topical themes. Typically expressionistic and intellectually provocative, these works may or may not feature a transformational character arc. Performance art draws from various mediums, including poetry, visual art, installations, music, and multimedia.

The End of the Moon by Laurie Anderson

› This one-person performance is part musical journey, part history lesson, and part personal experience. It examines the interconnectedness of loss, spirituality, and cultural trauma.

Other examples

› *Tongues* by Joseph Chaikin and Sam Shepard
› *The Artist Is Present* by Marina Abramović

14. **The Hybrid One-Person Show or the Combo Plate.** This type of solo show combines several of the above types such as dialogue, characters, and narration wrapped around a particular event.

700 Sundays by Billy Crystal

› The title refers to the number of Sundays shared by Billy and his father. This Tony-winning solo show shares the autobiographical story of his youth, portrays characters, and uses dialogue within the cultural context of the Jewish and jazz worlds.

Other examples

› *A Bronx Tale* by Chazz Palminteri
› *Latin History for Morons* by John Leguizamo

The Nuts, Bolts, and Buckles of Your Play

Seven Keys That Make a Solo Show Work

We have found that there are seven components that can support almost any one-person play. This chapter is a high-level overview of them, each of which is explored in detail later in the book.

It's important to understand that you will discover some of these elements along the way. You don't need to know everything about your show before you start writing—in fact, you probably shouldn't! Rather, circle back to these keys as you work and make discoveries.

You know you. Refer to this list when it will be useful for your process. Some artists like to have tips and guidelines early on, so the information can help inform their work as they create it. Other writers find that any type of suggestion too early in the process feels inhibiting to their exploration. If that's you—if trying to take all this on board right now is going to put you in your head and curb your creativity—page on past it. Come back to this chapter after you've got a messy first draft.

We've found that some of our students will refer to these keys before they begin writing and use it as a guide to develop their show. Others turn to it in the middle of their process to determine where these pieces might fit. Still others use it once they have a draft in order to troubleshoot, as a menu of possible fixes for elements that might need attention.

1. A Sturdy Arc—Beginning, Middle, and End

Solo pieces take an audience on a journey, and a journey starts in one place and ends in another. Sometimes the journey is geographical, but most of the time it's internal. The journey can be physical, emotional, spiritual, or intellectual, but some sort of transformation must take place in the course of the show. Making sure the progression of that transformation is specific and clear will make your show satisfying for an audience.

What happens in your solo play? What events take place that change you or your protagonist? Most one-person plays have a plot, which is simply a sequence of events: this happened, and this happened, and then this happened. Stories have tension or some sort of conflict that wants resolving. If we stop in the middle of telling a story—a good story—our listener will lean forward and ask, "But then what happened?" Theater is an art form of action, events, things happening moment to moment.

2. Narrative Structure

Narrative structure is the order in which the events of your show are revealed to the audience. Humans experience life chronologically, and the stories in many solo plays are sequenced that way. This is how we have told stories since we were children, and it's very effective. However, you may choose to roll out the plot of your solo play in a different order, which will affect the audience's experience and influence how they understand your story.

Narrative structure frequently develops organically as you work on your show. Other times, once everything is written down, you can start thinking about structure and making decisions about what will best serve your show. Maybe you want to hook the audience by starting in the middle of your big story, in a moment of high drama. Or perhaps you want to start at the end and circle back with the audience to let them experience how you got there. Whatever you choose, your show will still need rising tension and some kind of resolution, but there are lots of ways to do that. We encourage you to make deliberate and thoughtful decisions about this element of your play and not just let it happen.

3. An Essential Question

As you are working on your solo play, you'll begin talking to people about it, and they'll ask, "What is your show about?" You may respond with a sentence about the events of the show: "It's about my two years in the Peace Corps in Panama." Or your response might be the theme of the show: "It's about discovering myself" or "It's about patriotism" or "My show's about inequality."

Notice how definitive and finite those statements feel, as if you've got it all figured out. Questions invite exploration. Questions leave some breathing room. Questions beget more questions. And that's good.

Essential questions give us something specific to wrestle with throughout our piece. A well-formed essential question helps to prevent the play from drifting or feeling thematically scattered. A show may or may not end up answering the essential question. Many times, it won't. The point of an essential question is not to find the answer, but to explore possible answers.

Notice how the following questions feel more alive than the statements above: "What does it mean to help others?" "Who am I when I'm a stranger?" "What does it mean to be American?" "What does it mean to be a good person?" "How can helping be nontransactional?"

Of course, a writer may not know what their theme or essential question is before they start. We often don't know what we're writing until we write it! After we have done quite a bit of writing or we have a full messy draft, we read through it and ask: What am I, as the artist, grappling with in this show? What am I trying to figure out? What is the big question I am trying to answer? The answer might be the basis for your essential question. (Can your show have more than one essential question? Sure. You may have a handful of questions you're wrestling with.)

4. Theatrical Elements

Your solo show is a play with one performer. There may be multiple settings and characters, but you (or someone else) will be the only person onstage and, typically, the only voice your audience will hear. You may be asking, "But how am I, alone on a stage, going to capture and hold an audience's attention for 60–90 minutes?" (If you are not asking this question, please start now!)

"Theatrical elements" is the answer. Or it's part of the answer, along with a captivating story, excellent writing, and a kickass performance. Theatrical elements are components of your show that heighten the text and help you tell your story. These are often technical elements, such as lighting, sound, set design, slide projections, puppets, or costumes.

We can also build theatrical elements into our performance. Consider utilizing dialogue and scenes, portraying multiple characters, using vocal variation, singing, dancing, pantomime, or chainsaw juggling. You might incorporate film techniques, such as building a montage of experiences, fast-forwarding, using slow motion, or quick cuts. Theatricality in performance includes moving our body and using our voice in ways that we don't typically do in our everyday life. Musicals, for instance, are inherently theatrical because we don't generally break into song when we are in the midst of an intense moment in our lives.

Even if you will be performing your show in the tiniest of venues, know that a theater audience has a built-in expectation that they will see something other than talking or "just real life" when they go to the theater. Let theatrical elements help you.

5. Something at Stake

Another way we ensure audiences care about our story is to be clear about what is at stake. Does it feel important? What's at risk for the main character?

Stories, plays, and movies are not written about our typical days—the days when everything goes according to plan. We make art about the days when something is different—when a relationship, a job, or our view of the world changes forever. The event has to mean something for the main character, if no one else.

This doesn't mean that every one-person show is written about an earth-shattering event. The reality is the event only needs to be important and impactful to the main character. We may not know you or care about science fairs, but if we understand how desperate you were to win the seventh-grade science fair, we'll care about that story. If we understand that winning the science fair was a way for you to get your father's scarce attention, we'll care even more.

High stakes can add levity to our stories as well. If you understand how invested a character is in growing a vegetable garden, you'll understand her mounting frustration as she is unable to keep the neighborhood cats from pooping in it. You'll understand how this woman ultimately finds herself staking out the backyard in the middle of the night with a super-soaker water gun.

Vulnerability and truth-telling are other ways we make sure the stakes feel high enough in a piece. Does the performer really let us in through their performance? Does it cost the main character something to tell this story?

6. A Strong POV

Most solo shows are told in first person—using pronouns such as I, me, we—even if the characters in the show are historical or fictional. A show about Winston Churchill may feature an actor playing Winston Churchill or his wife, but those characters will be talking about themselves and their own attitude about events. The more specific, clear, and distilled your protagonist's point of view, the better.

Consider a story you might write about your first kiss. We have all read or heard first kiss stories, but your story will be distinctly *yours*. The details about where you were, who the kiss was with, what you expected it to be, and how you felt about what happened will be unique. The reason listeners will care is that they are getting the story with your attitude about the events, your inner monologue, and how you felt at each moment. All these details create a strong point of view.

Another important aspect of point of view relates to you as a playwright. It can be daunting to think that any play we are creating must say something brand new or ask a question that has never, ever been asked before. It's not so intimidating if we understand that we can say or ask something that has been said or asked before, but in an entirely new way. That is done through point of view. Letting your personality shine through your writing will make your stories sound like you are the only one who could have written them.

That's the good stuff.

7. Never Just Tell

If you are coming to solo shows from the storytelling world, you may have the idea that a solo show is simply a longer version of what you already do. Good news: in some ways this is true.

However, solo shows are part storytelling and part theater. At live lit events storytellers can get away with talking about an incident in a story without showing it. We might describe the kind of kid we were when we were eight years old or talk about what Grandma's voice sounded like after forty years of Pall Malls.

Plays, however, are about action. In the theater, we want to observe events unfolding in the moment. In a play, we watch characters work something out right in front of us, and the most important moments in the story happen onstage. (It's true that the Greeks way back when were fond of resolving wars and having characters die offstage. A messenger would tell the audience about it in a looooooong monologue. But theater doesn't really work like that anymore . . . thank goodness.)

Playwrights know that there must always be forward-moving action, and that audiences want to see the big things happen. And you can do that in your play, too. To avoid the pitfalls of just talking *at* the audience, we generally suggest that in a solo show, at any moment, the main character should be doing one of four things:

- being "in scene"
- directly addressing the audience as the Contemporary Narrator
- directly addressing the audience as the Scenic Narrator
- actively discovering or struggling to work something out in front of the audience

We'll go into these four specific ways to make sure you're not just talking at the audience in our chapter "Four Ways to Never Just Tell."

Your Brain's Got a Soft Spot

Research tells us that our minds wander off an unbelievable thirty to forty-seven percent of our waking day. That's right. We have "monkey mind," a mind that won't sit still, like a monkey swinging from branch to branch in a tree. It happens constantly—when we're bored, not bored, in conversations, and even during sex. (You know it's true.)

Apparently, this is especially the case when we're listening to facts and data. While receiving this type of information, only two areas of the brain are engaged: the auditory cortex (for listening) and Wernicke's area (for processing words). Both of these areas are located in one small part of the brain, so, unless we're really invested in the facts and data coming at us, our monkey mind will probably start swingin'.

However, when we're listening to a vivid story with sensory details, many more parts of the brain are activated, triggering the release of hormones and neurotransmitters like cortisol, dopamine, and serotonin. These focus our attention and stimulate our emotions, making it more likely we'll store the experience in long-term memory. In fact, when we're truly engaged in a story, our brain waves start to mirror the storyteller's brain patterns, as if the events in the story are happening to us.

As a solo writer and performer, your job is to harness this brain stew, so that you're no longer hoping your audience stays with you—you're crafting an experience that quiets the monkey mind.

Start your story at a moment of tension, surprise, or curiosity. This triggers the brain's alert system and makes people lean in. Once you've hooked folks, keep them there with vivid sensory detail. Don't say, "It was hot." Say, "Sweat pooled in my waistband and my shirt clung like a cold second skin." That fires up the sensory cortex and puts the audience *inside* the experience.

To hold emotional focus, establish what's at stake early. If an audience doesn't know why it matters to you, they won't care. Emotional stakes build empathy, which releases oxytocin—the hormone that deepens connection. Structure matters too. The brain craves shape: a beginning, a middle, and an end. Use it. Pay attention to pacing. Speed creates urgency; slowing down lets a moment land. Last, don't forget vulnerability and transformation. These moments activate mirror neurons and invite the audience to imagine their own change. That's where the real connection happens.

Understanding the brain science behind storytelling is like being handed the keys to the control room. The more you know about how your audience's brain ticks, the more confidently you can guide them through a journey that matters.

TRY THIS!

1. The next time you go to a play or movie, watch the audience. What moments make them still? Make them shift forward in their seats? Laugh? Then analyze *why*. What brain buttons might the story or performance be pushing?
2. Build a brain map of your solo show. Highlight and color-code each section:

   Blue for sensory detail
   Red for emotional stakes
   Green for mounting tension
   Yellow for transformation

   This visual map may help you see the neurophysiological patterns of your show—and where you may need to turn up the engagement dial.

Story vs. Anecdote

We were driving our friend Natasha, a terrific solo artist, home from a live storytelling event. We agreed that some of the stories we'd heard were lackluster, even "blergh." As we parsed what worked and what didn't, Natasha, who's prone to delightful dramatics, shook her fists to the heavens and yelled, "Oh my God! Just because it happened to you doesn't mean it's a story!" And there it was—sweet and to the point. Some of the storytellers hadn't shared actual stories; instead, they offered anecdotes that left us thinking, "Eh, so what?"

While both anecdotes and stories are narratives, an anecdote simply recounts events without delving into their significance. They center on a single moment in time and are often funny or dramatic. They can illustrate a point, provoke thought or laughter, or support a broader narrative, but no matter how interesting or unusual an anecdote is, if it doesn't dig deeper, it remains unsatisfying as a story.

A well-crafted story goes beyond recounting events to find meaning. It provides greater depth and complexity, touching upon universal themes. Characters in a story reflect on their perceptions and delve into the emotional essence of an experience, revealing how it shaped the character's view of themselves and the world around them.

One way to make sure we're creating stories, not anecdotes, is by incorporating the process of reflective thinking. This practice of analyzing an experience allows us to gain perspective and come to terms with things that have happened. Without it, our lives become a series of isolated events with no connected meaning. Reflective thinking insists on honesty, vulnerability, and being connected to your own personal beliefs.

In a one-person show, reflection is the process of creating meaning from events that can often seem insignificant. It allows writers to craft the themes and messages that they want to convey throughout their piece. An audience wants to understand a character's perspective—they're dying to know why the protagonist acted as they did, what fueled their motivations, and what changes were sparked. Reflection acts as the bridge between personal experiences and universal truths.

Sometimes anecdotes can be turned into stories with introspection and by asking the right questions. It's certainly worth a try! But sometimes a humorous incident with a stranger or a madcap experience at the coffee shop is just an anecdote. Trying to inject a deeper meaning into such moments can feel forced, even if the moment itself is interesting.

During the writing process, be sure to reflect on the narrative and ask these questions:

- Why is this event important to my main character?
- What are their reactions?
- How did it shape their perspective?
- What have they learned?
- What is the deeper meaning behind the story?

For example, imagine a story about an eight-year-old who hears the bells of the ice cream man in the distance. With money already filched from her father's change jar, she's been roasting like a rotisserie chicken in the sun for what feels like hours. As the ice cream man comes into view, he unexpectedly heads off in the opposite direction. "No!" she screams, jumping to her feet and running toward the wide street.

Spotting an oncoming car, she thinks she can outrun it, so she steps off the curb. Adrenaline surges through every cell of her being, propelling her forward—until she realizes she's misjudged the car's speed. She freezes, thinking, "What should I do?" The car brakes and swerves, stopping just in time. Panting, both she and the driver acknowledge each other and the moment.

This story without reflection is simply an anecdote about a close call. But with introspection, the story can take on meaning depending on how the character interprets the event. Perhaps the girl was so shaken that she vowed never to put herself in a situation like that again, staying within her comfort zone for the rest of her life. Alternatively, it could be the story of a kid who realized that she loved the adrenaline rush so much that she spent her life chasing that high through extreme sports like solo ice climbing. Or maybe the incident left her with a phobia of cars and traffic, making it difficult for her to navigate the larger world. Or this close call might have caused such anxiety that even the thought of ice cream triggered panic, preventing her from ever going out with the cute Baskin Robbins employee—leading to a life of loneliness and day-old baked goods.

It's also important to note that characters can hold two conflicting emotions at once, adding complexity to a story. We've all experienced fear and excitement, glee and sadness, humility and schadenfreude simultaneously. Remember your story isn't about what happens to the character—it's about how the character reacts to those events and the consequences of those reactions. A story creates meaning from the seemingly meaningless, though the "ah-ha" moment may not come right away. The character might need years to fully understand its significance.

Last, here's a special gift. In our classes, we have both witnessed that the art of reflection is not just a tool but also a mighty, mighty process. It can help you, the writer, think about your own experiences and emotions and lead to a deeper understanding of yourself and your place in the world.

The Beginning (Once Upon a Time . . .)

At its most basic, a simple formula for a good story is the one used in Alcoholics Anonymous: "This is how it was, this is what happened, and this is how things are now." The beginning of a story sets the stage and introduces the characters and the conflict; the middle is where the action unfolds; the end brings resolution and closure.

There's no one right way to start a solo show. But, generally, you'll want the beginning of your show to draw the audience into the play, set the tone, and establish the story. Here are some ways to do it. Not every option will fit every show, so pick what feels right for your story and style. Choose one or a few.

Give 'Em a Dopamine Hit

Dopamine, that chemical the brain releases when we feel good, is also responsible for motivating us to continue doing something we've started. Get the audience on your side right from the start.

Choose a meaty, interesting piece of dialogue to open the show. Audiences love being dropped into a conversation that's already happening. Notice how the following opening lines grab your attention:

> "You boys are pulling a lot of boners out there! You're pulling a lot of gosh darn boners." And with that line, Mr. Mathews went down in history, forever etched in the memory of

> thirteen eleven-year-old boys as we sat erect on a baseball bench too embarrassed to look left or right.
>
> **—Tim G.**

Another option is to jump right into the middle of an inciting incident or ongoing action. Choose a scene that is a turning point in your story or a moment that represents your character's journey. Drop the audience into the heart of the action, skipping any extensive exposition or setup.

These suggestions hook the audience and make them pay attention. Don't worry about starting at the very, very beginning of your story; you can always provide the necessary background information later through exposition or time jumps. The key is to begin with a scene that has energy, emotion, or conflict.

For example, *Romeo and Juliet* opens with a fight scene between the servants of the warring families, the Montagues and Capulets. The brawl gets out of hand as more people from both sides jump into the fight. We might not understand the reason for the fight at first, but as insults fly and punches are thrown, it becomes clear that they've long been feuding.

Introduce Your Main Character

One way to do this is to have the main character break the fourth wall to share their thoughts or feelings in a direct address to the audience. This personal interaction creates a sense of intimacy and fast-tracks your relationship with the audience.

Another option is to show the main character doing things or interacting with other characters in a way that reveals their traits, relationships, or the world they live in. Actions can speak volumes about a character and their situation.

The movie *The Godfather* starts with a family wedding scene. An unassuming man approaches the imposing Don Corleone—the protagonist and head of a powerful crime family—to seek help in avenging his daughter's honor. He is forced to beg and show respect by kissing Corleone's ring, promising to return the favor someday. Corleone then gives his blessing and embraces the man. This early moment establishes Corleone's status and power.

Let the Audience Know What the Play Is About

Find a way to introduce the main idea or central theme of your play so the audience knows what's important and what they should be paying attention to. In a typical solo show there may be several stories and themes, but the opening should communicate the filter through which the audience can see the play.

In the opening moments of the solo show *The Year of Magical Thinking* by Joan Didion, the audience is hooked by the protagonist's warning that what she is about to describe will also happen to each of them. That it's inevitable and there is no way to prepare for it. We soon learn that the protagonist is talking about death, and that she is dealing with the sudden loss of her husband. In the first five to ten minutes of the play, she introduces the concept of "magical thinking," a form of denial and hope that the impossible might be reversed.

In Mike Birbiglia's *The New One*, the show begins as observational comedy about furniture, specifically a couch. The couch becomes a metaphor for fear of change, personal space and ultimately, the experience of becoming a parent. The theme is not introduced with a direct declaration, as it is in *Magical Thinking*, but revealed through metaphor.

Hit Them with the Quest

Your character's quest should be front and center in your play. What does the character want? Introducing the character's quest early is important because it gives the audience a filter through which to see the play.

The quest creates conflict and transformation, driving the story forward. It reveals the character's motivations and aspirations, making them more relatable. If the audience doesn't understand the quest, the play's structure and purpose can become wobbly and confusing. When an objective is clear, the audience becomes invested in how the character will overcome their challenges. Is the main character trying to get pregnant? Looking for God? Searching for an identity that defines them? Seeking a soulmate?

In the opening scene of the solo show *Latin History for Morons*, John Leguizamo breaks the fourth wall, directly addressing the audience and telling them to listen up because he's got a lot of ground to cover and not a lot of time to educate and empower them. Using dialogue, he jumps into a scene of a racist schoolmate bullying his son. Trying to help his son, he realizes that he knows very little about Latin American history himself. This sets the stage for his quest to uncover and reclaim his heritage.

Set Up the Tone of the Play

Establish the atmosphere and mood early so the audience knows what to expect. Is it a serious drama? A lighthearted comedy? A dramedy? Satirical or experimental? If the play combines moments of comedy as well as drama, it's important to establish a light tone or include something amusing early to give the audience permission to laugh throughout the piece. Introduce humor too late and the audience may be unsure whether they are allowed to laugh at all. Additionally, if your solo show contains devices such as dialogue, multimedia, imagery, symbolism, music, or circus arts, we recommend including them early so that it doesn't feel like a new element is coming out of nowhere later.

In the first two and a half minutes of *Latin History for Morons*, we see all the devices we have mentioned. John Leguizamo sets the tone by entering the stage with a broad smile and acknowledging the audience. The stage is set with a chalkboard, a messy desk, and cluttered bookshelves. He's dressed in a rumpled suit, wearing high tops, and carrying a box and backpack. Using the intonations of a schoolteacher with a hint of humor, he then addresses the audience by saying, "Settle down, settle down, because we've got a lot of work to do here . . ."

The lights shift, and he starts talking in a conversational tone, sharing an anecdote about coming home and hearing the bed creaking in his son's room. He imitates the sound of the squeaky bed frame, making the audience believe that there is some kind of sex going on. Instead, he finds his son jumping up and down on the bed playing a video game. The audience laughs.

TRY THIS!

Take a scene, story, or anecdote from your solo show in process and experiment with ways to begin your piece:

- Open with a meaty, interesting piece of dialogue.
- Start in the middle of an inciting incident or ongoing action.
- Begin with a strong multisensory detail or image to set the tone.
- Use a question or a bold statement related to your theme to spark curiosity.
- Start with a physical action that reveals something about the character.
- Open with a moment of vulnerability, where your main character reveals a private fear, secret, or doubt.

EXPERT ADVICE

In many of your projects with Tellin' Tales Theatre you work with brand-new writers. What are some of the concepts you find are important to cover?

When people are developing a solo piece, I believe it must be about a subject they are deeply passionate about. One prompt I often use is "What is something that happened to you that you cannot forget?" If I'm teaching a class for people with disabilities, I like to use the prompt "When was the moment you realized you were different?" One of the most common mistakes I see people make is trying to tell their entire life story. The key is to focus on a single event that can launch the story.

Intention is another way to begin. Intention answers the question "What do you want from the listener?" I advise students to express this through action or an action word. Do you want them to give you a job? Do you want to convince them of something? Or do you want to reveal something to them?

Another trick I like to use, especially for people who are new, is to talk to the audience and identify what their relationship to you is. Is the audience a neighbor? Or maybe a tableful of old classmates at your high school reunion? This will change the story, the tone you use, and how you relate to them. And I always suggest writing a strong opening and closing line—for example, "I didn't come out as a little person until I was twenty-six years old" or "When you're younger, having a disability is like being a celebrity. It ain't that hard. All you gotta do is look cute."

Last, I encourage people with disabilities to go deep and share their full experience. Otherwise, it's easy for people to write you off as simply a disabled person. The audience needs to truly understand what you are going through mentally, physically, and psychologically to connect with you.

Tekki Lomnicki
Solo Artist, Master Instructor
Founder and Artistic Director of Tellin' Tales Theatre

The Middle (Lordy! This Is What Happened)

Occasionally, when we're at the theater, and without realizing it, we let out an audible sigh; it typically happens during the middle portion of the show. The middle is where stories can lose the attention of the audience, resulting in fidgeting, glances to check the time, and, worst of all, people falling asleep in the front row. It has happened to us, and it's as awful as it sounds, especially when they snore. That person may have had a martini with a Xanax chaser after a heavy meal, but, most of the time, it's the actor or the material.

The middle of a solo show delves into the character's journey by exploring their emotions, struggles, and desires. Avoiding a saggy, confusing, and boring middle can be challenging because so much is crowded into this portion of the play.

Here is a quick and dirty way to think about this. There should always be two intertwined stories happening at the same time—the journey of events and the journey of emotions.

The journey of events is what happens to your main character. It's the backbone of the story. The main character faces different problems and challenges while trying to reach their goal. As you craft the plot, you should be able to isolate every major event that happens to your main character during the play.

One example of a journey of events can be outlined in the following way: The main character, Amari, is a man who wants to be a father. It's always been his heart's joy to have a big family like the one he grew up in. After three years of trying, he finds out that he and his partner can't have children. They try medical intervention after medical intervention until they can't afford it anymore. They weigh the pros and cons of the adoption route. Then something strange and serendipitous happens . . .

Combining this journey of events with the emotional journey of the main character gives an audience a full experience. The emotional journey might begin with a feeling of assurance and expectation that morphs into disappointment, then guarded hope, followed by frustration and devastation, and then perhaps surprise. Throughout this process, Amari experiences a myriad of emotions—from the initial excitement of parenthood to the heartbreak of infertility, the uncertainty of their options, and finally, the unexpected turn of events that may offer a new path forward.

As you can see, the emotional journey is about the feelings and reactions characters experience as they navigate the events of the play. The audience is interested in events, but probably even more interested in how your character experiences the world internally.

The Big O: Obstacles

Understanding the obstacles your main character encounters on the way to achieving their goal is crucial to crafting the middle part of your one-person show. These challenges add depth and tension to the narrative, engaging the audience and keeping them invested in the outcome.

The writer Kurt Vonnegut famously said, "Every character should want something, even if it is only a glass of water." The middle of a story is where things get sticky and where the writer must answer the questions "What are the obstacles that get in the way of the character reaching their goal and getting what they want?" and "What does the character do to get what they want?"

In the last chapter, we talked about what comprises the beginning of the play, where the audience becomes aware of the character's wants, wishes, or expectations. The middle part of the story reveals the character's struggles to attain their goal. The character must overcome some obstacles, which provide that necessary element in a story: conflict. Obstacles can be external or internal.

External Obstacles

An external obstacle is a challenge that comes from outside the main character. The obstacle might take the form of a villain, rough terrain, or cultural barriers. External obstacles can also be events or situations the character has to deal with, like financial challenges or a cancer diagnosis. An external obstacle is something that happens *to* the character. Overcoming it shapes the plot and moves the story forward, leading to the character's growth and the resolution of the story.

Here are some examples of external obstacles in books, plays, and movies:

Societal or cultural barriers and injustices. In the movie *Hidden Figures*, the three main characters strive to overcome racial and gender discrimination in NASA during the early years of the space program.

Physical challenges. In the movie *The Martian*, an astronaut who is stranded on Mars struggles with physical challenges as he tries to survive and find a way back home.

Conflict with authority. In her solo show *Notes from the Field*, Anna Deavere Smith portrays various characters based on interviews. The play explores systemic oppression in education and criminal justice in America.

Lack of money and resources. In the play *Sweat* by Lynn Nottage, the lives of factory workers are explored as they struggle with financial hardships and the lack of job opportunities.

Relationship and interpersonal conflicts. In Tracy Letts's play *August: Osage County*, a feuding Southern family faces terrible revelations and rifts in their relationships when they return home after the patriarch goes missing.

Time and deadlines. In *Every Brilliant Thing*, a solo show by Duncan Macmillan with Jonny Donahoe, the main character tries to save his mother from depression and suicide by creating a list of "brilliant things" to bring joy to her life.

Internal Obstacles

Internal obstacles are in the mind of a character. They arise out of the character's psychology or beliefs and impact the character's thoughts and actions. In short, they are the psychological and emotional struggles that everyone deals with. For instance, a character who is afraid of failing might stop themselves from going after what they want, such as becoming a solo artist. Long-held anger toward a brother can lead to incapacitating guilt after the brother disappears at Burning Man. These kinds of internal challenges shape the development of the character and add depth to the narrative.

Here are some examples of internal obstacles in books, plays, and movies:

Guilt and regret. In Arthur Miller's play *Death of a Salesman*, world-weary salesman Willy Loman regrets his past choices, which have impacted his life and relationships with his family.

Moral dilemma. In the movie *The Dark Knight*, the inner conflict centers around whether Batman should break his moral code and ethical boundaries to protect the city from the villain, the Joker.

Loyalty vs. betrayal. In the book *The Kite Runner* by Khaled Hosseini, the main character, Amir, struggles with the need for his father's approval and whether to remain loyal to his childhood friend or to betray him by staying silent.

Fear of change. In the movie *Ratatouille*, the main character Remy, a rat with a passion for cooking, faces the fear of change and societal expectations. He wants to break free from the traditional role of a rat.

Struggle for acceptance. In the movie *Mean Girls*, Cady Heron, the new girl, struggles with the need to fit in with the popular girls, which makes her compromise who she truly is.

Self-doubt. In the musical *Wicked*, Elphaba struggles with being misunderstood and judged for her green skin. She strives to find her purpose and place in the world.

Pay attention to the middle of your show! A journey of events and a journey of emotions, along with strong obstacles for your protagonist to wrestle with, can help you keep an audience engaged.

The End (This Is How Things Turned Out)

We've all been there, leaving the theater after watching a movie or seeing a play, scratching our heads and asking ourselves, "What was that all about?" It's frustrating when a resolution feels confusing or is abrupt, or when a story has multiple false endings—not to mention those loose ends that leave us wondering, "What happened to the parrot? Did the aliens turn him into an energy source too?"

Endings are important because they stay with us. Done well, they give us a chance to reflect on the main character's journey and the overall narrative. A good ending provides closure and helps the audience parse the themes, messages, and character arcs that were explored in the play. Quite simply, the end of your solo show should give the play meaning.

The last scene of your solo show is like dessert after a meal. If it's not memorable, it can ruin the whole experience. You know how it goes—you say, "The food was great, but the dessert was just OK. I mean, it was a really good meal if you don't count the dessert." But let's be honest. You always count the dessert. For some of us, the dessert is the only thing that really matters.

A strong ending has three components: the Wrap-up, the Transformation, and the Takeaway.

The Wrap-Up

A well-crafted ending should give the audience a sense of completion and fulfill the contract that the writer makes in the opening of the play. The ending should say, "Hey, thanks for joining me on this journey. Here's a reward for your time and emotional investment."

The conflict and obstacles that the main character faces throughout the show should be addressed by the end, be it through reaching their goal, facing the consequences of not reaching their goal, or finding some other kind of resolution. The ending should allow the audience to think about the full arc of the main character's journey.

Bourne Identity: Was Jason Bourne able to recover his memory and discover his true identity?
The Wizard of Oz: Did Dorothy find her way home?
The Matrix: Did Neo overcome his fears and doubts and become "the one"?
The Color Purple: Was Celie able to find her voice and regain control of her life after years of abuse?
The Joy Luck Club: Can immigrant mothers and first-generation children bridge the cultural gap between generations and find understanding?
Brokeback Mountain: Did Ennis and Jack find a way to be together and live their lives openly and out?
In The Heights: Did Nina reconcile her aspirations for a college education with her loyalty to her family and culture?

The Transformation

Throughout your solo show, the main character should be driven by the quest established at the beginning. It's important for you as the writer to track the protagonist's development as they face conflicts and obstacles throughout the play and convey how they are changed by them.

Here are some questions that may help you draw a line connecting your opening to the closing.

- What did the protagonist want?
- Why was this "thing" important to the character?

- What changed in the protagonist?
- What did the protagonist learn about themself?

A solo playwright needs to allow these changes and transformations to unfold by the end of their show. The resolution in a solo show can happen in a moment of realization, an act of courage or righteousness, or a decision that reflects the character's transformation. One way to do this is to use the Contemporary or Scenic Narrator who can offer insightful commentary and additional perspectives. As the writer, ensure that your main character has a shift, no matter how small, in their values, thoughts, words, deeds, or understanding.

For example, in the movie *It's a Wonderful Life*, the main character, George Bailey, feels stuck and unfulfilled in his small town and working at the family's bank. He dreams of excitement and working as an architect out in the world, but his financial problems become so difficult that he contemplates suicide. He believes his life is worthless and that others would be better off without him.

When an angel shows George what life would be like had he never been born, George realizes the true value of his life. This journey brings George from a place of hopelessness to acceptance and gratitude for the life he has. He understands his significance and his place in the world. At the end of the movie, we are left to think about the impact we can have on others and the importance of appreciating our own lives.

It's important to note that an "ah-ha" moment of insight or inspiration does not need to happen within the forward-moving action of the play. There doesn't need to be a flash of enlightenment in the last scene. The protagonist often comes to a gradual understanding years later of how they changed because of an experience, with narrative distance from the events. For some, this revelation happens through the act of writing the solo show itself.

When Arlene wrote her autobiographical play *What Does the Sun Sound Like*, her transformation didn't happen suddenly, within the events and temporal confines of the show. The play explores being a CODA (hearing child of Deaf adult) and growing up in a Deaf family and culture. The narrative revolves around her being the prodigal daughter, leaving her Deaf family and community to find where she fits in the hearing world, only to return home with the realization that she is a Deaf girl living in a hearing body. She was the bridge between the two worlds and living in both gave her gifts, languages, and a deep understanding of two cultures that only a few have. It took her years to fully understand and articulate this dual cultural identity and integrate that "ah-ha" into her life.

The Takeaway

The end of your solo show is your opportunity to craft a resolution that resonates with the audience emotionally, intellectually, and thematically. It should lead them to think about the universal truth of the show and invite investigation for deeper meanings within your play. The audience may or may not leave thinking about the theme you had in mind for your show, but your job is to be as clear as possible for yourself in terms of what you hope to convey.

Crafting the end of a play is like finishing a puzzle, where all the pieces fit together to form a clear image. A strong ending should cement the meaning of the play, providing the audience with a key to unlock the play's intended point. When it comes to leaving an impression, a short, powerful sentence can be incredibly effective. It can be a moral lesson, a realization, a thought-provoking question or idea, or a call to action.

Endings don't need to be (and shouldn't be!) telling the audience, "So, what I learned was . . ." or "How I'm different now is . . ." Giving a character lines of dialogue in conversation can show, rather than tell, how they have been transformed by the events of the play. Sometimes a strong ending doesn't involve words at all. An ending can be a gesture, image, or action that leaves the audience with an understanding that something has changed in the protagonist—a character finally walking through a door, or taking off a wig, or throwing a consequential object into a garbage can.

Julie's first solo show, *The Half-Life of Magic*, wrestled with issues of parenting, what we choose to tell our children, and facing the unknown. The last image of the play, the moment before the final blackout, is Julie in Rome, tentatively and breathlessly extending her hand into the ancient Mouth of Truth.

The 1961 and 2021 film adaptations of the musical *West Side Story* also offer examples of a suggestive ending. The 2021 version features culturally appropriate Puerto Rican actors. The film has a darker, more dangerous atmosphere as compared to the 1961 version. Both films end with the same chain of events: Tony is killed by a rival gang member in front of Maria while they are planning to escape together. The dialogue is the same in both films, but the final images differ, which may impact some viewers' interpretations.

In the 1961 version, after Tony's death, his gang picks him up, but only a few members of the rival gang join in to carry him. They struggle with the limp body that hangs awkwardly. The camera pulls up and away from an empty abandoned lot, suggesting a feeling of hopelessness. However, in the 2021 version, all members of both gangs lift Tony in a manner similar to that of a fallen soldier. The closing music is the same as in the 1961 version, but with subtle differences that affect the tone. In the 2021 version, the same expansive camera move occurs, but the vacant lot is viewed through the bars of the fire escape, the place where Tony and Maria first fell in love. This suggests a focus on love as the most essential element of the story.

One ending is not preferable over the other, but each of these small choices are purposefully crafted to affect the audience's emotions in a specific way and suggest different interpretations. Keep in mind that there isn't a universal formula for crafting a powerful ending for your solo show. Don't be afraid to experiment and discover what works best with your narrative.

We want to be clear that a satisfying ending is not necessarily a happy one, or one where everything gets fixed. Sometimes the protagonist comes to terms with a situation that cannot be resolved or changes their mind about what's important or what their goals are. Whether the ending is happy or not, it's important to circle back to the initial quest or conflict of your play and address it in some way.

TRY THIS!

Take five minutes and review the ending of your current manuscript. Consider what you want the audience to leave your play thinking about. Can you convey those ideas through a resonant scene, a callback, an image, or a dramatic line? There is no right or wrong way, only choices. Try three different endings.

EXPERT ADVICE

How do you help storytellers find an ending for a piece?

For me, an ending is all about how you want to leave your audience feeling, so the search for an ending is a heart search, asking yourself, "Does this feel right? Does this create the feeling that I want it to? What if I did this instead?" That's the litmus test I think is the most useful in terms of if an ending is "right."

In terms of tools or tactics, that can mean a lot of different things, depending on the piece of writing. I frequently point folks toward trying to end a piece in scene, i.e., landing it in space and time with characters, rather than telling the audience what a piece is about. On the other hand, 2nd Story just shared a story recently where the storyteller ended with a very clear "Here's why I told you this story" because the writer, when thinking about that "how do I want people to feel?" piece, really wanted the audience to leave with a charge around women's rights in the current political atmosphere.

I think it can be helpful to look for themes or words, something you've set up earlier that you can then land for the ending. If you've set up a question for yourself early in the story and then the last line actually answers that question, or you set up a question early in the story and the last line changes the question, or you realize in the last beat of the story that you were asking the wrong question. And an ending doesn't have to be puppies and rainbows. It can be a question, a gut punch, a devastation. A lot of times, people think, "Oh, an ending has to be happy. I have to *wrap this up* for the audience," and we've been socialized to think that feels a certain way. That it has to be positive. But that's not true. The question is more: "What is the close I want for this particular piece at this particular time?"

Amanda Delheimer

Artist. Advocate. Facilitator. Artistic Director of 2nd Story.

Something at Stake

Picture Andres. He went to a website and bought a ticket for your one-person play, turned off Grand Theft Auto, put on a clean shirt, and fought his way through congested traffic or the subway to get to the theater. He may not have been hungry when he left home, but he probably is now. This is a real theater, so the snacks consist of pricey gourmet cookies and tiny bags of gummy bears for $9, which he washes down with a $10 beer. He waits for his friend who is late, and they rush into the theater at the last moment, where he will sit on a somewhat uncomfortable chair for ninety minutes, no intermission. There's a mouth breather with terrible breath in the seat behind him. He begrudgingly turns off his phone as the house lights dim. How will you provide an experience for Andres that's worth everything he has gone through?

Hopefully, your piece will have a spellbinding, well-crafted text and a rehearsed, skilled performance. It will have a big idea or a compelling question for the audience to wrestle with, theatrical elements, and visual interest. In addition to all that, you'll fulfill your contract with the audience by making sure you have some "skin in the game." You'll take emotional risks and assume some vulnerability as you share your show, both in the writing and performance. You'll keep audiences engaged and caring about your story by making sure there is something at stake. What's at risk for the main character? Does it feel important?

Solo shows are written about life-changing moments—moments when characters are changed irrevocably, in large or small ways. These life changes are physical or material, or the character's view of the world changes forever. The events in a solo show don't need to be big and important in and of themselves, as long as they have a lasting impact on the protagonist. Sometimes the stakes will be life or death, and sometimes they'll just feel that way to the main character. If the audience understands that, the stakes will feel high to them, too. The key to raising the stakes in a solo show is ensuring that the audience fully understands the emotional journey and point of view of the main character.

In all our lives, seemingly small things can have a big impact, and those moments make great stories. If locking yourself out of your car leads you to a recognition of how similar you are to your mother and a greater acceptance of that fact, which you had been fighting for years, that small moment is a big deal. If it feels important to you, it can feel important to an audience as well.

We may not know or care at all about skateboarding, but if we understand that you were a clumsy kid sorely lacking in athletic ability, and being able to skateboard was crucial to fitting in with the kids in seventh grade, we'll care. And if we understand that your parents had just moved you across the country and this was a brand-new school and you were terribly lonely and desperate to fit in, we'll really care about whether you can skateboard or not because the stakes will feel even higher.

High stakes aren't just about serious drama, though. High stakes add levity to our stories as well. *Seinfeld* built nine seasons of comedy television around ramping up the importance of relatable, banal moments (finding a parking spot, personal slights, losing a sweater) to a level that was almost—but not quite—ridiculous, with hilarious results. We cared because we believed the characters cared.

Vulnerability is an important way to ensure that the stakes feel high enough in a piece and the audience cares about what's going on. Does it cost the main character something to tell this story? Does the storyteller or soloist really let us in?

You may be asking, "But *how*? How do I *do* that?"

In the writing phase, embrace vulnerability by telling the truth—the uncomfortable, sometimes ugly truth, which can be hard if your piece is a first-person narrative. It can be hard to resist the temptation to make yourself look like the hero at every moment of your play. If necessary, be willing to "look bad" in front of an audience and admit your flaws. Take responsibility for the things you did in the story, even if you have a different view now.

As a performer, whether you're playing yourself or another character, vulnerability means letting your guard down and staying in the moment. It means mustering the energy to go back and "re-experience" tough moments in the story with the audience, even if it feels exhausting to do that on a particular night, instead of just reporting or telling about them from a distance. That's what good performers do. It's hard at first, but it gets easier with practice. And it's worth it because it pays off in a much better show.

The example below is an excellent demonstration of vulnerability in writing. When we saw this actor perform the piece, she brought another layer of unguarded honesty to her performance as well. Notice how the soloist puts us into the scene with her, in all its uncomfortable reality.

> It was halfway through the meal when one of the tall silent waiters appeared at my elbow and tapped me lightly on the shoulder. He carried a highly burnished silver tray and on it was a small, folded piece of pink paper.
>
> "For you, mademoiselle," he said softly. Immediately, all conversation at our table stopped. For a confused moment, I thought he was giving me the bill.
>
> "What is this?" I asked.
>
> "It is from the gentleman over there," he said, gesturing to a bearded man seated behind me who I could only vaguely see in the mirror.
>
> I stared at the paper as if it would bite me, until my mother said,
>
> "Well read it."
>
> Silently, I read, "How do you do. I wish I could say that I knew you, but since I don't, I would very much like to meet you." It was signed—oh I'll never forget this—Peter Livingston. I keep the note still, fifty years later, pressed into the travel diary I kept of that trip.

> I was, at age fifteen, completely unequal to the task of making any response. The adults all laughed and prodded me to reveal the contents, but I folded the note and put it into my purse.
>
> It was as if the mask of homeliness that covered my once perfectly acceptable face had been pulled off at last. If a complete stranger thought I was pretty enough that he would make such a bold move, then maybe I was an attractive girl after all.
>
> **—Stephanie M.**

To be clear, we never encourage a soloist to write about or perform events from their life before they are emotionally ready to do so. It's important to approach any difficult experience from a place of healing and growth rather than focusing solely on the pain and suffering. There are subjects you may never feel comfortable writing about or sharing with an audience, and that's fine. Also, we're not suggesting that a vulnerable performance consists of weeping or raging or doing something humiliating or any of the things that make an audience feel vaguely unsafe.

Write and tell the story that only you can tell, without flinching, and make sure the audience understands what's at stake. This is one of the ways to create a solo piece that folks connect with and care about.

EXPERT ADVICE

How do you go about raising the stakes of a story and making sure an audience cares?

While working on my show, because it was about my life, there were moments of my feeling "This is not a story, this is not a show, this is not . . . whatever." And then my director would reflect back to me what she heard, what she felt, and why she thought it was important. She would ask questions, and I would get more and more specific, and dig deeper, and share more. And the more specific I got, the more it affected me, and the more I, as the character in the show, changed in the piece. And that raised the stakes.

Penelope Walker
Actor, Solo Creator & Performer, Director

Essential Questions

Another way to approach developing an arc or raising the stakes in your work is by identifying an essential question. This might be an open-ended question your protagonist is wrestling with throughout your play or a question your show raises and leaves the audience pondering. A useful tool in so many ways, an essential question can also help you focus your theme and make it more active.

Let's say, for example, that you already know your solo show is going to be about the time you moved back to your hometown of Mount Dora, Florida, and opened a doomed snowmobile dealership with your lay-about sister. You've got the characters, events, and a setting—a strong who, what, and where. The absolute absence of snow in central Florida provides a strong obstacle. It's lining up to be an intriguing story.

At some point, however, you'll need to ask yourself, "But what is it *about?*" Or, if you have writer friends, they might ask, "But what is it *really about*?" What is the broader, more universal theme your show is exploring? What's the big idea you're poking at?

Your answer may be "It's about failure" or "It's about family" or "It's about dashed dreams." Your play may actually be about all of those things. But notice how definitive and settled those statements sound, like you've already got it all figured out. Do we really want to see a show about how you've already got it all figured out?

Questions, on the other hand, leave some breathing room. They beget exploration. Notice how these questions feel a bit more dynamic and alive: What is success? What does it mean to go home? When is an impossible dream still worth dreaming? How culpable am I? Is anyone? How do humans pick up and go on?

Questions will keep you curious, seeking, and trying to figure things out. And that will keep an audience interested. If you feel like you already have a theme in statement form, what questions are you asking around that theme in your show? What is the Big Question you are trying to answer? If you can distill the theme of your show into one essential question, you will have a spine for your show.

And yes, sometimes a show has more than one essential question. You may have a handful of questions you're wrestling with, though you might find over time that one of those questions will come forward as the most important.

Essential questions propel your story and serve as a unifying idea. It's also important to note that your show may not end up definitively answering your essential question, but your protagonist should gain some sort of clarity and resolution regarding it. Your solo play may not have an answer to the question "What is success?" But the main character will have a deeper understanding of their own idea of success.

Folks frequently ask Julie, "When are you going to write another solo show?" Her answer is always "When I have something that's keeping me up at night." For Julie, the essential question is what she is trying to figure out. It's the "Why am I writing this?" In some ways, it's not only what she's grappling with, but what she wants the audience to be thinking about and examining too.

When Julie was writing her solo play *Good Enough*, she was well into the process before she realized that her essential question was "What does it mean to be a good person?" Her show didn't have a title at that point either—the title came after the discovery of the essential question. Obviously, there isn't an answer we can all agree on to the question "What does it mean to be a good person?" and the question may not even be interesting to some people. But it was interesting to Julie, and even though it was never spoken aloud in her play, it served as her North Star.

On the other hand, the essential question for a different play of Julie's was "What's the difference between religion and magic?"

This question *can* be answered through a simple process of looking up some definitions. However, ultimately, the show was investigating something a bit less literal, with subthemes around parenting and honesty. Julie's essential question was never explicitly named or referred to in the play, but it helped her keep her focus on what the play was about.

Of course, the audience will take away various things from your show based on their individual life experiences, priorities, and how they see the world. That's great, actually. However, it's crucial for you as a playwright to be clear in conveying your intention. When you know the main question your show addresses, you can build in images, foreshadowing, and clues that support the story you are telling.

When Arlene wrote her solo show *Aiming for Sainthood*, which focused on her mother's cancer and recovery, she initially thought the essential question was "How do you transform the grief associated with loss?" After completing the first draft, however, she realized the play answered the essential question "Where is God?" Arlene, being an intuitive writer, allowed the play to guide her toward its true focus. She then revisited the work, incorporating specific vocabulary, religious iconography, dialogue, and stories that better served this essential question. It also led her to the show's title.

Here are a few other examples:

Jane Wagner's solo show *The Search for Signs of Intelligent Life in the Universe*: What does it mean to be truly human?

Mike Daisey's solo show *The Agony and the Ecstasy of Steve Jobs*: What is the cost of our technological devotion—and who pays it?

Suzie Miller's solo play *Prima Facie*: What happens when the law is built to protect power, not people?

Give yourself the gift of an essential question. It can serve as a guiding light when you're in the editing phase of your process and help clarify what does and doesn't need to be in your play. Anything that doesn't lead back to your essential question should be cut. Sometimes your essential question can even give you compelling copy for your marketing materials if that's the direction you want to go.

TRY THIS!

Essential Question Octopus: Write what you think is your essential question in the center of a page as the body of an octopus. Then draw tentacles reaching out from it—each tentacle representing a related subquestion or idea connected to the main question. For example, if your essential question is *What does it mean to be successful?*, your tentacles might ask: *Is success measured by others or by ourselves? Can failure be part of success? How does the meaning of success change over time?* Write down as many questions as you can come up with, understanding that these questions may change.

Your Work Is Going to Suck (for a Little While)

Someone asks, "How did it go today?"

You gaze into the distance and reply, "What, the writing? It's going well."

You smile knowingly to yourself. "Yeah, it's going really well."

"Tell me more," they say.

You absentmindedly pull a hair off your sleeve. "I wrote the perfect transition into the next scene," you say, but you don't want to sound too braggy. You continue, "And it just came pouring out of me. I mean, this might be my best work yet! Maybe ever!" You can't stop gushing and in the back of your mind, you think, "Yep, I was right all along. I am a really good writer."

Two days later you sit down, excited to dive back in. As you skim through the pages, your heart sinks. Wait. What? This is awful. But . . . but . . . just the other day, it was flawless. Now, the writing feels clunky, chunky, and incoherent. You knew it! You're not a writer. You're a fraud, and this solo piece is going to suck.

Our advice? Don't panic. Pause, take a breath, and say to yourself, "This is just the first draft. That's all. It's just a place to start."

All writers have bad first drafts. Even famous ones! Anne Lamott calls her first attempt a "shitty first draft." And Ray Bradbury just "blurted" his drafts out. The whole point of a rough draft is that it lets you get your raw ideas out. Even in the horrible messiness, you'll create valuable material to work on and refine later. The process of writing a first draft will lead you to find unexpected connections and happy accidents in the work.

The bottom line is that a first draft is like a first kiss. You're not sure what you're doing. Sometimes your aim is off. You may bumble and stumble through it, and it's always sloppy and messy. However, first drafts are the most important work you'll do because they allow you to start the creative process.

And please, when writing a first draft, don't get sidetracked with editing. Not yet. Creating and editing are two very different operations that are best approached separately. Gently but firmly banish both your editor and inner critic, assuring them that they will have their moment—just not right now. Fixating on the quality of the writing too early in the process can mess with your creativity, and that's the last thing you want when you're trying to generate material.

Later, when reading back through a first draft, focus on what works. Scenes that hum. Characters that are interesting. Places where you surprise yourself. This is the beginning of your show. Remind yourself, "Hey, (*insert your name here*), you did the hardest part; you wrote something, and that counts for everything."

People Your Play

Building Characters

Developing the characters that populate your play is absolutely critical to writing an effective solo show. Characters drive a story, and if a main character can't hold the audience's attention throughout an entire play as they pursue their quest, the play will fall flat.

Effective characters need to feel authentic whether the genre is sci-fi, horror, drama, comedy, or superhero. Whether the story takes place in a medieval castle, Tiffany's, the Midwest, or on the moon, the protagonist needs to ring true within the world of the play.

Characters feel believable when we can identify and connect with some aspect of their humanity. Even when they are very different from us, we should be able to connect with the character on a human level. In John Leguizamo's *Freak*, even if you are not male or Colombian, even if you don't come from a loud, contentious, broken family, anyone can relate to a character who is searching for identity, family, and a way to express himself in the world. Even Batman, a fictional character who wears a cape, employs a butler named Alfred, and works out of a batcave, somehow feels relatable—perhaps because Batman spent years overcoming his grief and childhood pain and because we can empathize with his vulnerability.

Specificity Is important

It has been said that the more specific something is, the more universal it feels. This concept applies when creating a character for the stage. The more detailed, unique, and particular a character is, the more truly human they will feel to an audience. You can give specificity to them through physical details, personality traits, the language they use, their actions or reactions, or their inner thoughts. You get to decide what's important for your audience to know.

In her solo show *Aiming for Sainthood*, Arlene describes her father in this way:

> My father is the George Clooney of the Deaf world, and his Deaf voice sounds like a foghorn echoing off still waters. It's a voice that he hides away because the hearing world has convinced him that it was hideous, but when he signs, his hands paint masterpieces.

Because Arlene's father is a major character, and she believed that it was important for the audience to understand the cultural context, she combined several of the options above to create this description.

Here are some examples of how our students have described characters in their work:

> If Mary Poppins and Santa Claus had a love child, and who's to say they didn't, that was Aunt Mary.
>
> **—Jackie M.**

> One might expect she would make snide remarks, but Mary C. is not that kind of girl. She's pretty with wide cheekbones and dimples. Her hair is brown like mine but not in sausage curls—in a neat ponytail. She's better than I am at math, certainly, and is usually named if a smart girl is needed for some demonstration by the student teachers. She lives on a successful dairy farm, which makes her different from us town children.
>
> **—Joyce H.**

> During my goth period, I was extremely averse to being labeled or categorized, yet I spent most of my time mentally sorting adults into crude binary categories: hip or square, amazing or pathetic, young or old, nice or mean.
>
> **—Angel D.**

Characters Should Be Multidimensional

Characters are people, and people are complex. Humans are full of contradictions, complicated emotions, flaws, and aspirations, and our characters should be too. Take the protagonist in Phoebe Waller-Bridge's *Fleabag*. She's sarcastic, snarky, emotionally detached, and self-destructive. Yet, in her moments of sorrow, we see a sensitive, vulnerable woman who longs for connection and redemption. This reflects the dichotomy of a character who appears to be callous and unfeeling but is also compassionate and has a great well of emotion. In both the play and the series, the main character frequently breaks the fourth wall to provide exposition, internal monologues, and a running commentary on events, giving us a clear picture of her emotions. (*Fleabag* began as a solo show at the Edinburgh Fringe, became a British TV series, and won Emmys, Golden Globes, and BAFTAs. So start writing!)

No person is one-dimensional. A person who volunteers every weekend might also ignore their family's needs. Someone might be kind to strangers but ruthless in business. That's because people carry the capacity to be both selfish and generous, often within the same day—or the same scene. These opposing instincts exist side by side in real life, and when they show up in our writing, they give characters complexity. They make characters resonate, not just because they feel real, but because they are a reflection of the messy nature of being human.

If you're writing an autobiographical piece, you may find it difficult to portray your weaknesses and mistakes, because as humans we always want to lead with our best. No one wants to think of themself as a villain. It takes courage to tell the truth about ourselves onstage, and it can leave us feeling very vulnerable.

One idea that was helpful to us when we were writing our first autobiographical shows was to understand that every character is a hero in their own story. Almost every character can justify their actions and do what they think is best in that moment, and that's true of you, too, even when you've made mistakes. This is an important lens through which to understand human behavior, character development, and the complexities of moral decisions. Even when a choice may seem objectively wrong or harmful, in the character's or narrator's mind, it can be justified considering their circumstances, quests, needs, or desires.

We worked with a solo artist who was writing about assuming the role of the responsible child for a father who was dying. The writer upended his life, moving from cosmopolitan France back to his small farming community, and learned the mundane duties and worries of being a caregiver. It was a compelling story; however, the son's portrayal in the play depicted him as a saint, making the character feel flat and one-dimensional. So we asked him, "When were you not the perfect son?" He hemmed and hawed and sputtered. Then we lovingly encouraged him to explore the question, with no requirement to put it onstage.

The following week, he didn't come to class, making us wonder if we had driven him away. As it turned out, he was just sick. We were never so happy that a student was under the weather. When he returned, he revealed that at times he'd wished his father would hurry up and die so he could get back to his life. He shared how hard it was to admit it to himself and say it out loud.

Boom. This one sentence cracked the entire play open. The empathy coming from the class was palpable. As the performance got closer, he was concerned about how people would see him. We encouraged him to trust his story, himself, and his audience. We also reinforced that if he wasn't happy with those lines in the show, he could always take them out after opening. However, following every show, people hugged him and shared that they too had felt anger and impatience in caregiving situations. He was embraced for sharing his tangled emotions about a difficult moment.

Creating complex characters is equally important when writing fictional characters or a biographical solo show. For years, Mother Teresa was known as a saint-like figure devoted to caring for the poorest in India and was often portrayed in a one-dimensional way. After her personal diaries were published, it became clear she experienced years of spiritual crisis yet remained devoted to her faith and work. The diaries also revealed her belief that enduring physical pain could bring people closer to God, and that she may have allowed people to suffer unnecessarily. All of this information adds complexity to her legacy, and its inclusion in a solo show about her would make it even more interesting.

Most people have a way they like to show up in the world and be perceived, and a way their flaws are exhibited when they're under pressure. People have large or small secrets that they're not proud of, which emerge in tough situations and events. Give your audience characters that reveal themselves over the course of your play, the same way humans reveal themselves as you get to know them. Your play has a plot, and the conflict will allow your protagonist to be seen as both their best and worst self.

How to Reveal Character

There are many ways that an audience can learn about a character. Characters can be revealed by their actions—for example, *He held the baby as if it were a lost treasure.* They can also be revealed in what they say about themselves, such as, *I've always dreamed of loving a child in this way.* Additionally, characters come to life through what others say about them, like, *He is happiest when he is holding that baby.* How do you reveal character through action? Let us see how their emotions, opinions, and attitudes show up through their behavior—for instance, *He threw the PlayStation on the ground and stomped away.*

We've found that audiences respond to characters who are employing agency and making active choices. The play itself will be so much more interesting if, instead of reacting to everything that comes their way, your character also makes decisions based on their quest, strengths, their history, and, most importantly, their weaknesses.

By the way, not all the characters in your play need to be multidimensional or have a character arc. Some characters may simply serve the function of providing information or moving the story forward. They are the proverbial "spear carriers," and giving them too much depth can distract us from where we should be placing out attention.

The Proust Questionnaire

We like using this tool to develop complex characters. This questionnaire originated from a parlor game in the Victorian era, in which guests filled out little booklets with preprinted questions. (We like to think about it as an antique version of a slam book. Remember those?) Many famous people from the era filled these out, most notably Marcel Proust, author of the novel *Remembrance of Things Past*, which is launched with a memory of a madeleine, and ends 1,267,069 words later.

We love how this questionnaire can invite a writer to think outside of the box! We've found it can inform material that's already written or act as a springboard to create new material. A small element can sometimes add a great deal of depth to a character. Other times, the answers may provide a multisensory or specific detail to include in the play. You can answer the questions for yourself or answer them for your characters. While there are many versions of this questionnaire, here is the one that Proust originally answered in 1890:

1. What is your idea of perfect happiness?
2. What is your greatest fear?
3. What is the trait you most deplore in yourself?
4. What is the trait you most deplore in others?
5. Which living person do you most admire?
6. What is your greatest extravagance?
7. What is your current state of mind?
8. What do you consider the most overrated virtue?
9. On what occasion do you lie?
10. What do you most dislike about your appearance?
11. Which living person do you most despise?
12. What is the quality you most like in a man?
13. What is the quality you most like in a woman?
14. Which words or phrases do you most overuse?
15. What or who is the greatest love of your life?
16. When and where were you happiest?
17. Which talent would you most like to have?
18. If you could change one thing about yourself, what would it be?

19. What do you consider your greatest achievement?
20. If you were to die and come back as a person or a thing, what would it be?
21. Where would you most like to live?
22. What is your most treasured possession?
23. What do you regard as the lowest depth of misery?
24. What is your favorite occupation?
25. What is your most marked characteristic?
26. What do you most value in your friends?
27. Who are your favorite writers?
28. Who is your hero of fiction?
29. Which historical figure do you most identify with?
30. Who are your heroes in real life?
31. What are your favorite names?
32. What is it that you most dislike?
33. What is your greatest regret?
34. How would you like to die?
35. What is your motto?

TRY THIS!

Here's a simple exercise we often use in our classes: First, identify four traits your main character reveals through the text. Then, open up a thesaurus and find antonyms for each of those traits. Now, ask yourself—does your play also express these opposite qualities in your character? If not, your character might feel one-note, and it's time to take another look.

Types of Narrators

If your solo show uses the device of the actor breaking the fourth wall and speaking in their own voice directly to the audience about events, your show is probably in the form we would call a narrative one-person show. This is how we share stories in our daily lives, and the basic concept is "Let me tell you about . . ." Many types of solo shows have some element of narration, meaning that the audience will receive certain information through a narrator. That narrator may be you if the show is autobiographical, or a different character if it is not.

We distinguish between two types of narrators in solo work—the Contemporary Narrator and the Scenic Narrator. We first encountered these concepts through the wonderful director and storyteller Mark Travis, author of *The Director's Journey*. Understanding the function each of these narrators serves in our storytelling gives us a tool that we can use to make our work even better.

Both the Contemporary Narrator and the Scenic Narrator are your protagonist. They are both you, if your show is autobiographical. The difference is in what the narrator knows and at what point in time the narrator is speaking.

Contemporary Narrator

When the Contemporary Narrator tells the story or gives information to the audience, they are speaking with everything they knew in the past as well as what they understand about the story now. They speak from a POV that knows what is going to happen. Addressing the audience as the Contemporary Narrator allows us to break out of a scene and share insights about what is taking place, craft intimate or humorous asides, and create moments of reflection. This type of narration almost always breaks the fourth wall and is a direct address to the audience.

Here is an example of the Contemporary Narrator from the solo play *Good Enough*:

> I know now that I could have put my hand out and pushed him away. I could have said, "Don't kiss me" or "I'm not interested." I wasn't an unconfident kid. But I didn't want to embarrass him. I knew that if you possibly could, the good thing was to put other people at ease. If I had any other tools in that moment, no one had shown me how to use them. When we got off the ride, without saying anything, I gave him the slip near the funnel cakes, walked across the highway to the Kmart, and called my mom to come get me.

Here is an example of the Contemporary Narrator from Lynnette Li's lovely piece *Mangoes*:

> Something I didn't fully realize back then is how my mom has a different energy, a fresh life source, every time she is with any of her three sisters. I only witnessed it every few years when we spent precious time with our extended family. A deeper breath, a laugh in her eyes, a bubbling in her voice. They signal that my mom feels at home, that she belongs. I think that's what made that trip so special.

Scenic Narrator

The Scenic Narrator is you (or the main character of your piece) talking to the audience from a different point in time. This type of narrator breaks the fourth wall and tells the story from within the scene, using only the knowledge and point of view they have in that moment.

There are points in a solo play when we need to give the audience context and exposition while we are in the middle of dialogue or action, and using the Scenic Narrator will allow us to stay right there, where it's happening. When you're the Scenic Narrator, you don't know what's going to happen next any more than the audience does. You're moving through the scene with them.

Here's an example from Arlene's show *What Does the Sun Sound Like*. The excerpt is from the POV of Arlene as a preteen and her beliefs about her teacher at that time. She speaks with a child's voice and language. It is a direct address to the audience:

> This is my teacher Sister Mary Concepta and she's the meanest nun in the whole school. I think she looks like one of those raptors from Jurassic Park, only with a habit on. She's about a hundred and ten years old and has been dying of cancer for decades. But everyone says that she's going to live forever because she's so mean not even God wants her. Sister Mary Concepta is one of those nuns whose beady little eyes roam the classroom all day for another victim, someone too fat, too stupid, too ugly, too poor, too different, or too weak, and then she breaks them. All in the name of the good Lord, of course. It's Catholic School Darwinism at its best.

And here is another example of the Scenic Narrator from Lynnette Li's *Mangoes*. Notice how, though the scene stops while she addresses the audience, she does so from within the limitations of the scene's time and place:

> My dad said, "I was on jury duty once with that judge who presided over Vincent Chin's murder trial. He called me up to the bench after court one day, and I thought, oh no, what's this guy going to say?"
>
> I waited for him to finish.
>
> "He said he was going to take a trip to China, and he wanted to know where to eat." He chuckled.
>
> This was not the rallying cry I craved. Why weren't they mad too? Where was their rage? Why didn't we ever talk

> about any of these things that happened to us? How could I have possibly come from these parents?

Many narrative one-person shows use both the Contemporary Narrator and the Scenic Narrator. Having this mix of moments when we hear from the all-knowing Contemporary Narrator and moments when the Scenic Narrator is speaking contributes to a rich experience for the audience. We can use the Scenic Narrator to hear about events close up—from the point of view of a character at the time the events took place. At other moments, we can use the Contemporary Narrator, who will have some narrative distance and a different perspective on events.

TRY THIS!

Choose a key scene or monologue where you are currently using one type of narrator. Rewrite that section from the other narrator's point of view. For example, if it's currently written as the Contemporary Narrator reflecting back, rewrite it as Scenic Narrator living inside the moment, or vice versa. Perform or read both versions out loud. How does changing the narrator's perspective shift the stakes, intimacy, or tone of the scene?

EXPERT ADVICE

Narrators allow for real connection and conversation with the audience. And that really creates a lean in. Breaking out as a narrator allows you to be fully emotionally present in the moment of your story, but then set it down for a moment and let the audience know that you, the actor, are OK. If the audience is worried for your character, that's good—they're completely involved in the show. But if they're wondering if you as an actor are OK, they can't watch your show fully because their nervous system is too activated. I want the audience to be able to just be in the story with me, so they have to know I'm OK. Narrators are an easy way to do that, I think.

Khanisha Foster
Director, Writer, Performer

Dialogue: Finding the Voice of Your Characters

If you think about it, except for the stage directions, every line in a solo show is dialogue. Dialogue is the exchange of spoken words between two or more characters. It's a tool that propels the narrative, gives insight into characters and their relationships with each other, and creates mood, conflict, and tension. And yes, everything the narrator says to the audience is dialogue, too.

In some solo plays, the narrator speaks to the audience like they are confidants, while in others, the narrator treats the audience as a character in the play. In *Late Night Catechism* by Vicki Quade and Maripat Donovan, the main character, a nun, treats the performance like a catechism class and speaks to the audience as if they are students. In *Every Brilliant Thing* by Duncan Macmillan with Jonny Donahoe, the relationship with the audience is that of a trusted friend. The audience participates in the play, interacting with the main character in a way that deepens their connection to the story. As the creator of your show, you have the opportunity to determine what kind of relationship you want to have with the audience and write accordingly.

Some writer-performers may use conversational speech, while others adopt more formal or period language. For instance, one of our students created a solo show about L. Frank Baum, the author of *The Wonderful Wizard of Oz*. This student crafted the show's language and vocabulary to mirror Baum's style from the late 1800s. In Joan

Didion's *The Year of Magical Thinking*, based on her book of the same name, the language is contemporary but literary, as Didion was a celebrated writer. In Diana Suarez Mucci's autobiographical solo show about race, *Spit*, there are two narrators that break the fourth wall. One is a sixteen-year-old from the late 1980s, complete with Madonna references, and the other is her older self, using vernacular and references appropriate to an adult in 2020.

Creating Authentic Dialogue

In our classes, many new writers find they are creating characters that all sound the same, which is simply not realistic. Differentiating speech for our characters, making sure that each one has their own distinct voice, takes work. This includes paying attention to speech patterns, wordplay, rhythm, cadence, word choice, style, and attitude.

Authenticity begins with you, the writer, knowing your characters. Understanding their background, age, education, quirks, and a dozen other qualifiers that will influence their language. A short-order cook and a college professor may have different vocabularies—their phrases and idioms will reflect their daily experiences. A thirty-year-old soccer mom from middle-class suburban America probably won't speak like a seventy-year-old retired prime minister from Britain.

Spend some time listening to the people you work with, friends, and relatives. Notice how their speech differentiates them from each other. Think about how each would refer to a male colleague that they worked with: one might say, "There was a guy I worked with," another, "There was a man that I worked with," or, "There was this dude that I worked with." Some might say, "There was like, this guy that I, you know, worked with," and in the case of Arlene's mother-in-law, "There was a fella I worked with." As you can see, each one of these phrases says something different about its speaker. Judy Blume, the author of one of our favorite books, *Are You There God? It's Me, Margaret*, said, "Nothing teaches you as much about writing dialogue as listening to it."

Below are some specific aspects of speech to consider when writing dialogue.

Sentence Structure

People speak in different sentence lengths. For example, young kids generally speak in short, simple sentences or long run-on sentences that may seem like a stream of consciousness, while many adults speak in complex compound sentences.

In a YouTube interview with Amplified 2021, the playwright/lyricist/composer Lin-Manuel Miranda spoke about developing sentence structures when he was writing lyrics for different characters in the musical *Hamilton*. He said that because Alexander Hamilton was an eloquent and verbose character, he wanted to write him "at least a four-syllable rhyme every time." Meanwhile, understanding that the George Washington character was the commander-in-chief of the Continental Army, he wrote lines and lyrics that were short, regimented, and military sounding.

Vocabulary, Word Choice, and Dialect

These factors can reveal gender, class, status, education level, geography, and age. One of our longtime students is a writer in his mid-seventies, a Vietnam veteran from a blue-collar family. He uses phrases like "Don't mind me—I'm just being a knucklehead" or "That guy is a wisenheimer." He calls his father "my old man" and the TV "the idiot box." A favorite friend who is a preschool teacher says, "Oh my goodness," while her sister throws f-bombs in the same situation. Each one of these examples demonstrates how vocabulary plays an important role in defining who a character is for an audience. People in the Midwest tend to use the term "pop," while those in the Northeast and West often say "soda." In Philly you'll eat a "hoagie." In Jersey you'll have a "sub." In the US, the sport is known as "soccer." In most other parts of the world, it's called "football."

Idiosyncratic Speech

Incorporating personal speech traits helps create realistic and distinct characters. Maybe one of your characters uses "upspeak," with its rising inflection at the end of a declarative sentence, which makes everything sound like a question? "Zuck talk" uses informal speech when more polish is expected and features the frequent use of "right?," which assumes agreement. (It was fantastically defined by John Hermann in *The New York Times* as a "linguistic hoodie in a metaphorical boardroom.") A mother-in-law might use the phrase "Now wait a minute" to ask a question, interrupt a conversation, gather her thoughts, or when she is talking to herself out loud. (You know who you are.) Some of us pepper our speech with "interstitials" such as "ummm," "like," "literally," "you know," or "I mean," especially when what we're saying does not have a purpose.

Authentic language is chaotic, full of fits and starts. Christopher Guest, the screenwriter of the classic mockumentaries *This Is Spinal Tap* and *Waiting for Guffman*, says in a 2004 interview with *The Guardian* that real people do not talk in written speech. "In real life, people fumble their words. They repeat themselves and stare blankly off into space and don't listen properly to what other people are saying." So, like, you know, you don't have to feel like you have to write in full sentences, or, you know, grammatically correct language. (See what we did there?)

Remember that a character's dialogue can change depending on the circumstances—their mood, their emotional state, and the person they are speaking to. A person may use different vocabulary when they are chatting with their friends at the corner bar than when they are speaking to a judge in a courtroom after they've been arrested for disorderly conduct at said bar.

Good dialogue isn't just about words; it can be about the spaces between them. We know many playwrights who include the word "silence" or "beat" or use punctuation like an . . . ellipsis . . . or a slash to indicate a break in speech. These can help underline the emotional weight of the story.

Here are our top tips for writing great dialogue:

1. Read your dialogue out loud. This will help you pinpoint any awkward or stilted phrasing.
2. Ask someone else to read it and simply circle the lines that feel inauthentic.
3. Set up a reading. Nothing will give you better information than to hear the work coming out of someone else's mouth. (Arlene loves this method. Once she gets over her cringing, she rewrites the dialogue.)
4. Edit. Edit. Edit. Avoid repetition and take out unnecessary words or phrases. Make sure the dialogue pushes the journey of events or the journey of emotions forward.
5. Listen and learn. If you want to be inspired, read or watch plays and films that are known for great dialogue. Some examples of notable plays include *Sweat* by Lynn Nottage, *Angels in America* by Tony Kushner, *Who's Afraid of Virginia Woolf?* by Edward Albee, and *Hamilton*, written by Lin-Manuel Miranda. As for films (noting here that the writers are credited rather than the directors), consider *Everything Everywhere All at Once* by Daniel Kwan and Daniel Scheinert, *Goodfellas* by Nicholas Pileggi and Martin Scorsese, *Glengarry Glen Ross* by David Mamet, and *Lady Bird* by Greta Gerwig.
6. Listen and learn some more. If you ever want to hear bad dialogue, watch Tommy Wiseau's cult film *The Room*. It's widely accepted to be one of those films that falls into the category of "It's so good because it's so bad." The dialogue and conversations are stilted, unnatural, repetitive, confusing, and full of non sequiturs.

TRY THIS!

1. Choose a stage play you like. Select a dialogue exchange between two characters and transcribe it. Why transcribe? Handwriting engages more brain regions—motor, visual, sensory, and memory areas—than typing, leading to deeper attention. The writer Thomas Ganey calls this "manuception." (Yes, he invented this word.)

   Analyze why this dialogue exchange works so well. Examine how the word choices and sentence structure reveal character traits or advance the story. Then, for fun, rewrite the dialogue from a different character's perspective.
2. Take a scene from your script and remove half the lines of dialogue. Replace those cut lines with silence—beats, gestures, or nonverbal action. What is still communicated? What becomes more powerful? What absolutely *has* to be said in words? Now go back and reinsert only the lines that feel essential. You may discover your characters say more when they say less.

Make a Scene!

In the last chapter, we talked about creating authentic dialogue. Now, let's look at how to put narration, exposition, and dialogue together to build scenes.

The storytelling company 2nd Story defines a scene as "characters in a place, with dialogue or action, unfolding in real time."

Let's break it down.

Characters in a place refers to specific people in a specific environment that is not the stage you are standing on—in a car, on a soccer field, in a doctor's office, at a café in Prague, or at the fryer behind the counter at McDonald's.

With dialogue means, of course, words being spoken by a character, such as "Go catch the ice cream truck before it rounds the corner" or "You can't handle the truth!" or "May I tickle your dog's tummy?"

Action can refer to what characters are doing onstage even if there is no dialogue. For instance, there might be an entire scene in which two characters use only actions and gestures to have an argument over where to place a chair. A scene may involve just one character, such as a person deciding whether to open a door or not. If there is meaningful action involved—movement toward and away from the door, the use of pantomimed or actual objects, expressive gesture—those actions constitute a one-person scene.

Unfolding in real time means that we experience the scene at the pace it would actually happen—no summary, no fast-forward. (Of course, we take many liberties in our writing and can feel free to cut and add words and actions. We may even jump ahead by saying, as narrator, "Two uncomfortable minutes passed this way.")

Generally, if a moment is significant enough to write into a scene, something is at stake, meaning that there is some import to the dialogue or action. That doesn't always mean life-and-death decisions or transformation. Sometimes what's at stake is subtle: a held-back truth, a shift in power, a glimpse of longing. Stakes create tension. They give the moment shape. Something is revealed—about a character's values, fears, hopes—even if they aren't fully changed by it yet.

Try reading aloud each of the following examples from Julie's play *Good Enough*. These are two different treatments of the same event—one told through simple narration, where the character breaks the fourth wall and speaks directly to the audience; the other in scene, with dialogue between two characters and a little narration woven in.

Simple Narration, Not in Scene:

> We are waiting to pick up our daughters when Sandy asks suspiciously if I give Gerald money every time I come through the intersection. I explain that no, sometimes I give him food or something else.
>
> She doesn't say much. I fill the awkward silence explaining that I know Gerald well enough that I know what his kids look like. Sandy is incredulous and confused, so I haltingly explain that one day, he had handed me an envelope of pictures he said he wanted me to see. And there was Gerald in one of those tall chef's hats. Another photo of younger Gerald, in a red sweater, looking like any other tourist or student. Pictures of his three kids back in India, on his mother's lap. I tell Sandy that the pictures seemed precious—and that I

made a special trip out later the same day to get them back to him.

Sandy thought that was weird, and when I argued that it wasn't like I was giving Gerald $50 or something, she ends the conversation by looking out the window and surmising that the congestion might not be so bad at the intersection if Gerald wasn't standing in the middle of the street.

In Scene with Dialogue (and a little narration too):

Sandy and I are in her Range Rover waiting for our girls.

"Do you give that guy money every time you come by here?"

"No . . . Sometimes I give him food or something."

"Huh," she says.

"I mean, I know him. I've seen what his kids look like."

[*Turning to me*] "I'm sorry—what?"

"Well . . . One day, he handed me this envelope of pictures he said he wanted me to see."

[*To the audience*] And he had. A photo of Gerald wearing one of those tall chef's hats, in front of a fancy table piled high with shrimp. A younger Gerald, in a red sweater, looking like any other tourist or student on one of the Chicago River bridges downtown. And there were pictures of his three beautiful kids back in India, on his mother's lap. I thought the pictures seemed too precious; I made a special trip out later the same day to get them back to him

"Wow. That's weird, Julie. He's a guy begging for money."

"It's not weird. It's not like I'm giving him $50."

[*Looking out the passenger window*] "Well, the congestion might not be so bad at that intersection if he wasn't standing in the middle of the street."

Notice how much closer and involved in the action we feel as we read the scene, as opposed to the descriptive narration. There's no need to describe *how* something is said, because it will be conveyed through the performer's delivery. We'll get a sense of how the various characters speak—clipped or laconically, high-pitched or guttural, with a dialect or not—and get a sense of how the characters might hold themselves physically, through the performer's characterization. The audience will have a visceral sense of who the characters are by the time the scene is over. Dialogue and scenes are one way to show instead of tell.

Also notice in the second example above that the section describing Gerald's photos is a break, or a time-out, from the scene. Those lines are a direct address to the audience as the Contemporary Narrator. Sometimes you may choose to pull out of a scene temporarily to summarize something, have a moment of reflection, or reconnect with the audience before going on.

What is at stake in this scene? Perhaps the main character is realizing for the first time that not everyone has the same view about giving money to unhoused people on the street. Perhaps she is questioning her own actions for the first time. In any case, after this interaction with Sandy, she won't be quite the same the next time she drives through that intersection and sees Gerald.

Scenes can be a few lines or a couple of pages long. Though some successful solo shows are written entirely without them, scenes can be thought of as the pillars supporting your story. Just as pillars are necessary in a building where there is the most weight, consider portraying the most important moments in your piece in scene. Scenes cause the audience to lean forward. They capture our full attention because something is happening *now*, in the moment, and we are invited to be part of it as it happens.

Again, there is no right or wrong way to write a solo show! Scenes are simply another tool you can use to create engagement and a sense of immediacy.

Scenelets

We think of "scenelets" as one, two, or three lines of dialogue that offer a dip into a moment in a story, when a full scene is not warranted. Scenelets are great for breaking up a too-long section of narrative, giving an immediate sense of a character's voice, or conveying a feeling. For example:

> I moved my tanning operation right up to the curb to avert disaster. The second I heard the mail truck clattering down the hill each day, I peeled my sweaty thighs from the plastic lounge chair.
>
> "Hi, Virginia!" I would pipe up, as she handed me the mail.
>
> "Hello there."
>
> She knew. She knew I was up to something, as I avoided her eyes and turned away to furtively rifle through the stack.
>
> **—Carly P.**

Can you picture this scenelet in performance? Can you hear the forced casual tone in the main character's voice as she greets Virginia? Do you hear the wry note in Virginia's "Hello there"? Perhaps even see the "side-eye" she gives the girl?

Here is another scenelet from one of our students:

> The priest gestured to come forward to the altar. Padding forward in my white patent leather mary janes, I knelt down in front of him and heard him whisper, "Will you move over? I'm doing two at a time here." This was not the spiritual counsel I had envisioned.
>
> **—Stephanie M.**

Depending on how the performer says the priest's line, the audience will be able to determine whether he is distracted, rushed, or sneering at the child. Putting this moment into a scenelet allows the audience to have the experience and unpleasant surprise along with the narrator. Think of scenelets as a tool to add texture and variety to your storytelling.

One more example from a student:

> Mom slipped away very quietly, twenty-five years later, at a North Side hospice full of other dying people. Near the end, she crooked her finger at me and I approached the bed.
>
> "Well, if I had it to do all over again," she whispered . . .
>
> "Yes, Mom?" I asked with tears in my eyes.
>
> She blurted loudly in my ear, "Yeah. If I had it to do all over again . . ."

"Yes, Ma?"
". . . I would have all Danish Modern furniture!"

—Connie S.

TRY THIS!

1. Think about a verbal interaction you had with another person in the last week, important or mundane—an argument, an interaction with a sales associate, or an everyday conversation that took place in your home first thing in the morning. Write the interaction in scene. In addition to recording the words, try incorporating any gestures as stage directions [*He placed the receipt on the counter* or *she wrinkled her nose and turned away*]. Though a writer may choose to not incorporate silences into their final script, try doing that here to make the scene very clear: [*Pause*].

   Now, read the scene aloud. Adjust any dialogue that feels "not quite right." Read it aloud again. Try to convey the intention behind each line of dialogue—pause where there are pauses and enact gestures where they happen in the scene. Notice how, even if the moment from your life was not consequential, it gains import when written and performed as a scene.
2. Look for a moment of narration in your play that might be more clearly conveyed in scene. This might be a moment that could use more amplification, such as a turning point. Or it may be the introduction or arrival of a new character, with their own vocal cadence and mannerisms. Or you may just find a block of text that feels long and might benefit from moments of spoken dialogue.

   Try writing this moment as a scene and reading it aloud with the surrounding material. What do you notice? Is the audience able to know more about your characters through hearing their voices?

Telling the Stories of Others

It's important to consider the ethics of storytelling as we begin our work on a solo play. We must acknowledge that our first-person narratives can only hope to tell *our* truth, a truth that ultimately may not align with the perspectives of the other folks we write about. We also need to ensure we're not, in the name of truth, personally "outing" folks with our work. We delve more deeply into these ideas in our chapter entitled "Truth vs. Accuracy."

Writing from another person's point of view also requires ethical considerations. You may be writing a fictional solo play, a character-driven show, a biographical piece, or any of the other fourteen types of solo plays we talk about in this book. You may be writing a play to perform yourself or writing a piece for someone else to perform. Whatever the case, we need to be thoughtful and sensitive when we decide to write other characters and give them a voice.

You, dear playwright, have a fabulous imagination, but you only have your own, singular lived experience. Each of us has a very specific set of intersectional personal identities that influence how we encounter the world. We all have biases and lenses that were ingrained in us before we could choose them. As adults we can examine those old ideas and make choices about them going forward.

Though that doesn't mean we can only write characters who have roughly the same identity as our own, when we plan to portray characters who have identities we don't share, it's essential that we bring sensitivity and deep consideration to the work. Certainly, it's critical that everyone hears stories of Native people and folks with disabilities and migrants but, if that is not our own story, we have to consider whether we are the best person to tell that story. No one means to engage in damaging cultural appropriation, but impact matters more than intent.

In solo work, our bodies convey the text. Our stories are delivered to the audience through a body, and that body matters. Solo artist Melissa DuPrey urges us to "be aware of our own vessel, especially when we're talking about decolonized storytelling. We don't want to shed what we have inherently or externally, but to actually lean into that and use all of it." We need more artists of color bringing their experiences from the margins to main-stage performances, and that work needs to be done by artists of color themselves. The rest of us can help by creating space for that work, funding that work, and supporting that work.

You may think that writing and performing the definitive solo piece on Harriet Tubman is an excellent idea because you have spent years researching her life. You now want to bring her story to an audience in a biographical solo play. If you are Black, there is a good chance your physical body and possibly your lived experience support Harriet Tubman's story. However, if you are a white woman (or man), there are excellent arguments against this plan.

Race is a social construct, not a biological one. This simply means that the idea of race is a human invention that is not based on scientific facts. However, invented or not, discrimination on the basis of race, skin color, and ethnicity is very, very real in the United States. Skin color has been assigned meaning, while ear shape and eye color have not. The prejudice and discrimination white people inflicted on Harriet Tubman are central to her story, and while an actor of color will not have had her specific experience, they may have an identity that is more appropriately aligned with Harriet Tubman's. Many roles in the theater are not dependent on the race of an actor, but this role most certainly is.

Color-blind casting was once widely embraced as a movement toward equity but is now being questioned. Though many theaters continue to cast actors in roles outside their originally written identities, there is a growing movement toward identity-conscious casting, a practice that considers how race, gender, disability, and other facets of identity shape meaning onstage. It shows a growing understanding that the identity of the actor playing a role always matters and always has.

What if you are white but want to write this play about Harriet Tubman and have another, more culturally appropriate actor in mind to perform the role? This could work if you have real relationships with writers of color who can read your work and give you feedback. But this is not a project that should be embarked upon lightly.

We don't know what we do not know, and all of us, with the best of intentions, make assumptions based on our own personal identities. We're not arguing against writing characters of other ethnicities, cultures, or religions—but we are urging you to carefully consider how you are giving voice to those characters. Surround yourself with expertise as you embark on the project. If you seek advice or feedback from anyone, you must compensate them for their work and expertise.

Part of the joy and obligation of writing is telling the stories of others, crawling into their heads, and bringing them to life. We're not suggesting that you can't write or portray characters who are in the midst of a mental health crisis or who are Muslim or queer or use a wheelchair, if that's not your experience. But bring knowledge and curiosity to the task.

Julie has a scene in her play *Love Thy Neighbor . . . Till It Hurts* in which she is being egged by some neighborhood children on Halloween. The fact that Julie was white and the children were not is a crucial element of the story. In the writing of the scene, Julie took care to make sure she was not portraying the children as "bad kids," which they weren't. They were kids in Halloween costumes doing the same thing lots of kids do in neighborhoods everywhere. She also wanted to be clear in her writing and performance that the encounter never felt like a dangerous situation. When it came time to perform the scene, which contained a lot of dialogue from the children, Julie didn't want to do a straight-up imitation of the voices of the Black children, but they did have their own very specific speech pattern, which couldn't be ignored. In the end, she focused on portraying the kids as children, with a suggestion of the speech pattern. Julie is a professional performer with the acting chops to calibrate her performance. In the hands of a more novice performer, the scene might have felt very different, veering toward stereotype or ignoring identity altogether.

This type of consideration should also be extended to the portrayal of disabled characters. While Arlene self-identifies as a disabled artist, she does not identify as autistic. She has taught autistic students and has collaborated alongside autistic artists, but she came to understand that proximity alone does not grant the depth needed to fully comprehend or authentically represent an autistic perspective.

While working on *Whampo!*, a satirical comedy about a reality show, Arlene enlisted the feedback of a neurodivergent disability consultant and a focus group of autistic individuals. The focus group discussed topics related to language, including identity-first references, as well as the attitudes and reactions of other characters toward autism. Arlene was happy to learn that she got some aspects of the play right, but she also gained insights into where she went wrong. The final piece of the puzzle was the ability to cast an actor with authentic lived experience, whose input brought depth to the workshop process.

This kind of collaboration is important across all kinds of representation, such as a gay man crafting dialogue for a trans woman, or someone writing from outside a cultural or religious tradition who may miss the emotional weight of ritual or language. Yes, there may be shared values or overlapping experiences—but those overlaps don't replace lived nuance.

Representing Our Own Culture and Identities

Some of the writers in our workshops have shared concerns about speaking for their own culture. They wonder whether they have the right to tell these stories. In many cultures, certain beliefs, attitudes, or behaviors are often kept quiet. Writers might feel pressure to avoid these sensitive topics out of fear of backlash, betraying their community, or revealing secrets that have been kept hidden for a reason. There can also be the fear of misrepresentation. You might worry that talking about these issues could paint an inaccurate picture of your culture as a whole. Breaking that silence can feel like crossing a line.

In any social identity group, there will be a wide range of views and experiences. As an artist, you have an inherent right to tell your truth. Whether you're writing fiction, biography, memoir, or something in between, your lived experience makes your work authentic. You don't need to speak for everyone who shares that identity—your responsibility is to speak for yourself only. When approaching sensitive work like this, be honest, even when addressing difficult or uncomfortable cultural truths. Highlight the diversity within your culture, respect traditions, and avoid stereotypes. Consider how your writing might impact your community, both positively and negatively, and when in doubt, ask for feedback from folks in the community.

We support art-making that is explicitly or implicitly about social issues and justice. Ask for and accept honest feedback, be willing to admit that you may get things wrong or fail to anticipate an audience's reaction, and offer feedback when asked in good faith. Understand that language changes, and our understanding of race, gender, religion, age, and disability continues to shift and change over time. Don't create your show in a vacuum.

EXPERT ADVICE

As someone who works with many emerging artists, how might you guide a playwright who is trying to write about situations or cultures where they lack lived experience?

If a young or new writer is trying to tell a particular story outside their culture or lived experience, I advise them to first do their research and then seek partnerships with another artist to write from their experience and cultures, creating a unique story that embodies both. Writers telling stories about cultures other than their own has long been problematic. I've had conversations with playwrights about approaching subjects in a way that is equitable and inclusive. I might say, "I'm noticing you're always writing about a culture other than your own. Have you explored that? You might be interested in that culture, but what is it about your own story that's not as satisfying or interesting to you?" We want to hear stories in first voice, or in the authentic voice of a culture. But there are ways to compare your own journey to another person's journey as a way to bridge understanding and create dialogue around what we share.

Ilesa Duncan
Director, Theater Maker, Arts Educator, Producer, Arts Administrator

Making a Good Show Better

The Power of POV

In writing, we understand point of view to be the narrator's position in relation to a story. If you had a decent composition teacher in high school (we didn't), perhaps you learned that stories can be written in first person ("I" or "we"), second person ("you"), third person ("she," "he," "they," "it"), or fourth person ("oneself," "someone").

Most solo shows are told in first person, even if the characters in the show are not meant to be the performer. The solo actor, as themself or any other character, generally speaks as that person, and we see the world through their very specific and particular worldview.

When we are talking about the importance of a *strong* point of view in a solo play, we're talking about characters who bring to every situation particular experiences, ideas, and beliefs that shape how they see the world. It's not just *what* they think—it's *how* and *why* they think it. When it comes to solo work, being able to feel and understand your protagonist's particular point of view is crucially important.

Writing POV

Consider a story you might write about the death of your grandmother. Many of us have had the experience of losing a grandparent, but even if our experiences have some details in common, your story will be unmistakably yours. Perhaps, coincidentally, we both lost our grandmothers in the same hospital, but still, what that hospital smelled like and felt like to you will be unique. Your relationship with your grandmother; her endearing idiosyncrasies, quirks, and flaws; and your opinions about her will be yours alone.

The reason listeners will care and connect with you is that they will be getting the story with your attitude toward the events, your inner monologue, and how you felt at each moment. All these details create a strong point of view, resulting in a bond of intimacy with the audience because you will be letting us in.

The solo playwright Dael Orlandersmith is a gifted and tenacious actor, so she writes solo plays in which she often portrays several different characters involved in an incident. Her play *Until the Flood* examines the actions and inner life of various individuals involved in the social uprising in Ferguson, Missouri, after the shooting of teenager Michael Brown. The characters in the play speak as themselves, in the first person, about their experiences and opinions. Dael's plays are so astonishing because each of these characters has a distinctly different, distilled point of view that is made very clear to the audience. Understanding each character's POV makes it impossible to dismiss or vilify any of them, regardless of our own political beliefs.

Think about what your protagonist's goals, values, and deepest motivations are. These aren't things that need to be spoken aloud in your play, of course, but they're the driving force behind the character's actions. Socioeconomic level, intellect, education, past successes, and failures—all these factors influence a character's point of view. The more honest you can be about how a character views the world, the more intimacy you are offering the audience.

Physicalizing POV

In a solo show, POV is typically conveyed through the language of the characters, whether it's shared as the narrator or through dialogue. However, POV can also be conveyed through physicality.

The way a character receives information and responds to an event can be shown through their reactions, facial expressions, and body language, providing insights into their emotional state without the need for explicit verbal expression. Make a note of scenes and segments in your show where your character's attitude about something might be portrayed wordlessly. This could be a facial expression that is a quick aside to the audience, the way your character handles a prop, or the way they hold their body as they observe an offstage event. This kind of physicality has the potential to introduce another layer of depth to your play.

TRY THIS!

1. Take a scene or section from your solo draft and see if you can pinpoint moments that convey your main character's unique point of view on the world. Underline descriptions, phrases, or dialogue that reveal where your character is coming from. Are we getting a glimpse of what this character values and holds dear? Are we getting a sense of what is beautifully weird about this individual?
2. Choose a scene from your solo draft where your main character interacts with another character. First, read the scene and ask yourself: What does your protagonist believe is happening here? What do they want? Now flip it. Write a short internal monologue (just a few lines) from the *other* character's point of view in the same moment. What do *they* think is going on? What do *they* want? Then compare. Where do the perspectives clash? Where are the characters completely missing each other? These differences in POV are where real dramatic tension lives. Finally, sharpen the moment: tweak a line, an action, a beat of silence—something that highlights that disconnect for the audience. Let us feel the gap between two truths.

Make It Multisensory (See, Hear, Taste, Touch, and Sniff It!)

It's been said that, as artists, our job is to pay attention, to notice as much as we can with each of our senses—easier said than done in a world where there is so much stimulation and so many opportunities to be distracted. Most human beings learn about the world through using the five senses we learned about in school and four others that we don't usually think about. (That being said, all humans are different! Those of us with a disability may be having a different experience.) Our solo writing must convey enough of the sensory details we have experienced to hook an audience so that they feel what we feel. Where specifically do you feel the cold in your body? What does a particular dog's bark sound like? How is that singular sunset beautiful?

Research says that when we listen to a story full of sensory details, describing the physical sensations of swimming against a riptide, for example—limbs being violently yanked back and forth, the sting of icy water—our motor cortex is activated, and we can feel as if we're in the middle of the action, as if it is actually happening to us. Incorporating multisensory details—that is, layering and stacking several of them—can also evoke deep emotions in the audience, providing a more powerful and memorable impact than ordinary words. Sometimes these details appear naturally in your first draft. Other times, you can weave details in when you are finished with the first draft, while rewriting the piece.

Our Five Senses and a Couple of Others

When it comes to writing multisensory scenes, we can expand beyond the traditional five senses to create an even richer experience for audiences. We've included an example for each sense based on a summer spent down the Jersey shore.

1. **Sight.** Describe visual elements of the scene, using colors, shapes, and movement within the environment.

   Example

   Maybelline lip gloss melting in a beach bag stuffed full of Tolstoy novels, Cosmopolitan magazines and near-empty wallets. Blistering looks from skittish mothers as they dragged their children away from the melee.

2. **Hearing.** Incorporate the sounds of the scene. Use specific sounds associated with characters or objects, including ambient noises, voices, music, and nature sounds that make the scene come alive.

   Example

   The rhythmic crash-crash-shhhh of the surf at high tide. The high-pitched squawk of greedy seagulls eating Cheetos out of our hands.

3. **Taste.** Introduce taste sensations, describing flavors and the texture of food, objects, or liquids.

   Example

   Sticky lips and salty teeth biting into a gritty salami and mustard sandwich. A long, endless pull of an icy Diet Pepsi under a razor-hot sun.

4. **Touch.** Explore tactile sensations by describing how things feel to the characters' skin or fingertips, including textures, temperature, and the overall physical experience.

   Example

   The sting of a shaved bikini line in the salty surf. Chapped lip kisses in the dark.

5. **Smell.** Bring in the sense of smell by describing various odors in the scene, such as smells of nature, food, or objects.

   Example

   The smell of the ocean and the boardwalk tar. The scent of salt-water taffy that followed us everywhere.

6. **Kinesthetic Sense.** Capture how bodies move—gesture, posture, and presence in space.

   Example

   Trudging through hot sand, legs burning, flip-flops slapping against heels, towel dragging behind like a defeated flag.

7. **Enteroception.** This is a fancy word for the internal sensations of a character, such as gnawing hunger, nausea, exhaustion, stinging pain, or a racing heart. While we may not always think of enteroception as part of the sensory world, it adds a visceral component to our work.

   Example

   The rumbling of your stomach because you skipped breakfast to sqeeze into a tiny swimsuit.

8. **Time.** Consider how you can incorporate the sense of time passing in your work, such as the ticking of a clock, the lengthening or shortening of shadows, or other indicators that can create a time-related experience.

   Example

   The weak light of dawn signaling a new day and a new adventure. The last golden sliver of sun over the bay telling us to go home for a shower.

9. **The Sixth Sense.** Don't be afraid to explore your characters' gut instincts, intuitions, or perceptions, which can provide subtle cues, extending the boundaries of the traditional senses.

   Example

   The tingly feeling that the late-night bonfire holds something magical. The sense of being watched by the cigar-smoking grandpas on the dock.

Multisensory details can create vivid, memorable images, making the audience feel immersed in the story. Notice how the descriptors in this example give us a sense of movement.

> There it is. The Pirates' treasure chest. Disguised as a rotting log. We run to it. We raise our mighty swords. Begin our brutal work. The chest explodes, filling the blue sky with brown rot and green moss. We increase the intensity of our attack, intoxicated by the musk smell that reminds me of Grammy's basement. We are lost in this moment. We do not see the motherlode of gold as it falls from the chest. As it rises above us. Not yellow coins. Yellowjackets. In a flash the air is on fire. Angry bees are covering me like the fur of a golden bear.
>
> **—Tim G.**

Multisensory descriptions can also be used as information carriers. They can immerse an audience in an experience as well as reveal and inform a story. When we hear a cupboard creak open to show a few boxes of mac and cheese and instant noodles, we don't need a narrator to explain financial strain. Our hands can feel it on the arm of the threadbare corduroy sofa. Likewise, the crisp unzip of garment bags and the gleam of a dozen designer purses in a cedar-scented walk-in closet instantly place us in a world shaped by money, status, and appearance. These aren't just props, they're entry points into character, context, and story.

Writer Michele Weldon tells her students at Northwestern to take mood into account when writing multisensory details.

For example, let's consider a description of your fifth-grade classroom:

> Five rows of desks, six deep. A gleaming whiteboard, first thing in the morning. The 4×5-inch piece of wood that functioned as a hall pass. The background sounds of shuffling feet and sighs from the kids as they work a math test.

However, when you incorporate the mood of the scene, those descriptors may change to serve the story. If that fifth-grade class is combined with an embarrassing incident, as the writer, you may include different details. What happened in the room and how you felt about it will affect which sensory details you take note of:

> The view of your shoes on the brown tiled floor as you hang your head. The flush of heat in your face. The blood rushing in your ears. The one look of sympathy from a kid named Wheels.

Understand that multisensory descriptions may not come quickly. Be patient, take a moment, and if necessary, close your eyes. Some writers find it helpful to look at photos or listen to music from that particular time. Everyone has a different experience, and you want the audience to understand your particular point of view. Push yourself to think outside the box.

Be Choosy!

It's important not to overwhelm your audience with *too many* sensory details. Choose the senses that are most relevant to each scene and use them strategically to immerse the audience in the story. A teaching colleague says, "Write fat and edit thin." We love this directive because it encourages you to generate many multisensory descriptors and later go back to choose the ones that best serve your story.

Writing fat is like having a pantry fully stocked with beans, pasta, pancake mix, tuna, chicken stock, salsa, cereal, and honey. When your pantry is brimming, you, as the chef, have the opportunity to pick just the right ingredients that will work for a particular dish. In the same way, the more multisensory descriptors you've identified, the more choices you have to intentionally incorporate into your writing those that will provide important information about the character, the scene, or the arc of your story.

Here is a paragraph from a story by a writer in one of our workshops, Louise F. In the first draft, the paragraph was written without multisensory details:

> I arrived at the funeral home late, just as the services were coming to an end. I walked up the aisle. I gave the rose to the undertaker, who placed it in Mr. Beauchamp's hands. He then secured the casket, and the pallbearers came forward.

After receiving feedback on the paragraph, the writer's next revision had *too many* details:

> I arrived at the funeral home late, just as the services were coming to an end. I stepped into the sanctuary, my legs feeling like jelly. The funeral director had started preparations to close the casket, but when he saw me rushing down the aisle, holding the rose in my hands, he stopped and waited. A hushed silence fell over the room. A dozen displays of lovely pink and white flowers surrounded the bronze casket, and their sweet scent filled the air. Mr. Beauchamp's remains lay upon a plush silk lining in the casket, looking so natural and dignified. I found myself blinking hard to keep back hot tears. I kissed the rose and handed it to the undertaker. The solemn-faced man took the flower and placed it in the lifeless hands of Mr. Beauchamp. I smiled. Then the undertaker secured the lid on the casket with a click and motioned for the pallbearers to come forward.

Her last revision got it just right for her particular story:

> I arrived at the funeral home late, just as the services were coming to an end. I took a deep breath and stepped into the sanctuary. My legs felt like jelly. The funeral director had started preparations to close the casket, but when he saw me rushing down the aisle, holding the rose in my hands, he stopped and waited. A hushed silence fell over the room. I found myself blinking hard to keep back hot tears. I kissed the rose and handed it to the undertaker. And then he secured the lid on the casket with a click.

Notice how each of the paragraphs makes you feel. How did you respond to each? How were they different? What did you "see" in your mind? How did the material in each draft change your relationship to the scene? How did it change your understanding of the story?

Remember, writing fat gives you options. Editing thin gives you focus.

TRY THIS!

Pick a specific scene from your solo show that takes place in a clear location or moment in time. Close your eyes and plop yourself right in the center of it. Settle into your memory or imagination and take inventory using all nine senses. Don't censor or evaluate, just gather. Then, go back into your material. Which of those details create vivid pictures? Which ones suggest emotion, backstory, or meaning? Keep those, trim the rest.

EXPERT ADVICE

We've always admired the interesting and original multisensory details in your work. Tell us about your approach.

I always consider opposing senses for the sensory details I've just noted. What color is the scent? What does the sound taste like? What does the touch smell like? Then, what emotion should the detail convey? Is it chilling or calming? Sinister or serene? Is the traffic light an exploding flower or the slow wink of an eye? Is the light from the television a warm cup of milk or a braying donkey? I'll give the grass, the chandelier, the car a personality, or conversely turn the character into a bale of hay, a discarded bag of trash, a seedling. I know I've got it when I've scared myself or find myself wondering, "Where did *that* come from?"

Elizabeth J. Gerard
Writer, Author, Storyteller

In General, Be Specific

We've urged you to incorporate multisensory details into your work because they create an immersive experience for the audience. Another strategy you can use is specificity. Writing with specificity means identifying particulars such as brand names, products, addresses, names, cultural references, locations, or institutional or group affiliations. This labeling helps the audience experience your story in a more vivid way.

Once, when Julie asked a student in her class how their writing was going, they said, "Last week, I got a lot of suggestions about adding details and specifics, but I don't want to. I want my story to feel universal so the audience can really relate to it."

This gave Julie a squiggle of excitement. Specificity is one of her favorite topics. She understood exactly where her student was coming from—they worried that including specific details about their 1990s kindergarten classroom, drinking strawberry Nesquik, and the Furby in their backpack would prevent the audience from connecting with their own kindergarten memories. But it doesn't work that way. Specifics, like a magic trick that challenges our assumptions, provide a context that helps the audience connect the dots and create their own images. These images spark memories and emotions, even if the details aren't an exact match.

When Julie was a kid, Missouri winters brought a lot of snow. After a big storm, she and the neighborhood kids would pile the snow up to the roof of her house, making a ramp to sled down into the street. This description may not conjure a picture for the listener. But if she tells you that she and Curt Meyer used silver Snow Disk Flying Saucer sleds to hurtle off Julie's low-slung '70s ranch house, landing in the middle of Darby Lane, until Mr. Bova came out yelling because they might crash into his Ford Escort, those details prompt the brain to create a visual. Specificity invites people to fill in the blanks, making even unfamiliar details feel personal, relatable, and memorable.

Your childhood might have been different—maybe you didn't have a grumpy Mr. Bova who lived across the street, or maybe you grew up where it never snowed. But the details Julie provides can still connect you to your own childhood memories. Through these specifics, you can share in her experience, creating an empathic connection.

Specifics reveal more about characters' backgrounds, attitudes, class, and the time period than generic nouns ever could. If Mr. Bova drove a Cadillac, it paints a different picture than his very middle-class Ford Escort.

These labels can be an extra layer of information for your audience. They focus the lens in all sorts of ways. Think about how a specific grocery store can signal where a character lives or their socioeconomic status—for example, a Piggly Wiggly, Ralphs, or Whole Foods. Labels can also reveal politics—a Black Lives Matter T-shirt or a MAGA hat—or suggest someone's age, like AXE body spray or Mr. Bubbles.

The two excerpts below convey the same information. One is more general; the other is more specific. See how they change the way you experience the material:

> Wearing the one-piece bathing suit I'd brought for the trip, I headed down to the beach behind the motel each afternoon. The suit hit me below where my actual breasts would have been, had I actually had breasts, and I looked utterly ridiculous as I gingerly navigated the grass wearing my dad's loafers.

> Wearing the only bathing suit I'd brought for the trip, a one-piece strapless my mother had unearthed at Filene's

Basement, I headed down to the beach behind the Sea Aire motel late each afternoon. The diagonally striped suit hit me about three inches below where my actual breasts would have been, had I actually had breasts, and I looked utterly ridiculous as I gingerly navigated the prickly clumps of sea oats separating the motel from the beach wearing my dad's ten-sizes-too-big loafers.

—**Melisha M.**

TRY THIS!

Choose a memory from your life or imagine a fictional moment from your protagonist's life. First, write a short paragraph describing the moment generically. Then rewrite it using labels and specificity: add street names, product brands, the exact music playing, the specific scent in the air, what your character is wearing. What does that version reveal that the first one doesn't? Finally, read both aloud. Notice how the specific version sparks imagery and feeling.

Untangling Tenses

"The past, present and future walk into a bar. It was tense." We use this silly little pun so often in classes that someone gave Arlene a paperweight with the saying emblazoned on it. We love it because it underscores a powerful tool we can put in our toolbox when crafting a one-person show.

The choices you make regarding tense can affect the narrative voice, alter the audience's involvement, add a sense of immediacy, or change up the rhythm of a piece. Understanding how each tense functions allows you to manipulate your material to tell the story in the most impactful way. We encourage you to experiment with five tenses: past, present, past continuous, present continuous, and future perfect.

Here is an example of a true-life experience written in different tenses. Read them out loud and notice how they land.

1. **Past tense**

   I sat at my desk and waited for inspiration to strike when suddenly I sensed something odd. The hairs on my scalp tingled. I turned slowly, and there I saw the poltergeist outside my window. I panicked and dropped to the floor.

   The past tense is the most traditional and common way we tell stories. It's how we've been sharing narratives since we were babies—stories about our families, adventures, and fairy tales. When you tell a story in the past tense, you look back on the events with the knowledge of what came after. Past tense allows the teller to reflect on past experiences and actions and have the option to add context to them. In a one-person show, using the past tense enables the storyteller to share their reflections and their analysis of the events.

2. **Present tense**

> *I sit at my desk and wait for inspiration to strike when suddenly I sense something odd. The hairs on my scalp tingle. I turn slowly, and there I see the poltergeist outside my window. I panic and drop to the floor.*

If you want your play to feel more alive and dynamic, try putting your material into the present tense. It puts the audience right in the middle of the action, as if everything is unfolding in that moment. The present tense brings the story to life, ramps up the urgency, and keeps your audience leaning forward.

3. **Past continuous tense**

> *I was sitting at my desk and waiting for inspiration to strike when suddenly I sensed something odd. The hairs on my scalp were tingling. I turned slowly, and there I saw the poltergeist outside my window. Panicking, I dropped to the floor.*

This tense is used to describe actions that have happened in the past using the words "was" and "were," often with the addition of "-ing" to verbs. Using this tense in a solo show is a more active way to tell a story that happened in the past. It allows you the opportunity to add backstory and context, similar to the simple past tense, with the added bonus of making the audience feel like they are having a more immersive experience.

4. **Present continuous tense**

    I am sitting at my desk and waiting for inspiration to strike when suddenly I'm sensing something odd. The hairs on my scalp are tingling. I turn slowly, and there I see the poltergeist outside my window. I panic and drop to the floor.

    The present continuous tense is one of our favorites to use in a solo show. It describes ongoing actions or events happening in the present moment. This tense helps the audience feel connected to the action by capturing the energy and essence of a scene. Writing in this tense allows the performer to bring the story to life right before the audience's eyes.

5. **Future perfect tense**

    Unbeknownst to me, this time next week, I will sit at my desk and wait for inspiration to strike when suddenly I will sense something odd. The hairs on my scalp will tingle. I will turn slowly, and there I will see the poltergeist outside my window. I will panic and drop to the floor.

    This is a fun, interesting, and odd little tense to play around with. It describes an action that will happen in the future. It can add a note of anticipation or foreshadowing or simply be a different way to narrate the work to change up the rhythm of the play or make it more interesting.

(Oh, by the way, Arlene's run-in with the poltergeist turned out to be a grocery bag caught in a tree and quivering in the wind.)

Can you use more than one tense in a play? Yes, you absolutely can, as long as it's done with care and clarity. As a matter of fact, we encourage it. Shifting between tenses can introduce dynamic contrasts within the narrative. While some solo shows use only one tense, it's important to know that you have options to vary the pace, immediacy, rhythm, and interest of your material. So don't be afraid to experiment and find what works best for your one-person show.

For example, many of our students opt to use the past or past continuous tense when breaking the fourth wall and directly addressing the audience. They then transition into a more active present tense or present continuous tense when creating scenes with dialogue, which can make the performance come alive and feel more dynamic.

Notice how the script below changes from past tense to present tense before going into a scene.

> When I told my mother I was going to have a home birth, she gave me one of her looks: Eyebrow arched in a perfect upside-down V, mouth in a straight line. I never know for sure what she's thinking, but that look has never said, "Good idea."
>
> I know Mom doesn't quite understand the newfangled ways her children are having babies. I guess she thinks what worked for her should work for us.
>
> By 11:00 a.m. the next day, I am in labor!
>
> I think to myself, Can I have this baby before my mom gets here? Mom's plane gets in at 9:30, with driving time, that's 10:30. 12 hours of labor with the first, 22 hours with the second, divided by 2 is 11 . . . I can have this baby by 10:00 tonight!
>
> **—Francesca S.**

The first sentence, in past tense, provides context and background that enable us to more fully understand the scene that the narrator begins to unfold in present tense in the next sentence.

Sometimes, we want the audience to feel immersed in a scene as it's happening. Other times we want more distance. For example, we worked with a student on a one-person show about surviving an abusive relationship. She wrote the play using scenes crafted in present tense and driven by dialogue, often presenting a blow-by-blow account of the abuse as it unfolded. During a workshop reading, she received feedback that one particular scene—depicting the moment her protagonist decides to leave after watching her abuser choke her dog—was too intense. Several audience members said they emotionally dropped out of the play at that point. The solo artist realized this was not the effect she wanted to evoke, so she began experimenting with a more distancing tense, and ultimately found that the future perfect tense created an eerie scene that was more to her liking. The use of this unusual tense changed the tempo of the scene and signaled a shift in the character's experience, marking one of the most interesting moments in the play.

TRY THIS!

Experimentation is a critical part of creating a solo show—especially when discovering the tense that best serves your story. Take a short section from your script and rewrite it in each of the five major tenses: past, present, past continuous, present continuous, and future perfect. Read each version out loud and pay attention to how the change in tense affects tone, pacing, and emotional distance. Then, share your favorite versions with someone else and ask how each one landed for them. What felt immediate? What felt reflective? What surprised you? Let these discoveries guide how you use tense to shape time and intimacy in your piece.

Universal Truth

A universal truth is a deeper meaning in your play that will resonate with folks because it speaks to the human condition. It's the BIG story told through the vehicle of the little story. It answers the question "What is the story *about*?" versus "What *happens* in the story?"

At its most basic level, "what happens in a story" often refers to plot—the series of events or the immediate conflicts. However, understanding "what it's really about" involves mining beyond the surface into the heart of the narrative and its deeper meanings. Themes like loss, identity, or moral conflict are important, but they become universal truths when they are expressed as specific insights about human experience. For example, *There are some losses from which we never recover*, or *The version of ourselves that we hide can be the one that saves us*, or *Change is inevitable*. These truths go beyond general subjects—they articulate something deeply felt and recognizably human.

A well-articulated universal truth transcends culture, background, geography, and class, allowing audience members to empathize and connect. It can act as a tuning fork between the story and the audience's own life experience. Identifying a universal truth will also help ensure your show has depth, coherence, and purpose beyond the anecdotal.

Take, for instance, *The Wizard of Oz*, the tale of an unhappy girl named Dorothy who lives on a farm in Kansas with her uncle and

Auntie Em. Following a cyclone that takes her, along with her dog Toto and her house, into the Land of Oz, she's told by a good witch that the only way to get home is to follow the yellow brick road, meet the great Wizard, and destroy the Wicked Witch of the West

Originally written as a children's novel in 1900 by L. Frank Baum, *The Wonderful Wizard of Oz* was based on stories he told his own children. It was adapted into a stage musical in 1902 and a film in 1939. It was also the basis for *The Wiz*, and it inspired *Wicked*, a novel that became a Broadway musical and film. Dorothy has even gained status as a gay icon. The book has been translated into over fifty languages and is in the Library of Congress.

Each semester, when we ask about universal truth in *The Wizard of Oz*, people mention several that resonate with them. Some say it's the line "There's no place like home." Others point to the idea that friendship is a powerful force or that everything you need is already inside of you. Some are struck by the warning to beware of the man behind the curtain. Each of these names a specific insight into the human experience—more than just themes, they function as universal truths: personal revelations that speak to something bigger, deeper, and widely felt.

However, when we analyze the film, we come up with a different universal truth: the journey home is often a journey inward. Dorothy is lost, both physically and emotionally. There is an actual yellow brick road that serves as her guiding path. In the end, Dorothy finds her way back home, with a new understanding of herself, what is important, and her place in the world. This truth—that the search for home often leads us to a deeper sense of self—is one that resonates across cultures, ages, and experiences. But that's just our opinion.

A well-crafted play may contain multiple universal truths, and audience members might walk away with a different one depending on their life stage or personal experiences. Still, as the storyteller, you should write with clarity and intention, understanding the truth you want your piece to carry.

Symbolism and Motifs

Symbolism can enhance the universal truth in your solo work, adding depth. For instance, the colors for a rose can carry symbolic meanings—romance (red), gratitude (pink), or friendship (yellow). A motif is a recurring element, theme, or idea that can serve to enhance the universal truth. One of our students used the repeating motif of calendars, seasons, and clocks to convey the passing of time. Motifs and symbolism can function as Easter eggs, inviting audiences to interpret and uncover messages within the story. Remember, a universal truth doesn't always have to bash the audience over the head. Instead, it can be a subtle thread throughout the play.

Sometimes the universal truth develops during the construction of the piece. Other times, the story or play tells you what it is, and you may need to go back and weave the universal truth throughout the entire play during revisions.

If you've written a complete draft, it might contain a universal truth that you don't yet see. Review it from one of these perspectives:

- **Look for patterns.** Are there major ideas or themes that run through the story? Ask what your material is telling you. Break down each small story within your play and ask what each piece is really about.
- **Track the plot.** Reflect on the journey of events and how the main character reacts to them. There may be a belief or principle that influences the character's choices.
- **Identify the essential question.** What is your protagonist wrestling with? What is their quest? Your character's decisions, weaknesses, and transformations may point you to the universal truth.

The universal truth in Thornton Wilder's classic play *Our Town* is that life's most precious moments often go unnoticed until they are gone. In Heidi Schreck's solo show *What the Constitution Means to Me*, we see that democracy is not a fixed ideal but an ongoing negotiation; the universal truth is that it must be challenged and redefined by each generation. *In the Heights*, a musical by Lin-Manuel Miranda, reminds us that dreams may lift us to the future, but it is our roots, our people, and our language that define us. And in *Moonlight*, a film that began as a university solo show by Tarell Alvin McCraney, we see that the parts of ourselves we hide in childhood often wait to be reclaimed.

Pablo Picasso said, "Art is a lie that makes us realize the truth." A solo show that lacks a discernible universal truth can come across as shallow or lacking in depth. For us, nothing is more satisfying than leaving a theater and having a thoughtful discussion about the meanings behind a play we've just seen.

TRY THIS!

What's your main character's quest? What are they longing for, chasing, avoiding, or trying to become? Identify the obstacles in their way—both internal and external. What might the universal truth be? Don't worry if you're not sure yet—just guess. What does your character know at the end of the play that they didn't know at the beginning of the play?

Four Ways to Never Just Tell

In this book, we're using the terms "solo show" and "solo play" interchangeably. Both of these phrases have something to offer us. "Show" reminds us that we don't want to be standing in front of an audience just talking to them—we need to show them events. "Play" reminds us that solo work has its roots in theater, where audiences watch characters work things out right in front of them with scenes and rising tension. The action doesn't happen offstage—it happens right there, in the moment. Every solo show is to some degree a theatrical play, so you'll want plenty of forward-moving action.

We generally suggest that in a solo show, at any moment, you'll want to be doing one of four things:

1. Be "in scene."
2. Directly address the audience as the Contemporary Narrator.
3. Directly address the audience as the Scenic Narrator.
4. Actively discover something or struggle to work something out.

Let's break this down a bit.

Be "In Scene"

You'll find a whole chapter on writing scenes and some examples of scenes elsewhere in this book. Briefly, we think of a scene as *characters in a place with dialogue or action, unfolding in real time.* Scenes allow us to show action and dialogue rather than telling about them. Instead of telling an audience about what you were like when you were eight years old, we can watch you in a scene with your grandma and get the sense of your constant motion and hear how you talked at that age.

We'll get your take on your grandma's voice through your point of view. We'll get to hear her idiosyncratic vocabulary and see her peculiar habit of cocking her head when she smoked. We may see you jump in and out of the characters. Maybe your grandma will reveal information about herself or you or other characters through the dialogue. We may even get details about your childhood living room throughout the scene, as you help her onto the brocade couch covered in plastic.

Scenes capture an audience's attention because they are happening right now, in front of us. We are invited into the middle of the action. We feel like we're really there, and we start to care about the characters in a deeper way.

Directly Address the Audience as the Contemporary Narrator

One of the wonderful things about solo shows is that we can talk directly to the audience. One of the most potent ways to do this is as the Contemporary Narrator. The Contemporary Narrator is you (or your protagonist), in this moment, talking to the audience with the knowledge of everything that you know right now. Addressing the audience as the Contemporary Narrator allows us to break out of a scene and share insights about what is happening, craft intimate or humorous asides, or create moments of reflection.

The Contemporary Narrator might say to the audience, *What I didn't know then is that my grandma had $65,000 hidden under her mattress in hundred-dollar bills,* or *It's probably obvious that I did not pose a threat to my bodybuilder neighbor,* or *Later, I would discover the* *car had a cracked carburetor and a rusted chassis, but that day I drove off the lot marveling at my good fortune.*

Like a scene, directly addressing the audience with information in the immediate now can feel dynamic, depending on the tenses you use in the telling and the acting performance.

Be careful, however, not to write the bulk of your solo play in the Contemporary Narrator voice. If you discover you have large chunks of text directed at the audience, and if those chunks of text are telling—rather than showing—the events of the story, consider whether some of that information can be conveyed through scene or dialogue instead. While it's true that some one-person shows are written entirely in this style, we encourage you to experiment to create a more dynamic play. All tell and no show can be a death knell.

Directly Address the Audience as the Scenic Narrator

The Scenic Narrator is you (or the main character of your piece) talking to the audience from the point of view of a certain time and place, in present tense, with only the knowledge they have in the scene. It's you talking to the audience as that eight-year-old in a scene with Grandma, turning to us and saying: *Grandma smells like perfumy soap and cigarettes*, or *My favorite thing in the whole wide world is my Barbie Dream House*. This kind of narration feels compelling because we get a strong sense of who you were at a different time—before you knew everything you know now.

There are moments in a story or solo play when we need to give the audience context and exposition. Providing this exposition through the Scenic Narrator allows the performer and the audience to stay in the time and place of the scene. For example, notice that following the dialogue below, the Scenic Narrator gives us lots of information through the voice and frame of reference of her twelve-year-old protagonist:

> In Sacred Heart Church, I open the door of the dark confessional and kneel.
>
> "Bless me, Father. It's been three months since my last confession."
>
> "My child, tell me your sins."

"I sneaked some hosts from the sacristy, and after I ate a bunch of them, I found out they had already been changed into the Body of Christ."

"How many did you eat?"

"Um . . . about 50."

The whole story swirls in front of me as I kneel there. I'm the church organist at Our Lady, where I'm also in the seventh grade, and they pay me fifteen bucks a week to play two Masses on Sunday, which is like, $7.50 an hour. I'm really good at convincing my teacher, Miss Gibbar, that I need to be let out of class early so I can walk across the parking lot to the church to practice the organ, but mostly I hang out back here, in the sacristy. I can use the priests' bathroom, and there's breath mints in this drawer here, and up here, in this cupboard, are all these boxes of unblessed communion wafers that they get from Catholic Supply in St. Louis. They don't have much taste, but I love how they melt on my tongue and stick to it.

—Julie Ganey, *The Half-Life of Magic*

You can see how the narration paragraph following the scene would be very different if it was delivered by the Contemporary Narrator, which would require the actor to step out of the scene and give exposition as their present-day self:

When I was in seventh grade, I was the church organist at Our Lady, where I made a whopping fifteen bucks a week playing two Masses every Sunday. I spent most afternoons convincing my teacher, Miss Gibbar, that I needed to be let out of class early so I could walk across the parking lot to the church to practice the organ—even back then, I knew I wasn't very good. Mostly I'd hang out in the sacristy. I'd use the priests' bathroom, help myself to their breath mints, and snack on the open boxes of unblessed communion wafers bought from Catholic Supply in St. Louis. Looking back, I can't believe they never noticed—I mean, I ate stacks of them. They didn't have much taste, but I loved how they melted on my tongue and stuck to it.

Only you can determine which narrator is right for any particular moment in your play, depending on the effect you are aiming for. Both approaches are effective but will deliver different results.

It's important to note that most narrative one-person shows have a mix of both Contemporary and Scenic Narrators throughout the piece. In this way, we can hear about events from the point of view of a character at the time those events took place and also hear from the character much later, with a different perspective on the events.

Actively Discover Something or Struggle to Work Something Out

This last guideline ensures that we are not simply ruminating or regurgitating in front of an audience. It keeps us from filling our work with rhetorical questions and rambling monologue.

In most solo plays, there are moments of reflection, when we pull back from the action and explore what it all means. That's great! These moments provide depth to our work. The trick in those moments is to ensure we are really wrestling with an idea or making an actual discovery in front of the audience, *with* the audience. This idea of actively discovering in the moment is something that is ideally done through both the writing and the performance.

Here is an example:

> Even in this moment, I can't understand why my sister lied. Maybe some people are not built for telling the truth, no matter how much they want to. Or maybe I was too young to understand what was at stake. I think that was the beginning of the end, though.
>
> **—Madison P.**

These lines have the potential to feel electric for an audience actually witnessing the performer on stage trying to discern the truth. They will be less effective if the performer is just musing or asking questions the answers to which she already knows. The last sentence is the moment the struggle is put aside and character's thinking changes, which can be conveyed through the delivery of the line.

Consider the line *I saw that she didn't love me the way I loved her.* This is a line that could simply be stated to the audience as information, maybe delivered as an aside, by the Contemporary Narrator. Another choice would be for the actor to discover this fact for the first time in the scene and share this new information with the audience as the Scenic Narrator. Perhaps the actor's eyes widen with the surprise of the realization. The line could be even more strongly written as *For the first time, I saw that she didn't love me the way I loved her.* However, even in its original form, the line could be delivered as a complicated realization that needs to be unpacked.

The idea of actively struggling to work something out in front of the audience is especially useful when we are asking questions in our shows, such as *Should I have made a different choice?* or *Does it matter that I left without saying goodbye?* Let the audience in on your attempt to figure things out by sharing the struggle with them.

TRY THIS!

Scan through your script. Do you have large chunks of text directed at the audience? Consider conveying some of that important information through scene, meaning characters in a place, with action and lines of dialogue. Or, change the narrator from Contemporary to Scenic, or vice versa. Which of these options best serves the story? Do you have moments where your character is thinking aloud to the audience? Aim to shape the moment through the writing or performance to make sure the character is truly discovering something or wrestling with an idea.

Write from the Scar

When creating an autobiographical solo show, we may explore challenging or traumatic experiences from our lives, which can be an intensely personal endeavor. These experiences, especially if we are still in the process of deciphering and understanding them, carry high personal stakes. However, even when the material is very difficult, it's crucial that the play ultimately presented onstage is written from a place of healing, or written "from the scar, not the wound."

If a playwright hasn't moved past the raw intensity of a moment, having made sense of the experience, they may have a very difficult time presenting it to an audience in a way that is effective. Autobiographical material that is too fresh can feel unsafe for the performer and the audience both. However, just as a physical wound heals over time, and eventually the scar that takes its place reflects the history of the wound, artists can find a way to present traumatic material in a way that highlights their recovery and resilience.

Getting to that place requires time. We're human! It's often impossible for us to make sense of big events in our lives while we are in the middle of them. Trauma might need to be processed with a therapist or friends, talking about the event over and over before we can make sense of it. Obviously, this will be different for every person and every event. If we don't do this work—if we try to create a piece of art about a wound with no scar—we will simply be presenting a series of painful events. The show risks becoming just a trauma play.

We once worked with an extraordinarily gifted writer/actor who created a solo show about the abuse she experienced from her father. She ran away at sixteen, spiraled into substance abuse, and lived through more abusive relationships. Writing these stories in class was painful; she often sobbed as she read her work aloud.

We recognize that becoming emotional when reading or writing a story is common, especially when the work is in its early phase, for ourselves included. However, it was clear that this writer hadn't yet healed from these experiences and was writing from a place of rawness, uncovering memories she had repressed for years. We encouraged her to continue, but only if she felt ready to do so. The others in the writing group were compassionate and supportive, creating a safe environment for her to explore these experiences.

When we encouraged her to write about how she recovered and healed from these events, she struggled and ended her play with a few lines stating that she eventually made better choices, surrounded herself with better people, and survived. When pressed to elaborate on how she did that, she couldn't. That was a clear sign she was still caught in the riptide.

The art of crafting a story involves delving into the emotional heart of what the events meant to the main character and how the character changed as a result. We're not saying a writer needs to "move past" a painful experience before writing about it. For some, the act of writing itself can be part of the healing process. But it's important to understand that while writing a solo show can be therapeutic, it should never be therapy.

If you find yourself writing with active resentment, it's a sign you might need to reflect on the experience you're writing about. It can be entertaining to watch a performer villainize their jerky ex-boyfriend, but only if they are truly over the relationship and have moved on. It's hard for an audience to watch someone with a chip on their shoulder air grievances onstage. If you're struggling with personal, difficult material, we support your courage and believe that these kinds of stories are important to put out into the world. Make sure to surround yourself with a writing community, therapists, or friends who can offer support. Give yourself permission to write whatever comes up. If you find yourself getting overwhelmed, take a break; you may need to come back to that story later.

When you tell these stories, you speak for people who cannot speak for themselves. Sometimes audience members will see their own lives reflected back to them, maybe for the first time, and that is very powerful. Furthermore, these stories can be incredibly cathartic for an audience to witness. When you have not just a difficult experience to present, but also the experience of growth, your show can enable others to take this journey of transformation with you.

EXPERT ADVICE

Can you speak to your experience working with storytellers to help them tell difficult or traumatic stories?

My class at the DuSable Museum is a group of writers who have been together for more than seven years. Everybody in that group at some point or another has shared some kind of trauma through their writing. Writing is a cathartic process, and it's important to only tell a story when you're ready to tell that story. Don't try to make an event into something until you have enough emotional security and safety to be able to really dig into it. Never re-traumatize yourself to produce a story. Also, the folks listening to that story early on need to understand how to support that writer. Not just in the feedback around the construction of the story, but in holding the information and recognizing the depth of the trauma some incident has caused in their life. We need to support a person not just as a writer in that moment, but as a human being.

Willa Taylor
Storyteller, Dramaturg, Teacher, Activist

Humor and Levity

Think of this chapter like a Post-it Note—a reminder of something that you already know and want to make sure you don't forget.

Most plays will benefit from a little humor or lightness. We're not saying that every solo play is funny, or that every story has to have belly laughs. We're not suggesting that you should insert "funny stuff" in the middle of a serious moment. Ignoring tone and shoehorning laughs into a scene won't work. What we are saying is that even shows addressing the darkest, most serious topics can include levity, irony, or moments when the energy shifts. And those moments, in a piece that is tackling heavy material, can be an important part of making your show work because they can provide the audience with a momentary respite from the difficult, sometimes harrowing circumstances of your story.

Think of it like shifting gears in a car. No play should remain in third gear for the entire show—it risks becoming monotonous for the audience. Find ways to vary tension and tone, either through the writing or the performance. No play should be introspective or action-packed or emotionally challenging from start to finish. In the same way that even a farce must have some real emotion or human investment that the audience can care about, plays that deal with serious, traumatic issues probably shouldn't be tragedy from start to finish.

Here's what Kurt Naebig said about writing his show *Stove Toucher*: "Even experienced actors sometimes forget that if you don't bring your sense of humor to a piece, it makes the heavy stuff hard and the funny stuff not funny. I had some heavy material in *Stove Toucher*, but I didn't want to put that stuff up front. I wanted to make people laugh and feel relaxed by telling a nice, engaging story, so that when I finally tried to land some of that heavy material, they were open to receiving it. I didn't want the audience to feel like, 'Oh God, this is too much.' "

In any story, a writer is managing tension and release. If we ask an audience to be tense for too long without a breather, we risk them becoming bored or exhausted before the end. Humor or levity is one way to create that breather.

Physical Engagement

Physiologically, laughter has an immediate positive effect on the body. Our lungs take in extra oxygen-rich air, and the part of our brain that releases endorphins is activated (the ventromedial prefrontal cortex, if you must know). Laughter has been associated with increased levels of pain tolerance and a decrease in cortisol, a stress hormone. The limbic system seems to be centrally involved when we laugh (specifically the hippocampus and the amygdala), and the limbic system is all about behaviors essential to life. In other words, laughter is not just a reaction—it's vital to well-being.

Look, we're not scientists. Or doctors. But you get the point. A laughing audience is physically responding to your performance. That's a great thing. An audience doesn't need to constantly be laughing throughout your show unless you are a stand-up comic, but the right amount of laughter can enhance your story. Our friend, the comedian Ric Walker, explains that in stand-up, the story is serving the jokes, and in storytelling, the jokes are serving the story.

A Communal Experience

Julie toured all over the US with an improv troupe called Wavelength for a couple of decades. The group did comedy for educators at in-service professional development days, usually in school auditoriums and at conferences. Over years of performing for teachers and administrators, often at 8:00 A.M. or earlier, the group became experts at making their already funny show funnier. They discovered that getting the audience to sit close together, rather than scattered across a sometimes enormous auditorium, made a significant difference. Seating the audience in a concentrated area close to the stage made it possible for the audience to have a true communal experience together and for the laughter to "catch on" from one person to the next.

Laughter is infectious. It brings people together and helps dissolve barriers between individuals in the audience and also between the audience and a performer, creating a feeling of connectedness. Humor makes a performer more likable and relatable, regardless of the subject matter. Intentionally designing moments where laughter can happen during your show is a great way to exploit this wonderful effect. Be sure and construct a few opportunities for your audience to laugh early in your solo play—and then really give the audience a moment to do so. They'll unconsciously know it's OK to laugh from the get-go, and they'll feel like they have permission to do it.

Getting More Funny 101

Entire books—excellent books—have been written on comedy, so we won't pretend to encapsulate comedy writing here. But everyone, even you, "Little-Miss-Serious-Artist-Creating-A-One-Woman-Drama," can become more intentional about sewing some levity and lightheartedness into their work.

Start by slowing down and noticing the absurdities that inevitably occur in your everyday life. Pay attention to what makes you laugh. How can you bring a little bit of that into your work? Make note of the things you say and do that make others laugh. How can you capture some of that energy in your show?

You're probably already familiar with comedy techniques like the rule of threes, alliteration, and calling back to ideas you planted earlier. You can also think about incorporating running gags, satire, parody, exaggeration, irony, puns and clever wordplay, the element of surprise, witty repartee between characters, or slapstick and physical comedy.

Learning to land a joke, specifically using beats and pauses, can also help. One familiar formula in American humor, rooted in the Yiddish theater, has three key components: setup, beat (pause), and punchline. In our culture, we are often trained to hear jokes structured this way, making the pause critical to the delivery. There are many more techniques for delivering material that can turn something that doesn't appear to be a joke into a laugh line.

Exaggeration and Hyperbole

The excerpt below shows how exaggeration and hyperbole can add humor to your writing.

> It's June of 2004 and the wedding is at the coveted Perdoni Farms. Think Versailles decorated by *The Real Housewives of New Jersey*. There are chandeliers and glitzy gold statues peeing into murky fountains everywhere. And wedding guests have come in from all over the tri-state area which means there are tangerine spray tans, bedazzled nails, and so much hairspray that if somebody lights a match the whole place is goin' up like an arson fire.
>
> —**Arlene Malinowski, *Or Forever Hold Your Peace***

The excerpt below is an example of writing on a serious topic (children in a mental health facility), but the narrator does not take himself seriously. He pokes fun at himself and his own ineptitude.

> My first assignment at Children's was to lead a group of eight-to-ten-year-old boys. The bad boys of their home schools, they came to us for academics, therapies, and recreational activities. And I was their ringmaster, circus clown, and confidant.
>
> Now, the gold-medal Olympic event was trying to encourage ten highly active boys to transition from free time in the gym, up two flights of stairs, to math class. Herding cats? On catnip. On pogo sticks. Through a funhouse.
>
> One day my boys displayed a rare degree of cooperation—in seeing how far up the gym wall they could run. Concussions awarded extra points. It was a kaleidoscopic tumble of black and white and brown bodies with crew cuts and mullets and cornrows. And I was supposed to be in charge.
>
> —**Paul P.**

In this next example, the topic is also serious, but the humor is derived from the rhythm, alliteration, and repetition in the writing, as well as the performance.

> So my mom moved in with me, and we began. Glasses on, teeth in, hearing aids in. Walk her to breakfast. Get her pills, get her food, "Try to eat, Mom!" Can't eat, starts to cough, starts to choke. Calm down! Try to breathe! Try again. She says, "Everything hurts." So, it's glasses off, teeth out, hearing aids out! "I'm hungry." Glasses on, teeth in, hearing aids in! "I need a nap." Glasses off, teeth out, hearing aids out! "Isn't it lunchtime?" Glasses on, teeth in, hearing aids in. All. Day.
>
> **—Victoria P.**

The subject may be serious, but you don't have to take yourself seriously. That said, never sacrifice a character or a scene for a laugh. Don't dilute the most serious parts of your show for the sake of making people chuckle. Humor may not be appropriate for some shows, and that's OK. It's also true that some people are inherently funny, while others are not—they simply don't look at the world in that way. For those folks, trying to be funny may not feel authentic, so they'll find other ways to switch up the energy in their work.

TRY THIS!

Watch a stand-up comedy special, a sketch show, and a humorous solo show, such as John Leguizamo's *Freak*. See if you can identify these different forms of humor: hyperbole, the rule of three, rhythm and repetition, physical comedy or slapstick, and traditional setup and punchline. Analyze some of the funniest moments. Why did the audience laugh? You don't have to be a comedian to start to notice patterns and tricks and structures that occur over and over again. You can use them too!

EXPERT ADVICE

What suggestions do you have for someone who feels like their show could benefit from humor but isn't even sure where to begin?

Everyone can learn some techniques that can make their writing funnier, but more important than being funny is having a sense of humor. Start by being willing to show your real authentic self. If you can recognize your own shortcomings and process them in front of an audience, you have a really high chance of getting laughs through that, without using puns or word craft or jokes.

One useful technique is exploring and heightening the comic problem or conflict. The impulse of the beginner is to just solve it, but someone who is thinking about comedy will consider all the different ways you can try to solve this problem without success *before* solving it. Another comic technique I would encourage people to use is "Don't like it a little bit. Love it a lot." Hyperbolic thinking. Hyperbole isn't a lie; it's just exaggerating the truth to make it clearer to the audience. So, raise the stakes.

One thing I say to students is "Play to your own delight." Find out what's authentically fun and interesting to *you*. If it's fun for you, it's probably going to be fun for us. It might not be hilarious, but it'll be engaging and sometimes we just like watching someone deeply engaged in a thing even though we're not personally connected to it.

Ric Walker
Professor, Columbia College Chicago
Actor, Director, Solo Performer, Improviser

Truth vs. Accuracy

Time to talk a bit about truth and ethics in storytelling.

The only writing worth a damn is writing that tells the truth. As readers and audience members, we know that when it comes to writing and art, we're often referring less to an objective historical truth, and more to an emotional truth. A piece feels "true" if it captures something real and universally felt about the human experience. However, if the solo show you're writing is a biographical piece or a first-person narrative featuring stories and real characters from your actual life, it's worth spending a bit of time examining your relationship and responsibility to the actual, material truth.

Let's distinguish between accuracy and narrative truth.

Accuracy refers to factual, verifiable information. Accuracy is measurable and precise.

Narrative truth refers to the honest depiction of an event or situation, allowing for the interpretation of a particular individual and their point of view.

If I walk outside on a July day and say, "It's 90 degrees out here," that's either accurate or it's not. We could get a thermometer and check it. I might walk outside and say, "It's hot as hell out here." That's narrative truth (and also a simile and an opinion). It isn't verifiable.

No one knows how hot hell is, and not everyone's hot is the same. (Arlene's hot is 95 degrees. Julie's is 80 degrees.)

A depicted conversation in a show is accurate if it's lifted verbatim from a recording or transcript. We can prove what was said in the conversation, and a recording can even capture tone and inflection. That's factual truth. But this isn't the way most of us end up sourcing dialogue for our first-person stories. We use our memory and intuition and do the best we can. If we're lucky, we have some notes.

There aren't generally fact-checkers at our solo shows policing what we say, other than those individuals who were present at the events we are portraying. Storytelling isn't journalism and doesn't demand the same degree of accuracy. However, as storytellers, if we are presenting a story as "true" or "real," we should always do our best to check the facts and details we're talking about, understanding that the story around those facts will be largely influenced by the way we see and remember events. We have a responsibility to tell our truth and ours only, being careful not to reveal confidences that will cause hardships for other people.

A conversation we write from memory can be true in the sense that it is true as remembered by the storyteller, allowing some space for personal point of view and the fallibility of memory. It may be emotionally true and capture the truth of a relationship. It can have meaning and narrative truth. As Salman Rushdie put it, "Autobiography is not about the life of the author, but about the truth of the author's life."

But it's tricky, right? If your best friend is telling you about something that happened to them as a child, they only have their own interpretation of the event. They can only tell you the truth of how it was for them, and how it looked through their eyes and felt in their body. Their sister, present at the same event, might have different memories and a very different story about what happened. Any holiday dinner where families get to discussing stories from decades ago reminds us how mutable and personal memory is.

When writing first-person narratives, we try to represent events from our own point of view as best we can from our memory (and photos and letters, or whatever we have available to us). If we have enough narrative distance from the events we're writing about, if we've worked through the hard emotions and resentments that may be attached to the events, we can feel confident that we're not villainizing other characters.

One technique we offer when writing about others is to represent behaviors, actions, and words that we actually remember being said, as opposed to subjective opinions. The line "Aunt Liz thought she was better than everybody else" suggests that you can read her mind. However, showing us that Aunt Liz rolled her eyes and touched objects in the room as if they were dirty and kicked a cat out of the way conveys actual behavior and lets us draw our own conclusions about Aunt Liz. She will have her own version of the story, of course, but we don't have to worry about that. Maybe she won't come to the show.

Making Things Up

We often have students completely stymied by writing dialogue who say, "I can't put this part of the show in scene because I don't remember the exact words my mother said to me in this situation thirty years ago." Of course they can't remember. However, if they take a big breath and try to relax, if they sit down and marry their memory with their imagination while not trying to recreate the conversation perfectly, we find that writers can usually come up with something pretty close. They end up capturing the emotional truth of the situation and maybe even the voices of the characters involved. Writing can be made up and also true.

Mark Twain is often attributed with saying "Never let the truth get in the way of a good story." We wouldn't go that far, but this might be a good place to mention that some of us, on occasion, take artistic license in the crafting of our stories. If you're writing a story about the time you and six friends got caught toilet papering cars in the high school parking lot, you might include only four friends in the version you share with an audience. You might consolidate the two characters who thought it was a bad idea from the beginning and eliminate the one who never said much. Eight or nine characters in a story is usually too many for a listener to keep track of.

We have also, on occasion, condensed timelines or locations to make a tighter, better story, as long as it doesn't feel like we're compromising the truth in any significant way. In one of her solo shows,

Arlene took two true, funny events that happened a year apart and incorporated them into the show as if they occurred on the same weekend in order to heighten the comedy. While not factually accurate, the show still conveyed the emotional truth of the events.

Another approach when dealing with first-person narratives is to simply acknowledge your uncertainties. You can employ language like "I think the only thing we had to eat that night was beef jerky, but I can't be sure" or "I can't recall the exact model of car, but I do remember that he washed it with the care of a mother bathing her infant for the first time."

Options for Telling Sensitive Truths

What if you want and are ready to share a sensitive truth—*your* truth—and you're worried that it will hurt (or piss off) people in your life when they come to your show?

First of all, before putting an uncomfortable truth in your play that involves others, think about why you want to include it. Ask yourself if the information can be written around or left out. Is it too important to ignore? Make sure your motive isn't about hurting someone or seeking revenge. In the end, stories that vilify others had better have a good reason for doing so. When you're ready to go forward, we've found there are a couple of ways to go about truth-telling, and only you can decide what's right for you and your story.

Do It Later. There's a writer we know who has plenty they want to say concerning their parents' relationship and divorce, but they suspect the writing would hurt their parents deeply, so they've made a commitment to wait until they're no longer around to do so. It's not that the writer has nasty things to say, but the divorce caused a lot of emotional pain for the writer as a child, which they predict would be very difficult for their parents to hear about. For now, this particular writer plans to write about other subjects until their parents pass on. This may or may not work for you.

Do It Now, Limited Release. We've sometimes written stories and shows that we feel confident will have a limited, in-person release and discouraged certain family or friends from attending with phrases like "You're not the target audience" or "This play might make you feel uncomfortable." This only works if friends and family members will actually take the hint. If you think this technique will work for you, it can also give you some room to tell stories about your sex life in public without worrying about having your parents in the audience (if that's even the sort of thing that bothers you).

Do It with Witness Protection. We often suggest to storytellers that they change names of real characters in their stories. In fact, this is a best practice if you haven't gotten explicit permission from folks to use their names, regardless of whether you think they will dislike the content or not. If you're concerned that someone might actually be hurt, embarrassed, or offended by your story, changing names and small details can mitigate audience members' ability to identify themselves.

If you think about how you would feel hearing an unflattering story featuring you not being your best self, you can understand how changing names is often the right thing to do. You can also create composite characters to represent multiple individuals in order to mask their identity.

Ask Permission. If you aren't sure that the people in your story would appreciate the story being shared, you can ask permission. Even if they wouldn't be portrayed in a bad light, they might not be the kind of people who want to be in the spotlight at all.

When Julie was writing her show about her neighborhood, she approached all her neighbors who were characters in the show and discussed how they wanted it handled. Some felt fine about her using their actual names, others wanted names and identifying details changed, and some didn't want to be mentioned in the play at all. The drawback of this option, of course, is that, if you're going to ask for permission, you have to be willing to makes changes if people don't grant it.

Give a Heads-Up (But Don't Ask for Permission). Use this option when you are committed to telling the truth in a story and would like to mitigate uncomfortable feelings and preserve relationships by having a discussion with folks beforehand. A respectful and well-considered conversation can sometimes craft a soft landing for our stories.

Julie's play *Good Enough* included a story that featured a heated argument with her father about politics. She had done her best to paint a well-rounded picture of her father as a human with many good qualities and also some flaws, and she had tried to represent herself honestly as an imperfect person as well. She presented the written story to her father before the show opened, saying, "I want you to know how much I love you. I realize that this story is my perspective and experience only. I'm including this piece in my solo show, and I want you to be aware of it before you decide to sit in the audience and see the show." It worked. He came and saw the play, holding court in the lobby afterward like a real celebrity.

Do It (Without Apology!). In her beautiful book *Bird by Bird*, Anne Lamott says, "You own everything that happened to you. Tell your stories. If people wanted you to write warmly about them, they should have behaved better." Sometimes we just have to make our art. But be prepared for differing perspectives. Understand that others may have their own interpretations and recollections of events and be open to engaging in constructive dialogue if conflicts arise.

Consider the Risk of Legal Action. Be aware that, in a worst-case scenario, writing about others carries a potential risk of being sued, especially if the information could be seen as defamatory or an invasion of privacy.

For an excellent examination of truth and dishonesty in storytelling, we recommend a *This American Life* episode in which Ira Glass interviews Mike Daisey about liberties he took in his solo show *The Agony and Ecstasy of Steve Jobs*. Daisey manufactured characters and dialogue to heighten the impact of his show, which, as we've said, sometimes is and sometimes isn't an issue in theatrical work. But when the piece was featured on *This American Life*, a radio show classified as journalism, the lack of veracity was definitely an issue.

These are questions for you to wrestle with. It's up to you to determine how far you are willing to push the boundaries of factual truth to serve your solo show.

EXPERT ADVICE

How have you navigated telling stories that feature people you love, and the concept of truth vs. accuracy?

I like a clever and playful structural mechanism that lets the audience know I'm not the be-all and end-all of a particular moment, but that I do have my own real experience of it. I wrote a story about my mom, and I called it *Things My Mother Says Never Happened*. Structurally, I was able to approach the idea that "this is *my* truth," as opposed to "this is *the* truth." Another thing, I would say, is to not be too precious with yourself. There are different ways we tend to tell stories, the triangulation of seeing ourselves as the hero or the victim or the bystander in a situation. And I have to admit that I generally see myself as the hero. That was a way to survive in my life. That doesn't mean I've truly been heroic every minute, but when I tell my story to myself, that's who I want to believe I am. But I have to be as fair to other people as I am to myself in order to tell a balanced story. I have to think about my mistakes and when I've messed up and failed. Sometimes, when I'm writing a piece and remembering myself only as my hero self, I'll put on a song I was listening to a lot during the time the story took place. That opens up a different muscle memory, and I immediately remember all the embarrassing things about a moment. It reminds me that I was *me then*, not *me now*.

Khanisha Foster
Director, Writer, Performer

Putting It Together Bit by Bit

Who Needs Narrative Structure?

We think of narrative structure as the order in which the events of your show are revealed to the audience, which may or may not be chronological. (Do not Google "narrative structure." There are many definitions out there!)

Think about a string of multicolored holiday lights. Each separate light is an event, or plot point, of your story, and you can switch the order of the lights around to create different effects. Maybe all the red lights will come first, or maybe you'll create a pattern, interspersing them throughout. Maybe you want to lead with the green lights. You get to decide. This is your narrative structure.

Narrative structure sometimes develops organically as you work on a show. Other times, once everything is written down in one order or another, you can start looking at structure and making decisions about what will best serve the needs of your story.

You may be familiar with the classic narrative arc or five-point plot structure: Exposition, Rising Action, Climax, Falling Action, and Resolution. (You can go ahead and Google this if you want.) We're not suggesting you throw this arc out the window. In whatever way you choose to arrange your show, you will still need rising tension to a climax and a resolution of some sort. The audience will probably still need some exposition about the characters or circumstances.

Here are eight kinds of narrative structure and examples of each.

1. **Chronological.** A chronological or linear play starts at the beginning and moves forward from moment to moment or scene to scene in the order things actually occurred. This structure is the simplest and most common, and many classic plays follow it. Don't discount this structure just because it's popular—many stories will be best told this way.

   Examples
   - Play—*The Boys in The Band* by Mart Crowley
   - Film—*Schindler's List* by Steven Zaillian, based on the book *Schindler's Ark*, by Thomas Keneally
   - Book—*To Kill a Mockingbird* by Harper Lee
   - Solo Show—*Remember This: The Lesson of Jan Karski* by Clark Young and Derek Goldman

2. **Nonlinear.** This storytelling structure presents the events of the story out of order, going back and forth in time. It may incorporate devices like dreams, dance interludes, moments of fantasy, or a plot within a plot line.

   Examples
   - Play—*Angels in America* by Tony Kushner
   - Film—*Pulp Fiction* by Quentin Tarantino
   - Book—*The Sound and the Fury* by William Faulkner
   - Solo Show—*How I Learned What I Learned* by August Wilson

3. **Ouroboros.** The play begins in an intense, dramatic, or off-beat moment near or at the end, and then goes back to the beginning to reveal how the situation developed. This structure is also called a circle story or circular narrative. The story's starting and ending points are the same and mirror each other, but the main character is transformed.

   Examples
   - Play—*Lookingglass Alice*, adapted by David Catlin from *Alice's Adventures in Wonderland* and *Through the Looking-Glass*
   - Film—*Fight Club*, adapted by Jim Uhls from Chuck Palahniuk's novel
   - Book—*The House of the Spirits* by Isabel Allende
   - Solo Show—*Nanette* by Hannah Gadsby

4. **In medias res.** Meaning "in the midst of things," this structure opens without any introductory information or exposition. The action has already begun. Like the ouroboros structure, this narrative technique captures the audience's attention, bringing them front and center into the fray. Necessary exposition is then sewn into the plot as events move forward.

   Examples
   - Play—*The Pillowman* by Martin McDonagh
   - Film—*Goodfellas,* adapted by Nicholas Pileggi and Martin Scorsese from Pileggi's book *Wiseguy*
   - Book—*Gone Girl* by Gillian Flynn
   - Solo Show—*Krapp's Last Tape* by Samuel Beckett

5. **Bookend.** A show begins with a framing story and flashes back in time (or forward, or sideways) to a different, separate story or incident that flavors the first story. Once the second narrative is told in its entirety, the framing story picks up where the beginning left off and continues. Generally, the meaning of the overall story hinges on the juxtaposition of the inner and outer story.

   Examples
   - Play—*Our Town* by Thornton Wilder
   - Film—*Forrest Gump,* adapted by Eric Roth, from the novel by Winston Groom
   - Book—*Frankenstein* by Mary Shelley
   - Solo Show—*Antonio's Song/I Was Dreaming of a Son* by Dael Orlandersmith and Antonio Edwards Suarez

6. **String of pearls.** A series of scenes, vignettes, or self-contained small stories are strung together, so that, while they might each be very different, they form a complete play that has a sense of unity, even if the scenes do not build on each other.

   Examples
   - Play—*Metamorphoses,* adapted by Mary Zimmerman from Ovid's stories
   - Film—*Love Actually* by Richard Curtis

- Book—*Everything I Never Told You* by Celeste Ng
- Solo Show—*Santaland Diaries* by David Sedaris

7. **Parallel narrative storytelling.** This type of narrative ties together multiple perspectives, stories, or plot lines that are connected by a shared event, character, or theme. In a solo show, this is often accomplished by the performer portraying multiple characters.

   Examples
   - Play—*The Ferryman* by Jez Butterworth
   - Film—*The Joy Luck Club,* adapted by Amy Tan and Ronald Bass from Tan's novel
   - Book—*The Hours* by Michael Cunningham
   - Solo Show—*In & Of Itself* by Derek DelGaudio

8. **Hero's journey.** This structure has specific components, including a call to action, a decision to venture into unknown territory, facing adversity, and ultimately returning home with treasure and transformed. Often told chronologically, it doesn't have to be. If you have a protagonist facing a series of hardships in your play, do some quick research on Joseph Campbell's *The Hero's Journey* and see if a loose application of this structure is helpful.

   Examples
   - Play—*The Lion King,* music by Elton John, lyrics by Tim Rice; book by Roger Allers and Irene Mecchi
   - Film—*Star Wars* by George Lucas
   - Book—*The Hobbit* by J. R. R. Tolkien
   - Solo Show—*No Child . . .* by Nilaja Sun

There is overlap among these structures, and some stories, plays, shows, and movies use more than one. Keep in mind that these are just examples of some of the narrative structures we've encountered. There are many other options, including those you may need to invent to fit the needs of your show! We offer these as inspiration, as a place to begin.

TRY THIS!

If you haven't settled on a narrative structure for your solo play yet, be aware that some structures will work better than others. To make sure you have a good fit, start experimenting.

1. Write down the major plot points or sections of your solo play on index cards. Begin reordering them in various ways.
2. If you were to share your play chronologically, can you identify the Exposition, Rising Action, Climax, Falling Action, and Resolution?
3. Paying special attention to the climax or turning point of your show, can you reorder the other sections to create more tension up to that moment?

An Organizing Framework

This concept can be a little hard to grasp at first. Do what we have to do every time someone tries to explain "Higgs boson" or "the multiverse" to us. Take a deep breath. Don't panic. There's more than one way to cook a turkey, and an organizing framework is just one tried and true tool we offer.

Think of an organizing framework as the lens, storytelling device, or overall container through which your solo show is told. Distinct from narrative structure, which has more to do with the sequence of how your plot is revealed, an organizing framework is a unifying design and can give your show a distinct identity. It can be the superglue that connects everything together in a meaningful way.

The Tony and Drama Desk–nominated *The Search for Signs of Intelligent Life in the Universe*, a character-driven solo show with a string of pearls narrative structure, by Jane Wagner, centers on Trudy, a bag lady who communicates with extraterrestrial beings. These aliens ask her to observe and explain human behavior to them, which serves as the framework or skeleton for the story. Trudy tells the aliens that, although humanity is flawed, she believes humans are capable of great compassion and goodness, even if they sometimes lose sight of it. The organizing framework of a conversation between a human and an extraterrestrial provides a way to explore and answer the essential question "What does it mean to be human?"

Heidi Schreck's solo(ish) play *What the Constitution Means to Me* examines how the Constitution has and has not protected the rights of women, specifically the women in her family. When Heidi was a teenager, she participated in Constitutional debate competitions all over the country to earn money for college. She uses the rules and format of debate as an organizing framework in her solo show, even holding an actual debate in front of the audience about whether the Constitution should be abolished or simply amended to better serve all Americans. The show is a cultural autobiography that uses a string of pearls narrative structure, and the organizing framework does the heavy lifting—it unifies tone, gives shape to the narrative, and offers the audience a way in.

Lady Day at Emerson's Bar and Grill by Lanie Robertson is a solo show with music about the jazz icon Billie Holiday. This play is a biographical cabaret solo show, with a chronological narrative structure. The organizing framework is a fictionalized performance at a bar in South Philadelphia. While the play is inspired by real events, it reimagines one of her last performances and combines historical facts, monologues, and Holiday's music to tell the story of her life, struggles, and career.

An organizing framework can elevate a show by adding layers of meaning and theatricality while giving the audience a way to interpret and understand how all the pieces of a show fit together. However, not every solo show has—or needs—a formal organizing framework. Many successful solo shows, like *Fleabag*, *Remember This*, and *Grounded*, rely strictly on narrative structure.

Using an organizing framework is also different from having a theme. A theme is a central idea or message that runs through your show—like love, justice, or coming of age. A theme may provide meaning or inspire the story, but it won't offer structure. An organizing framework, on the other hand, is what gives your show its container, regardless of whether you are starting your play in the middle of the action, telling it chronologically, or bouncing around in time.

For example, the organizing framework of the Pulitzer Prize and Tony–winning show *I Am My Own Wife*, by Doug Wright, is that of an extended interview between the playwright and Charlotte von

Mahlsdorf, a transgender woman who survived the Nazi and Communist regimes in East Germany. This is a dialogue-driven solo show, and the play's interview framing device made the play not just about Charlotte's life but also about memory, identity, and how history is reported and recorded.

We have seen many organizing frameworks we love. Arlene structured her solo piece *Kicking the Habit* around the four mysteries of the rosary, using them as a device to explore her experiences with her grammar school nemesis, Sister Mary Concepta. Each mystery became a portal into a specific memory, helping the audience track both the story's spiritual and emotional arc. This structure added depth to the play, intertwining her personal story with religious symbolism.

We've also seen a solo play about a student's gap year that was framed through the seven deadly sins, offering an interesting perspective on personal growth. Another play explored a series of dreadful jobs, with each scene introduced by an HR memo or stipulation. One of our students used the frame of cleaning out an attic after their parent died. We've seen a solo performance using songs and music to create a narrative structure aligning with that of an album, with distinct A and B sides for framing the stories. One of our students took audiences on a cosmic journey using astronomy as a storytelling device to delve into trauma and grief. Finally, one of our inventive clients structured her solo show using the organizing framework of the reality show *Survivor*. Through the competitive and strategic lens of the game, she examined themes of trust and endurance.

In each of these cases, the organizing framework deepened our understanding of the playwright's message and also gave the audience a container that felt both familiar and surprising. We looked forward to and delighted in the *way* we were experiencing the story.

Sometimes you may not discover your organizing framework until you're deep into the writing process—and that's perfectly fine. Other times, you'll know from the very beginning how you want to tell the story.

When Julie was developing her solo show *Love Thy Neighbor . . . Till It Hurts*, she knew it would be the story of moving into a neighborhood she didn't know and building relationships with her new neighbors. She already had a first draft and lots of material when she heard an episode of *This American Life*, the long-running public radio show. In this episode, host Ira Glass described her very block in Rogers Park as "shabby." Julie's director and cocreator, Megan, suggested structuring her solo piece as a *This American Life* episode with four titled acts—as a kind of counter-argument to Glass. Suddenly, Julie had an organizing framework. The narrative stayed mostly chronological, but the radio-show format gave the piece identity, cohesion, and momentum.

Sometimes an organizing framework appears at the beginning; sometimes it shows up late. But when it clicks, you'll feel the difference.

Would an organizing framework enhance your show? Experiment a bit. Don't be afraid to think outside of the box. The only absolute make-or-break thing you MUST do to create a solo show is actually write it. Beyond that we're simply offering tools—lessons we've learned about what can help a solo play work.

TRY THIS!

Take a high-level, pulled-back look at your script/ideas/story so far. Jot down any metaphors that come to mind. Are there any processes, lists, or devices that could be illuminating as an organizing framework? Is there something you are doing in one or a few scenes that could be extended throughout the piece?

Stitching, Knitting, and Using Narrative

Putting together a solo show can be a lot like creating a quilt, collage, or mosaic. In each case, the focus is first on crafting the smaller components that will become part of the larger whole. Once most of those pieces are created, the fun begins: experimenting with how to fit them all together. You may find that you need to create an additional piece for one section, that another piece feels too large, or that some sections you've made aren't necessary after all.

When you reach the point where you think you have written all or most of the stories, moments, and events that will comprise your solo play, you can start thinking about how you want to construct them into a unified piece. There are lots of ways to go about this! Follow your intuition. Trust your instincts! Do it any way you want.

Take Inventory

First, take a good look at what you have. This might mean opening all the documents on your computer, all the written bits and bobs, and reading through them. Or it might mean printing everything and laying the pages out on your living room floor. Either way, take a moment to be *very* proud of yourself. Look how far you've come. You've done a tremendous amount of work, and you now have *a lot* of raw material to work with. As you review the pieces of writing, notice whether you want to break some of the sections down into smaller chunks. Some writers find that numbering or labeling the chunks of writing with very simple titles is helpful at this point.

How Ya Gonna Roll It Out?

You might already have an idea of how you want to sequence all this writing. Or you might still be figuring it out, and that's OK! This would be a good time to revisit (or read) the chapter in this book on narrative structure. We think of narrative structure as the order in which the plot of your show is revealed to the audience. You can always present your show in chronological order, which is the order that you (or your protagonist) lived the events, but it's not your only option.

At this stage, we're experimenting. Decide on an order and loosely assemble the pieces in that way. What do you think? Maybe? No? Try something else. A quilter might at this point lay out all her pieces of fabric or loosely baste them together, decide she doesn't like them that way, and take them apart again. Arlene likes to write the title of each section or mini-story on index cards and tape them on the wall, arranging and rearranging them.

Julie's play *Good Enough* consists of four different stories around the theme "What does it mean to be a good person?" She and her director, Megan, tried putting the show together in many different ways—arranging and reassembling—before finally landing on chopping one story up and telling the other stories in their entirety within that one story. Finding the right structure for your solo show is a process. Give yourself permission to experiment and play.

Stitching and Weaving

Once you've found a sequence for the pieces of your show that you're excited about, you can get down to connecting them. There are many different ways of doing this.

If you've written a solo play that consists of stand-alone monologues delivered by various characters, you may not need to stitch your scenes together. You might simply change your physicality to take on a new character or scene. You might use lighting to signal a transition. You might put songs or musical cues between the pieces.

If you've written what we call a narrative solo play, you'll probably connect the various scenes of your show with narration, which usually entails breaking the fourth wall and speaking directly to the audience to guide them through the story. These shifts to narration between scenes can be made even clearer with technical support and staging choices. For example, different parts of the stage can represent different times—past or present. You might say, "This wasn't the first time I had found myself lost in Venice. When I was ten years old, my family had taken a trip there to celebrate my parents' anniversary," and then move to the part of the stage that represents the past.

A scene in Dael Orlandersmith's solo play *Forever* takes place at the grave of Jim Morrison in Paris. She describes the type of day, what the grave looked like, and the people who were there. She breaks the fourth wall and talks directly to the audience, providing narration and exposition. But this isn't just surface description—she inhabits the scene with full presence, allowing the audience to experience the graveyard through her gestures, voice, and silences. She then flashes back to a scene in which she is eleven years old, in Harlem buying a Doors album, and has a frightening interaction with a man on the street. She includes dialogue between characters, taking on the vocal intonations of the man and the vocabulary and delivery of the eleven-year-old kid. These contrasting yet connected pieces are stitched together by narration. The narration isn't filler—it's the thread that connects emotional beats and time travel and guides the audience through the layers of memory and meaning.

The narration that connects the sections of your show can be from the Contemporary Narrator or the Scenic Narrator, and it can consist of backstory, inner monologue, the main character's private thoughts, or a moment of reflection. We often tell stories this way in our real lives—a mix of a little dialogue, descriptions of events or locations, a bit of he said/she said, and some narration to explain what happened next or what we thought about it. Though we want to focus on showing rather than telling, weaving in some narration can give the audience an intimate view of what's going on.

Notice how Errol McLendon, in his solo play *Inner State Stories*, uses his mother's rules of the road to transition us to the past in this excerpt:

The next day, there's snow. The scenery is amazing through South Dakota—mountains, rivers, so much sky—and billboards and truck stops becoming rarer and rarer. I stay in the slow lane and enjoy my drive, stopping at dozens of unique diners and tourist stops. There's no rush. There's no agenda. The trip is the destination.

If I get the least bit sleepy, I pull over and nap, even if I just left my motel an hour before. I imagine my mother in the passenger seat saying, "When the road starts to swim in front of your eyes, it's time to get out of the pool."

Other rules of the road she mentioned while teaching me to drive: "Your blinker is not a cap holder. It is your way of showing the other drivers you are a gentleman." "Only animals being chased by other animals need to take off in a hurry." And my favorite: "Drive like you don't want to die."

Thanks to my mother's rules of the road and her teaching me to drive in the Presbyterian church parking lot, I passed my driver's license test the first time and never did take Driver's Ed.

The real driver's test happened four months later. On our summer drive to Dallas, as we were about to get on the interstate, my mother pulled over and said, "I'm a little tired. I'd like you to drive for a while. I need a nap."

I'd never been more flattered or more nervous. I think I drove for thirty minutes and never went over thirty miles an hour. My mother never encouraged me to go faster. She just sat in the seat next to me with her eyes closed.

After a while, she opened her eyes, gave a very dramatic yawn and said, "Thank you, Pumpkin. I needed that. Do you mind if I take over now?"

I didn't mind. I was a nervous wreck. My hands ached from gripping the steering wheel and my T-shirt was soaked with sweat.

My mother admitted years later that she had been just as nervous. She hadn't slept at all but had kept watch through squinted eyes, "playin' possum" as she called it.

I make it to Keystone in a blinding snowstorm. I stop at the first hotel I come to and the only chain hotel I will stay

> at in the entire trip, a Holiday Inn. The next morning, I see Mount Rushmore in the snow.

The rules of the road are used here to transition us to a flashback where Errol was a new driver decades before. We're eased into the scene seamlessly. Also notice how Errol brings us back to the present of the play with "I make it to Keystone in a blinding snowstorm." Jumps back to the present like this can be assisted by lighting adjustments, a change in physicality, or, as Errol did in his show, a different vocal attack.

Planting Seeds and Payoffs

One technique to consider as you put your show together and create a satisfying journey for your audience is to plant seeds early that will pay off later. For instance, imagine a scene in a solo play where a protagonist is terrified of bugs and there is a spider between herself and the door to her apartment. She croaks "help," and her neighbor Mrs. Cratch responds immediately, entering the apartment and removing the spider. OK, that could work. But imagine how much more impact the rescue would have if the protagonist had complained offhandedly early in the play that she thinks Mrs. Cratch is a busybody who tries to listen in on her conversations. We don't recognize the seed until it sprouts later.

Seeds can be small details, lines of dialogue, or even actions that seem unimportant at first. Done well, these moments make the audience feel like they've been let in on a secret, creating a rewarding experience when the connections are revealed later. For example, we worked with solo artist Jackie Maruschak, whose play *The Secret Life of a Baton Twirler* opened with these lines:

> The last words my mother ever said to me are, "Well, there's a lot I want to say." And then . . . she never got to say any of it.

Talk about a cliffhanger. Later on, in the middle of this solo show, the main character receives a packet of information with a neon Post-it Note from her mother. She is caught so off guard by the fact that these are beneficiary papers—tangible evidence that her mother is actively dying—that she pays little attention to the note. The play ends with these lines:

> My mother, Marie, never expected me to be perfect. She may have thought she failed me in many ways, but she taught me in so many more. I never regretted having her as a mother. I just hope she never regretted having . . . (light bulb discovery) OH MY GOD . . . I know exactly what I needed my mother to say . . . It was there on the Post-it Note, the one I had forgotten about. It read, "I knew I had the right kid. Love you, Mom."

Stealing Film Techniques

When Arlene was developing her first solo show with director, filmmaker, and author Mark Travis, he encouraged her to apply film techniques to rearrange and refine various sections. Here a few film techniques that we like to invite our classes to experiment with.

- **Wide shots and close-ups.** Think of moments in your show where you are covering a span of years or giving an overview of a situation as a wide shot. Scenes, dialogue, and moments of narration that reveal our thoughts and feelings are close-ups. Just like in a great film, we want a mix of both, and we don't want to get stuck in either for too long.
- **Jump cuts.** In films, scenes can start and end in the middle of a dinner in a restaurant, in the middle of a phone call, in the aisle of a grocery store, or mid-swim at the pool. The same goes for scenes in your solo play. As long as the next scene conveys where events are happening and how much time has passed, it can actually be more dynamic to jump in or out of a scene rather than showing the audience unimportant details about how we got to or left a place.
- **Montages.** Think about a montage in a rom-com or one that conveys the drudgery of a menial job with repetitive tasks. In your show, you can create montages with gestures, snippets of scenes, or short, pithy lines to capture an experience. One example is the traditional love story montage in film. The

unlikely couple has a meet-cute, they accidentally get caught in the rain and duck into a doorway where they kiss for the first time, they share a romantic candlelight dinner, they blissfully fold clothes together at the laundromat, and—finally—we see them holding a grocery bag with a baguette sticking out of it while they are walking past the Eiffel Tower when one of them gets down on a knee. Boom! An entire love story in under a minute. Montages can also be effective at bringing levity and humor to our work.

Onstage, a solo performer could recreate this through a quick succession of physicalizations, snapshots of dialogue, changes in tone or tempo, or lighting shifts to signal the montage snapshots. They might step from one spot on the stage to another, making each location a new scene. They might use minimal props or costume pieces to suggest multiple quick scenes.

In *A Little Bit Not Normal*, Arlene's character experiences an escalating panic attack as she portrays a rapid-fire montage of voices that bombard the main character from all directions. She indicates this by directing her visual focus around the stage. The effect mirrors the sensory overload of the moment and gives the audience a visceral understanding of what's happening inside the character.

- **Fast-forward.** Solo plays can jump ahead in time just as films do. There's no need to say "fast forward." A sharp change of energy as we say "Six years later, I'm in a whole new city" works fine. The audience will follow you.
- **Slow motion.** A slow-mo sequence can add drama, suspense, or humor to a solo show, especially during an important scene, such as when the character is experiencing an emotional moment. For example, imagine your main character reliving a moment of dread, like having to go to the principal's office for cheating on a test. Instead of rushing through it, slow down the action and stretch out the character's movements. It's a great way to draw attention to details that might otherwise be missed in real time.

- **Rewind.** There are so many fun ways to rewind and flash back in solo work. Try simple techniques, such as moving to a new part of the playing space and saying "I'm five years old, and I've finally learned how to ride a bike without training wheels." Or try calling attention to your flashbacks by introducing them with "Rewind!" or "Hold on. Before I tell you this, I need to take you back." You can reverse the physical gestures, play with sound, repeat lines backwards or distorted. Then, "replay" the moment again, with new awareness.
- **Freeze-frame.** Creating a tableau pauses the action to heighten tension or add an emotional beat in your solo piece. The main character holds a pose, which can be paired with narration or an inner monologue, allowing the audience to reflect on the significance of what has just happened or what is about to happen.

If you take nothing else from this chapter, consider experimenting and trying lots of different techniques as you put your solo play together.

TRY THIS!

Play around with some film techniques.

- **Freeze-frame.** Choose a pivotal moment in your solo show—one that's emotionally charged or visually vivid. Perform the scene until it reaches its most intense point and then freeze. Now, speak directly to the audience from inside that frozen moment. What are you thinking? What can't you say out loud? What's really happening underneath the action? Use this "freeze-frame" to explore the inner life of your character. You can even return to the action after the freeze, as if nothing happened. Try it. Freeze. Speak. Unfreeze.
- **Rewind and replay.** Pick a short scene from your solo show (a conversation, a fight, a memory) and perform it once, all the way through. Now, imagine someone hitting rewind on a remote. "Replay" the moment again, with new awareness. Maybe your character sees circumstances differently. Maybe the stakes are higher. Maybe the same moment has a different meaning now. Rewinding gives you a chance to reframe a memory, correct a mistake, or show the gap between what happened and what you wish had happened.

Theatrical Elements

A solo show is a play with one actor. There may be multiple settings and characters, but you, or the actor, will be the only person onstage and, typically, the only voice your audience will hear. And that's great! You're going to have a tight, well-written, beautifully performed show that deserves to be heard. And incorporating some design elements can heighten and support your hard work.

Begin thinking about your show as a fully staged experience—not just a script. As you write, imagine how light, sound, and movement might support or amplify a moment. Ask yourself: What might the audience *see* or *hear* that supports what they feel? How might the space around you become a second character in your piece? These questions aren't separate from your writing—they're part of it. Start building those ideas in early. You're not just crafting words; you're crafting a world.

A scenic design that includes a simple backdrop, a structure, or a few furniture pieces can go a long way in creating a location or visual interest for your show. Platforms or blocks can provide places to sit and move around. We've seen a set consisting of a single bench that doubled as a bed, a child's fort, a stovetop, and a staircase. Another set was an entire wall made up of stacked packing boxes and a swing that hung from the ceiling. Each of these simple sets worked beautifully.

In our opinion, lighting design may give you the most bang for your buck. Lights are wonderful not just for suggesting mood but also for conveying changes in location throughout your show. An audience will catch on very quickly that a specific pool of light in a certain area of the stage is your bedroom or the neighborhood café each time you return to it. Similarly, you can alternate between a cool lighting wash and a warm wash to delineate past and present.

Like lighting, a good sound design can delineate locations and quickly switch up the mood of your show. Sound design is not limited to music or realistic environmental sounds (such as the sounds of a factory, seagulls, or a record scratch). Anything the audience hears that is supporting your text is sound design. To appreciate the possibilities, watch five minutes of a movie without sound and then watch to it with sound. Notice the difference!

A note about music and the use of songs. Research and understand fair use. Some folks want to sing three lines of a popular song in their solo show or use a recording or envision pre-show and post-show music. Some solo artists may think, "This is a tiny show that I'm producing myself, so I'm not going to worry about permissions" or "I'll use the material, and if I get a cease and desist letter, I will" or "I'll deal with it when I get to Broadway." Our advice is to investigate the guidelines and then make your own decisions. There are royalty-free music services and streaming platforms that have original music and songs for every genre and every era for free or a small fee. Just look online.

Because solo pieces have only one actor and it is so very awkward when they leave the stage, costume changes during solo plays are somewhat rare. This makes it essential for the performer's clothing to convey as much about the character as possible. Arlene has always opted to wear black on black on dark on black because it's a clean palate for doing character work. (Costumes look very different under the lights, so be sure to try out what you're planning to wear on the stage and have someone take pictures of you.)

Projections are a more cost-effective way to create a reality onstage than building a set. That doesn't mean they're easy to do, but the possibilities are endless if you have the right equipment and a talented designer. We love how projecting a photo, film, animation, or special effects can give the audience a world of information in an instant.

Puppets aren't right for every show, obviously, and they require real skill, facility, and practice. But we love them! They create an entire other presence onstage to interact with. We've seen a solo show in which a simple little hand puppet used as a child's toy in the early part of the play became a stand-in for a grandfather who was being lost to Alzheimer's later in the show.

A few well-chosen props can take on real power onstage, especially if the objects are symbolic or metaphorical in some way. We saw a solo piece in Chicago recently that featured a simple set and sound design, lots of projections, and only two props: a skateboard and an aluminum walker. They took on more and more meaning as the show progressed, becoming symbolic of the past and present.

Choreography can be an unexpected element in a solo show, allowing the performer to express a range of emotions through dance sequences or merely stylized movement. For example, one of our students incorporated traditional Indian dance to represent the emotional states of her main character. The same choreography was repeated in different moments of the play, varying the intensity to reflect the instability of her mental state. The dance was sometimes joyful, sometimes frantic, eventually completely out of control.

Stage makeup can enhance character portrayal through visual transformation. It can convey details about a character's personality, social status, age, or health. For instance, in one beautiful solo show, makeup reflects the main character's journey from childhood to adulthood and serves as a metaphor for the masks we put on in our lives. Using a frame to portray a mirror, the performer changed her hair and makeup in front of the audience throughout the show.

Who doesn't love spectacle? Special effects can be used to visually emphasize certain moments, create locations or atmospheres, or even help narrate the action. Special effects can range from strobe lights to flying objects and trap doors. One solo show we saw used a smoke machine during train scenes, and it also created the ground fog that the main character traveled through to escape the Gestapo. We're still waiting to see a solo show in which someone flies. Keep us posted.

Another person can sometimes add a theatrical element to a solo piece, though we realize that's counterintuitive. One of our students used two silent actors—one representing a demon of mental illness and the other the keeper of light and hope—who came onstage for a movement piece during a scene set in a mental health facility. Julie uses a live musician onstage for all of her solo works. The musician doesn't have lines but functions as a witness and confidant. Audience interaction can provide a truly interesting dynamic, as demonstrated in Duncan Macmillan and Jonny Donahoe's *Every Brilliant Thing*, where individual audience members are invited to play characters in scenes with the protagonist.

Of course, many one-person plays have been done with absolutely no technical support. The iconic image of a solo piece is a performer and a single chair on a bare stage, and that's worked well for lots of folks. Many of us end up performing in nontraditional venues like the back room of a bar or an empty storefront—places where you don't find backstage space or a lighting grid or any kind of sound system. You may not want to hire any designers for your show, and that's OK. You have a vision for your show. You're creative.

Practically speaking, if you're performing at a festival with a limited time slot to set up, perform, and strike your entire show, you're not going to be able to accommodate involved set pieces and numerous props anyway. You'll need something uncomplicated and portable.

Luckily, solo work's close association with storytelling means that the audience will be primed to suspend their disbelief and let their imaginations travel with you wherever you take them. That doesn't mean you have to do it all yourself. Theater is a collaborative art, and there are set and sound and lighting designers out there who know all about this stuff and can ensure your show feels professional if you want to work with them.

At this point, let's name the elephant in the room: money. We can't recommend asking someone to work on your show for no pay at all, so if you hope to use a designer or two, do your best to allocate some of your funds ahead of time toward paying them. If you can pay only a meager stipend, be up front about that. New designers are sometimes willing to take on projects to build their résumés. Always credit your collaborators. Designers are artists, and it's unethical to not credit them for their ideas and work.

When Julie was working on her first two solo shows, she had big dreams and a very limited budget. For her second show, *Love Thy*

Neighbor . . . Till It Hurts, she managed to get a couple of small grants to help her produce the show, and she decided she would earmark all of that money for a director and a composer/sound designer. That was all she could afford. She and the director counted on the theaters where they were going to perform to have a general lighting plot they could use, which worked out fine.

Julie's sound designer turned out to be a genius (not hyperbole). The underscoring and interstitial music that he wrote, along with the environmental sound effects, created an entire world onstage. The music signaled changes in location, time, and mood. The director had the idea of hanging a couple of wooden painted window frames from above to function as the set, along with a stool that could be used in a variety of ways. When it was all put together, the design felt professional and effective.

In the future, when some other theater wants to produce *Love Thy Neighbor . . . Till It Hurts* with a $60,000 budget, Julie can still have the revolving stage and the garden fence that disappears into the floor and the falling snow and the working oven onstage so she can bake a cake in real time and the big bubble machine (because Julie likes bubbles, not because the show calls for it). And you can bet she'll use the exact same sound designer, because he's a genius.

How to Go About Getting a Designer

First, think about which theatrical elements feel most important for your show. Perhaps you have your heart set on a particular aspect of your show being very professionally realized, and you want to make sure that element is well-produced. Great. Get a designer for that. If you know theater designers (set, costume, lighting, sound), they will know other designers, so that's a great place to start looking for folks who might be interested in collaborating with you.

If you—or you and your director—find a designer that you want to approach about working on your show, give them a copy of your script or invite them to see a rehearsal before committing. Have a conversation with them and ask what they are drawn to in your play. Don't put them on the spot and immediately ask what kind of design they envision, though you can certainly ask them what images your show brings to mind.

Share with them any ideas that you or the director have about the design, but remember theater is a collaborative art. You want to find someone who is on the same page as you, but they will have their own artistic ideas. This is good! Your designer may have ideas that surprise you and help you see your show in new ways. Inviting in collaborators and experiencing how they interpret your work can unlock all kinds of new meanings and ideas for you.

You definitely don't want to agree to work with someone whose vision is too far from yours or who can't hear you. Most designers worth their salt are pretty good listeners and collaborators. As you work together, proceed as you would in any relationship or collaboration that's important to you—with respect and honesty. Your director will also have experience working with designers and can be a great resource here.

YOU as Theatrical Element

As you are putting your show together, keep in mind that theatricality is more than stagecraft and design elements. Theatricality can also be built into your performance. Pantomime, singing, juggling, and unicycling are very theatrical because they involve specialized uses of the body and voice. Physicalizing film techniques, such as building a montage of experiences, fast-forwarding, using slow-motion or quick cuts feel theatrical because they involve moving your body and using your voice in ways that we don't typically do in our everyday life. Even scenes where we portray multiple characters and use vocal variation to differentiate them through dialogue feel theatrical—they literally feel like theater and capture an audience's attention.

In the end, folks don't go to the theater to see every day humdrum life. They go to see and feel *heightened* life. That doesn't mean fake and over-the-top, rather, intense and special. Don't shy away from that.

TRY THIS!

1. Start taking some notes on theatricality as ideas occur to you. When you picture your one-person play, what technical, theatrical elements feel most important? If you were getting your $60K production in a 600-seat house right now, how would your show look? If you could only have one—a set, lighting, sound, costume, or projection designer—which would you choose?
2. Look through your script or most current draft. Are there places to incorporate theatricality into your performance? What big, showy ideas would you try out if you knew no one would say no?
3. Go see solo shows in theaters and watch them on streaming platforms. Steal some ideas.

EXPERT ADVICE

I had very specific music that I wanted played at different moments during my show. I'd written everything with particular pieces of contemporary music in mind, and for my first production we had the rights to the music, because the venue had an agreement with ASCAP (American Society of Composers, Authors and Publishers). I included music by AC/DC, Joni Mitchell—music that added a lot to the show. Now I can't even put pieces of the recorded show online without risking being sued. If I had to do the whole thing over again, it might have been better for me to say to a sound designer, "In this section, I'm thinking about the song 'River' by Joni Mitchell. Is there something you can come up with that has that vibe?" I probably should have done that rather than using actual songs. I can't put any of my fabulous multiple-camera recording online, and if I take the show somewhere else, I'll have to have a new sound design.

Kurt Naebig
Solo Performer, Actor, Director

Create Some White Space

The only time the cable company has ever been right and on time is when they tell us to unplug and wait for ten minutes. Sometimes, the best way to move forward is to take time to step back. Your brain, soul, and creativity need a moment of white space.

In advertising, white space on a page of text and images is designed to give your eyes a place to rest. It's also a tool to declutter your brain, allowing clarity to emerge. Carving out white space means taking an intentional pause in the middle of your writing process. This pause can help you rediscover your work with a new perspective and a rekindled sense of commitment.

Artists of all kinds understand that creative breakthroughs happen when they allow for a respite. If you're feeling overwhelmed managing a busy to-do list or if you feel blocked approaching the next step of your show, we invite you to give yourself time to recalibrate and come back to the work with fresh eyes.

Creating white space doesn't mean that you stop willy-nilly. Commit to a specific length of time for your white space. It may be three days, a few weeks, or an entire season. This is an intentional time during which you'll remove the pressure of output without the guilt of coulda, woulda, shouldas. A defined time in which you let your solo show marinate, brine, pickle, cure, smoke, and ferment. Let it breathe. Other than that, time and living your life are the key elements of white space. Decide when you'll start and end and put it into your calendar.

Set forth the intention that you will use this time to be really present in your life. Taste your breakfast, appreciate your sleep, notice the Halloween decorations, take a different route to work, listen to your best friend's voice, get swept up by a movie or a great book, and value the small things. Think of this white space as a layover during your creative process and trust that it will help you with your solo show later on.

When your respite is over, take a deep breath, express gratitude, and move forward. Return to your solo work with gusto and verve. We know artists who have had magical experiences or moments of transcendence during these periods, while others just appreciate the relief of time off from expectations. Whatever it brings you, the pause is part of the process. Try creating some white space in your creative life and see what happens. Let us know.

Construction and Deconstruction

Writing and Rewriting (Ugh!)

The Japanese word "kaizen" is a compound of two words that together translate as "good change" or "improvement." More specifically, it means the making of small changes to bring about big improvements. One way to do that in your solo show is by rewriting.

When we talk about rewriting in our classes, some folks think it means they didn't get it right the first time or they're bad writers who should never think about doing a solo show ever again. Nothing makes us more heartsick than giving a solo writer some feedback on how to move their piece forward and finding they've abandoned the work because they think "it's no good." We invite you to look at it this way: many of us didn't do very well the first time we tried to ride a bike, make a free throw, or play the trombone. It took practice.

Rewriting is refining the work. It's where your ideas emerge more clearly and evolve into something stronger. Expect that a draft is simply that—a draft, not a comment on your talent.

The much-loved book *To Kill a Mockingbird*, by Harper Lee, was published in 1960. *Go Set a Watchman* wasn't published until 2015, though most scholars agree that it was written first. *To Kill a Mockingbird* was a reworked version of *Watchman*, with major revisions made to the storyline, plot, and characters.

Go Set a Watchman is written in the third person and takes place when the main character in *To Kill a Mockingbird*, Scout, returns to

Alabama as an adult. The infamous trial of a Black man accused of raping a white woman, which was the centerpiece of *Mockingbird*, is a small story told in flashback in *Watchman*. Scout's father, Atticus Finch, is not the idealized lawyer with a sense of justice that he is in *Mockingbird*, but a complicated man who must reconcile his racism with the law of the land. *Watchman* explores the disillusionment of a daughter returning home to a town and a father she doesn't recognize.

The Pulitzer Prize-winning *To Kill a Mockingbird* was written in the first person, from Scout's viewpoint as a child, and the events of the trial take center stage. Ultimately, *Mockingbird* looks at themes of racial injustice and moral growth from a more hopeful perspective.

When you go back to rewrite a piece, the ideas in the story or the bones of a good play are often already there. Approach rewriting like a treasure hunt. Your first draft is the map that leads you down a variety of interesting paths, and locating the spot to dig is the first step in rewriting.

You may find you have to dig a great deal, using different implements and tools. The dig may take weeks or months, sometimes even years. Stay patient and trust that your map is a good one. You may have to rest to catch your breath and have a sandwich. Having someone there to help with the excavating can be really helpful. The final phase of the treasure hunt is cleaning and polishing the gems and jewels, loot and booty. But that comes later.

The Treasure Map

Please write something, anything. Nobody's going to see it. Get your ideas down. Write fast. Don't get caught up in word choice or the order of events. Stuck? Brainstorm or do some idea mapping or list making. Just choose and go. Your only job in this part of the writing process is to keep the channel open. When you've done this, smile to yourself for having written anything at all.

Clear the Spot for the Dig

Do a gentle read-through of a section or the full draft to see the overall picture. Take it nice and easy and stay loose. Resist any temptation to start moving sections or conducting a line-by-line analysis. Your focus is reading for content. What themes emerge? What is the piece about?

As you're reading the section, make notes of anything that catches your attention—something that makes you pause, feels confusing, or requires revisiting later. Don't fix any of the material. Simply make notations. Julie uses green when making these notes because she says it feels less judgmental than using the dreaded red of the mean teacher.

As you read, try using the SMAF system of notation—snip, move, add, and fix:

- **Snip.** Mark unnecessary material—sentences, paragraphs, or entire scenes that do not progress or clarify the story, help to convey the universal truth, or that are redundant or overly detailed.
- **Move.** Identify sections that need to move to provide clarity. This might involve changing the order of scenes, shifting paragraphs or moving dialogue.
- **Add.** Identify areas that are too thin and need more depth, where your story could benefit from character development, descriptive details, or dialogue.
- **Fix.** Mark those sections, paragraphs, scenes, or sentences that need to be restructured or rewritten, including transitions that need to be improved.

Gettin' Dirty with the Deep Dig

The deep-dig phase of rewriting entails reviewing the notes you've gathered under "Snip, Move, Add, Fix" and working out some of those changes. This is where you get to have fun and experiment. Go ahead—change the tense. We dare you. Look at large sections of narration and consider switching them into scenes. Throw in some dialogue. Find creative ways to spin ordinary ideas. Shuffle the sequence of events. Speed up or slow down the pacing of a scene to build drama. Write a dream sequence, rant, or interpretive dance. This part of the rewriting process is where you can be absolutely creative.

Use Different Tools for the Dig

Research shows that reading material on paper and reading text from a computer screen activate different parts of the brain and engage different processing systems. Oral and silent reading also employ different cognitive functions. Experiment with lots of different methods to encounter and refine your work. Read it both silently and out loud from paper and your computer, and make changes as you go. As playwrights, we've found that reading the material out loud to another person—or having someone else read it to us—often gives us useful information.

Rewriting requires patience and trust. It will take time. The author and humorist David Sedaris explaining his process in a MasterClass segment, says that he goes through twelve to eighteen revisions of his essays before sending them to his editor. He then revises them further based on the editor's feedback. It is said that Tolstoy rewrote *War and Peace* at least seven times, sometimes revising individual scenes up to twenty-six times before submitting them for publication. (If you find that overwhelming, think of his poor wife, Sophia, the only one who could decipher his chicken-scratch. She had to copy all of his drafts by hand while raising their thirteen kids. We're not saying she's the hero of *War and Peace* . . . but we're not not saying it either.)

Hittin' Pay Dirt

The final phase of the rewriting process is to defend the work to yourself. Go through your draft and challenge every line in the play. What is this line contributing? Is this section necessary? Is any of this old information? Every scene, every character, every piece of dialogue or narration needs to clarify, define, move your piece forward, or have a purpose in the story.

A Heartfelt PSA About Cutting

We all have beautifully crafted sentences we love, urbane lines of dialogue, or passages that are bursts of brilliance. But if they don't serve the story, we have to cut them. Cutting a treasure can be hard because these gems confirm our talent to ourselves. However, we've learned that we cannot genuflect at the altar of the beautiful sentence. Most cuts result in a stronger and more compelling piece of writing.

Be sure to save old versions of everything you rewrite or create a new document for each draft, so you don't lose any material. This will ensure you can sleep at night. Both of us have a little file that holds these moments of revelation, and we've dipped back into them to use in other writings. We assure you that if you continue to exercise your writing muscle, these tiny moments of brilliance will come looking for you more and more.

TRY THIS!

Choose one section of your solo show, maybe a scene, a passage, or a small interaction between two characters that is sandwiched by some narration. Experiment with each of the techniques that are listed below. Notice which one was most helpful for this particular passage.

- Read the work out loud from the computer.
- Print it out on paper and read it to yourself.
- Read the material out loud to another person.
- Ask someone to read the material out loud to you.

Take what you learn and make some rewrites. Congratulate yourself on the effort and figure out where to put the Pulitzer.

EXPERT ADVICE

You're known for devising and developing material in front of an audience. How do you do that?

Spalding Gray said you can't tell a story without anyone to tell it to and I agree. I develop my shows the same way a stand-up comedian grows a special—in front of a live audience without a script. Often, I perform five to fifteen minutes in a variety show with improvisers, stand-ups, sketch teams, and people working on their SNL auditions. This process allows for more play, risks, and practice with audience participation. Filming the scenes allows me to study the live performance later, noticing tone and missed opportunities. When my longtime collaborator Sammy Zeisel and I began rehearsals for *Spank Bank Time Machine,* we reviewed seventy minutes of footage from six different cabaret performances I had done over eighteen months. We discarded fifty minutes of material; fifteen minutes became the beginning, and Sammy selected five minutes for the ending of the show. The rest of the show was easy to write because we knew exactly where we were headed. Apart from being a useful method to develop audience-focused work, using the comedy circuit makes me a better performer.

John Michael Colgin
Solo Artist, Trauma Clown/Health Educator

Getting Feedback (Eeeeek)

Let's get straight to the point. Do not create your solo show solo.

Yes, your show is your creation, and you get to make the final decisions about what's included and how you perform it. But feedback from others will help you make your play even better. After all, you're creating this piece to be performed for an audience. Getting some information about how the words you've written will actually land with an audience is a critical step. We sometimes discover along the way that elements of the piece which are really clear in our heads (for example, the play is obviously about resilience and hope) are not at all clear to a listener (who wonders why this play is so very bleak and why it induces curling into a ball and crying in a noncathartic way). It's difficult to discover those things without feedback.

You're at some point going to want to get some reactions to what you have been furiously working on all alone at your desk, or on your couch, or on your phone in the bathroom. There are all sorts of methods to get information about how your writing may land with listeners. Let's run through some of the main things to keep in mind.

When to Get Feedback

When you are ready to share your work and hear some responses to what you're creating is different for everyone. Some of us don't want to get too far into a project without running the main ideas by someone or hearing the writing aloud. Others of us don't want to hear responses to our work in the nascent stage when the ideas are still being developed. Those folks feel that feedback too early in the process, before everything is drafted, might cloud their vision. You get to choose. The *when* might depend on *who*.

Who to Get Feedback From

The answer to *who* should be giving you feedback depends on where you are in your process. Early on, we would suggest starting with people who have some experience with writing or theater themselves. These listeners may be playwrights, writers, or simply avid readers and theater lovers. We're talking here about folks who understand how stories and plays work, and who you suspect have your best interests at heart. Even after years of writing stories and sharing them aloud, writers can feel a specific type of tummy-quivering nervousness as they read a brand-new piece of writing aloud to someone else for the very first time. Start with some feedback from folks you trust enough to trudge gently through your process with you.

There's a reason artists refer to the work they produce as their "baby." We spend time dreaming about it, gestating it, and birthing it. If you're a mother, you may love your Aunt Tiff, but not necessarily trust her to watch your infant for an afternoon. The same can be said about your play. You may love your sarcastic friend Antonio, but you may not want him to be the person giving you feedback on your writing, especially if you are new to getting feedback. The opposite can also be true. It's frustrating to watch an overly attached mother so convinced of her kid's specialness that she refuses to hear any feedback about them. Don't be a person who is so in love with your work that you can't hear some observations from others that can actually improve it.

Feedback in a class or workshop setting can also be wonderful. In these cases, be aware that the feedback from a teacher can be direct and content-driven. The suggestions you receive from an instructor may be more specific and less open-ended than we will be outlining below. If you're part of a traditional class for credit, the teacher may specifically direct your work in an instructional way to meet the criteria of the lesson or learning goals. Don't fret. Throw yourself into that instructor's process with an open mind and know you can do what you want with your work when you're done with the class.

Whoever you choose to receive feedback from, protect yourself so you can feel empowered to continue working. You should never feel bad, othered, or less than in a writing group, class, or feedback session. If you consistently leave feeling worse than when you came in or feel like you are not getting the kind of support you need, stand up for your talent and leave.

How to Get Useful Feedback

Having some specific questions at the ready can help us get the feedback we need. Simply asking "So what do you think?" and sitting back with a hopeful and expectant air will only ensure that absolutely anything can now come out of folks' mouths. Also, a general question like that is a lot of pressure to put on our listeners. Here are some guidelines to frame our quest for feedback, inspired by Liz Lerman's wonderful critical response process (https://lizlerman.com/critical-response-process/):

- Always start by asking for some positives! This will help both you and your feedback-giver feel more confident. No matter where you are in your process, there will be plenty of positive things to say about your work. These questions will help get the ball rolling in the right direction. *What feels like it's working so far? When were you most interested in the story? Can you name a few of your favorite or the strongest moments?*
- Do you have any specific questions for your listeners? Are there moments in the play that you wonder about? Here are some examples. *Have I explained my work at the lab and the process of oxidation clearly enough, without boring you with too much detail? Do you feel like I'm too hard on my sister in that Meramec Caverns story? Am I making her a villain? Do you need more information about how I came to live with my grandmother in the bike story?*
- Ask a few problem-identification questions. *Were you ever confused? Was there a point when it took you a moment to understand what was going on? Did the story drag anywhere? Did your attention ever lag?*

- If you feel you've gotten thoughtful, valuable feedback from this person or group and you're interested in probing further, you can ask open-ended questions. *Is there anything else you think I should know or consider as I rewrite? Are there any general impressions you want to share?*

If you already have a full draft and you're doing some sort of invited performance for the sole purpose of getting feedback, consider asking someone else to facilitate. Have a discussion with the facilitator beforehand to determine the questions and time frame of the session. A thirty-minute session usually works well. The facilitator should also be in charge of keeping the guard rails on the discussion. If comments start to veer into counterproductive waters, the facilitator can gently herd the conversation back to the prepared list of questions. During a group feedback session, always beware of any feedback that begins, "You know what you should do?" or "If I were you . . ."

Be mindful of where you are in your process. For example, if your work is new, you'll want to ask general questions about the play as a whole. If the work is more mature, the feedback can be more granular. Finally, don't ask questions you don't want the answers to. For instance, if you're already in preview performances and you're not interested in completely rewriting the text at that point, don't ask for that kind of feedback! Ask about things you are actually able to rework, such as tech details or moments that need more clarification. (Additional questions to elicit great feedback are at the end of this chapter.)

Take Notes (or Don't!)

Whether you're getting feedback one-on-one or in a class, workshop, or writing group, set yourself up for success to hear what folks are saying. We generally suggest taking notes as you listen to critiques because feedback is information—valuable information. If note-taking doesn't work for you, record the feedback session or ask other people to take notes for you.

This is your work. You get to decide not only how you receive feedback, but when you have enough. If you feel at any point like the feedback session is going down a weird rabbit hole (and sometimes they do), feel free to stop. Don't be afraid to say "Whew! This is so great, and I have a lot to think about here, so this is enough for today" or "I'd rather not talk about that aspect of the show yet—I'm still figuring it out."

Be sure and thank folks who have taken the time to sit with you and do their best to share their thoughts. Even if you suspect that their feedback is not all that helpful, even if they disappointed you with their responses, say thank you.

Don't Get Your Boxers in a Bunch

We've heard it said that even feedback we think is way off base is worth examining to see if there is some small kernel of truth in there. As you are listening to the feedback you're receiving, consciously try not to judge whether it's good or bad, valuable or trash. Do your best to tame your defensive impulses and do some real investigation, especially around the hard-to-hear comments. Understand that it's perfectly normal to feel a little bit protective, uncomfortable, despairing, angry, and worse.

Listen deeply, ask questions to clarify if you don't understand, but be clear that this is a data-finding mission, and any determination about what feedback is true or not true, helpful or not helpful, can be done later. Listen and capture. Resist the temptation to respond to the feedback you're receiving. You can answer questions if you want to, but you're under no obligation to explain anything. Never feel the need to apologize for the quality of your work. We are all students of the art—all of us—and a well-facilitated critique focuses on the writing, not the writer.

Consider the words of the great Russ Tutterow, who held the position of artistic director at Chicago Dramatists for nearly thirty years: *It is not the writer's job to defend the work but to listen to how the audience experiences the material. In that way, the writer can take the information and decide if this was their intention for the play.* You're there to mine the audience—these well-meaning, imperfect listeners—for useful information.

After your feedback session is over, congratulate yourself. You're brave. You're a professional. Go get a drink. Celebrate. You've gathered your intel—you'll have time later to decide what's useful and whether so-and-so's idea about the ending is complete crap or not. After honest consideration, if you think a particular suggestion isn't helpful, you'll toss it.

More Feedback Questions

Choose from the questions below to address any specific concerns you might have about your draft. To make sure you get some positive notes first, we insist you always begin with one of the first two.

- Where did you lean in or feel most engaged?
- What images or moments stayed with you?
- What were the themes that emerged from the piece?
- What did the "greedy listener" in you want more of—and why?
- What did you want less of—and what made it feel unnecessary or repetitive?
- What is the story about? And what is it *really about*—the universal truth?
- Plot the journey of events: What happened, and in what order?
- Plot the journey of emotions: How did the emotional arc shift or build?
- Describe the main and secondary characters. How did they change or reveal themselves?
- Compare the beginning and end: What changed? What arc or transformation occurred?
- What are two questions do you have after experiencing the piece?

EXPERT ADVICE

How do you use audience feedback to further develop your work?

While the writing process is more personal, the performance is most certainly a partnership. I write the journey of both emotions and events, yet the audience and I decide in real time just how sad, bumpy, or exhilarating the journey will be. In that way, I rely on the audience feedback as much as the audience relies on my writing and performance for the work to be a success.

I host private readings in addition to performing public workshops to gather verbal and written reactions to my work. I then weigh audience feedback against my personal objectives to 1) educate the audience about something they may not have been aware of, 2) push the audience to examine and vocalize their own biases and fears as they relate to the topics I address, 3) create space for the audience to forgive themselves and others for any intentional or unintended pain caused toward self or others, and 4) give the audience an opportunity to exhale. If the feedback aligns with my core performance objectives, I find a way to include it, provided there is room in the script.

R.C. Riley
Playwright & Performer

Editing Techniques (Yikes!)

At some point, you will probably have to edit your show. For our purposes here, we'll think of "editing" as removing text from your show for any number of reasons. Even after your rewriting process, chances are you will still—to make your play better—have to excise some beautiful writing that you have labored over and felt proud of. Like doing your taxes or renewing your driver's license or getting your teeth cleaned, it's not always enjoyable, but you'll be sorry if you don't.

In this book (or in "Arlene and Julie World"), we think of rewriting as the process of taking an earlier draft—a first, second, or third draft—and making it stronger. You're honing and refining it. You might still be figuring out some major themes in the show and are often transforming the piece into something new.

The editing process comes after rewriting, which can also involve removing text from your play. Removing text when rewriting is intended to make the play different. In editing, the purpose is to make the play a better version of what it already is. It's the last step, tightening the writing and removing anything that might distract from what your play is about, after you know what your play is about. We love the image of distilling. When we distill something, we reduce the overall mass, but it becomes more potent.

We sometimes need to edit strictly for time. Most storytellers have been asked to fit their twelve-minute story into a seven-minute time slot—or five-minute slot—or to fit a ninety-minute story into a sixty-minute slot, particularly for festivals. Some stories cannot be told in five or seven or even sixty minutes, of course. You'll decide for yourself whether your shows can be effective at different lengths. There may come a point when you'll want to say no.

When it comes to editing your writing because you've been offered a certain time-restricted slot, know that *it is highly unprofessional to ignore a time restriction*. Honestly, it's just rude. If you truly cannot fit your show into the slot offered, say no. Don't be the performer who goes too long and pushes the entire lineup back. It doesn't matter if your piece is "good" and "worth it." Editing can be frustrating and emotional, but it's what separates the real writers from the hacks. (This the first time we've used the term "hacks" in this book because we want the tone to be encouraging. We know everyone is trying hard. But strong language is called for here.)

You've probably had the experience of watching a piece of theater or listening to a story that was much too long and meandering and was in desperate need of cutting. You felt restless and frustrated, held hostage by the self-indulgence of the performer. Perhaps there was simply too much in the piece and you couldn't decipher what was supposed to be important. Perhaps you got ahead of the story or simply stopped caring in the wake of your wasted time. Maybe you thought, "Why didn't anyone tell this person they needed to cut this piece?" In the same way that we wouldn't let someone walk around with spinach in their teeth or toilet paper on their shoe, we artists have to help each other find the courage to edit.

You've also experienced plays and movies that are tight and lean and completely engaging. You knew exactly what you needed to know at each point in the story. Your attention was held completely, and you were able to relax and lose track of time in the process of watching. That's what we're going for.

Specific Strategies for Editing

Once you have a full draft and you've done diligent rewriting, how do you figure out what needs to be trimmed? In your rewriting, of course, you've been cutting out scenes and paragraphs that you recognize as tangents. You've noticed moments where there's hefty description that needs to be thinned out, and you've done that. You've detected spots where you are repeating yourself or spending too much time in a specific scene. You may even feel like you have done all of this so thoroughly that the piece is finished. Usually, it isn't. Here are some approaches to editing. The first two bullets are about looking for whole sections or scenes that might need to be cut or condensed:

- Look at your show through the lens of your **essential question or universal truth.** With each scene and section, ask, "Does this lead back to my 'why' "? If you can't identify what your show is about, you won't have a North Star to guide you in your editing. Read through your play with the lens of your essential question or theme, asking, "Is this necessary? Does it attempt to wrestle with the essential question?"
- **Reading your show aloud** is a great way to start feeling for yourself what's unnecessary or where it's dragging. You may notice yourself thinking, "I need to get through this section faster." See what you can streamline. You could also record yourself reading your show and play it back. You might hear things you didn't hear before. Listening to someone else read your show aloud can be especially instructive. Settle back, take notes and try not to cringe. You'll be surprised what you learn.
- **Get feedback from others.** Find some folks to listen to your play and respond to what they are hearing. Be sure and ask, "Were there moments when you got ahead of the story?" "Were there any sections where your attention wandered?" "Did any parts of the show feel slow?" "Did you notice any place in the show where I gave you information you didn't need?"
- **Try reverse editing.** Start at the end of your show and read backward, sentence by sentence. You will more easily notice "fat" portions where you've used too many words. It can also help you identify where you have repeated yourself.
- **Micro-edit** by looking for words you can often eliminate, such as *that* (as in "I knew that I was wrong."), *very, just, about, almost, sort of, perhaps, while.* You can also cut unnecessary modifiers like *up* (as in "stood up"), *down* (in "sat down"), *long* (in "all night long"). Where there are three adjectives in a row, take out one or two. Most adverbs can be cut. Show us how

you are doing something rather than telling us. You don't need "she said angrily" if you can show the anger in performance. Get rid of actions that are explained by what follows. For instance, "She opened the door of the car and got in" could be "She got in the car."

- Editing is best done with **assistance from others**. Ask someone in your life who knows a little something about writing (or is just an avid reader) to go through your piece scene by scene and put a line through everything they believe could be cut without losing the meaning of the show. This doesn't mean you should cut everything they cross out, but it will help you see what's essential.

Try to think of the writing you are cutting out of your play as something you can save and develop later. Never delete! Trust that removing the parts of your show that are not 100 percent necessary will make the rest of your play more vivid. Like Michelangelo chipping away the marble that doesn't need to be part of his sculpture, removing what is not essential to your play will help the audience see with clarity what you've actually created.

TRY THIS!

As an exercise, take your show, or a section of your show, and edit it down by 50 percent. Then edit that down by 50 percent. You will be getting closer and closer to what is *essential* in your piece. You can put a lot of that back in, of course, but we bet you'll be able to see some things that don't need to be there.

EXPERT ADVICE

What kind of tips, advice, or wisdom do you have around editing?

I love editing. I think it's important to approach the editing step with love. And if you can't do that (maybe you really don't enjoy it, or you're too close to the piece), then it's good to find somebody who does, who can support you in that.

It's also important to note that we can edit with different things in mind—for clarity, word count, or a theme. I think the first step is knowing what the goal is—which thing I'm editing for at which point—because it's tough to edit for all of them at the same time.

Also, writers frequently try to edit too early, or they try to edit WHILE they're writing. This isn't possible! You can't edit a piece before you're done with it. It's important to really allow something to develop so that then you can have the conversation around "OK, so what do I have here? And what is the next best step?" Because the next best step might not be editing. If I have forty-five minutes of material and I'm aiming for a thirty-minute piece, that's more structural work that I'm going to have to do. I need to know, am I coming in with a scalpel or a hatchet?

I love cooking and baking, preparing beautiful (and delicious!) food for others. I think of editing like the finishing touches on a plate: how am I going to slice this beautiful piece of meat or frost this cake? Does this dish need finishing salt on the top or not?

Many times, I've seen writers cut something out before the piece is done. And sometimes it's a good cut, but *sometimes* it has to do with the writer not yet knowing what they're writing. They cut something out when it's the core of what they're actually trying to do—they just don't know that yet. It's important to just leave it all on the table until you have a sense of all the different ingredients that you have.

Amanda Delheimer

Artist. Advocate. Facilitator. Artistic Director of 2nd Story

How Do You Know Your Solo Show Is Done?

Your solo show is finished when you've told the story.*

* Not when you've said everything you want to say on the topic.

Rehearsing and Performing

The Great Script Debate

Solo Artists! Welcome to tonight's Mixed Martial Arts Cage Match throwdown, which promises to be a classic in every sense of the word. In the red corner, we have Arlene the Dream, weighing in with support for the Traditional Script Format, and in the blue corner, we have Julie the Juiced, with the Classic Prose Format. Let's have a clean fight, touch gloves, and let her rip, 'Tater Chip!

Where are we going with this? It's important to figure out a text format that will support both you and the style of your play. There is no hard and fast rule in the solo world in terms of how to configure your script. Arlene and Julie use their own styles for various reasons.

Arlene and the Modified Theatrical Script Format

Arlene formats her solo shows the way a theatrical script is generally written, with stage direction and character headings, even though all the characters and narrators will be played by Arlene.

An excerpt from *Life's Too Short and So Am I* by Julie D.

CONTEMPORARY NARRATOR

I have wanted to be so many things: Department store clerk, Peace Corps volunteer, and juvenile court judge. Specifically,

I have wanted to be Mary Tyler Moore, Lily Tomlin, Katie Couric, and definitely Oprah. But more than anything, for as long as I can remember, from as far back as when I watched Marlo Thomas in *That Girl*, I have dreamt of being an actress.

When I was eight years old at Mrs. Sharkey's Drama School, I memorized poems and tongue twisters . . .

JULIE, AGE 8

Betty Botter bought a bit of butter. But she said, "This butter's bitter."

CONTEMPORARY NARRATOR

At 17, I got my first dramatic role in a teenage-targeted TV show based on Verdi's opera *La Traviata*. I was Vicki, a prostitute who dies of (cough) consumption in the arms of her lover, Adam.

ADAM

Vicki, don't die. I love you.

VICKI/JULIE D, AGE 17

I love you Adam, I will always love you.

Arlene's a fan of this format for several reasons. It's standard in the theatrical world. Since she has used this kind of script throughout her career onstage, she doesn't have to mentally decode a new system. Visually, this format breaks up the material, so it doesn't look like a monolithic barrage of text. The character headings give her a quick visual cue as to which character is speaking next and make it easier for her to memorize. The white space within this format provides plenty of room to make blocking and acting notes in the margins. This configuration makes it easier for the director during rehearsals and for the tech crew during performances to follow the script. It gives Arlene an idea of how long the play is running. From her experience, a forty-five to fifty-page script, double spaced with fourteen-point font, runs about sixty minutes including transitions and acting and light/sound cues. When submitting to festivals, play competitions, and grant and residency opportunities, this is the preferred script format and makes a positive and professional impression.

An Example of Julie's Classic Prose Format

Julie formats her solo shows in the way a story or novel is generally formatted, with paragraphs and quotation marks or italics for dialogue. She uses space breaks between sections and stories, numbering each one.

> An excerpt from *Breaking Rules, Broken Hearts: Loving Across Borders* by Ada Cheng
>
> [*Sound cue: Lullaby from Taiwan*]
>
> I am six years old. In our living room at home in Taipei, Taiwan. I remember watching my mother walk to the door ready to leave. I run to her screaming: "No. No. Don't leave."
>
> [*Sound: Flight announcement: "Good evening. We are now boarding for Singapore Airline Flight 2537 to San Francisco. First-class passengers please step to the gate."*]
>
> It's 8 P.M. on July 15, 1991. My family and I are at Terminal 43 at Taoyuan International Airport, the main airport connecting the capital city of Taipei to the world beyond the island of Taiwan. My mother's eyes are swollen with tears rolling down her cheeks: tears of sadness. I am wearing an orange tank top, a jean skirt, and a pair of black boots: my usual outfit in my 20s. I reach for my two large suitcases. I am no first-class passenger, but I am ready to board.
>
> [*Mandarin/English*] "Take care of yourself. Call me every week." My mother reminds me. Again.
>
> "OK. You take care too," I say. Again, as well.
>
> I am thinking to myself: "This is it. I am never coming back."
>
> I leave my mother at the age of twenty-seven, like she had left me, again, again, and again.

Julie uses this format because she finds it simpler to read and work with. The formatting reminds her that she is simply sharing a story with an audience. It reminds her that there is no fourth wall; she is there to connect and be vulnerable and present in that moment, talking to an intimate companion. This formatting gives Julie a sense of how long her show is running. Generally, twelve double-spaced pages, in twelve-point font, runs about thirty minutes. This includes time allotted for scenes, transitions, and sound cues. When submitting her play to a theater or a festival, however, Julie will configure her show into a version of Arlene's script format. She agrees that it confers a bit more theatrical legitimacy.

Our Thoughts on Freeballin'

We've found a few solo artists who prefer to improvise, using bullet points to outline their stories as opposed to writing a complete script. These folks like to be loose with their language based on how they feel. In our experience, the freeballin' style is a herculean task to undertake for a full solo show.

While we've seen a handful of professionals do it well, we have more often seen solo artists meander, repeat themselves, wreck a joke, lose control of the emotional arc, and have a difficult time getting back on track if they get lost. Those who pull off the freeballin' style with consistency spend lots of time perfecting it behind the scenes. This style in the hands of a less experienced performer can come off as amateurish and under-rehearsed.

Here's one more bit of yellow caution tape. If you have lighting, blocking, or sound cues, your tech team will be depending on consistent text and blocking for their cues. We have never met a single stage manager who enjoys improvising calls in a show. Even if you develop your work through improvisation or devising, at some point make sure you get yourself a script and find a way to format it that works for you, and also your team.

Acting for Solo

If you're a professional actor, you already know that your voice and your body are your most essential tools for telling a story onstage. You may have spent years in classes or workshops honing these tools and understand that work never stops.

If you're new to performing, we want to be honest with you. This book alone cannot possibly teach you how to use these tools or how to perform onstage. There are some great books on acting (start with Uta Hagen's *Respect for Acting* or *The Power of the Actor* by Ivana Chubbuck), and the very best advice we can give you is to go take some performance classes. (Do it! It's fun!)

You don't have to be a professional performer with a union card to pull off a solo piece, but you'll need some basics in order to bring your text to life. Also, your physical body will need to be able to project your voice for a sustained period, and that doesn't just happen naturally. Maybe you've had the experience of arriving at the theater with tickets to a fancy play featuring a famous film actor, only to discover that the understudy is going on because the lead has lost their voice or generally run themselves down doing eight shows a week. We're always thrilled for the understudy, and not really surprised. Performing a lead role or solo show is akin to a vocal marathon. Our everyday voices are usually not ready for it—we have to work out and train for it.

If you have experience performing in traditional multicharacter plays, you may be amazed to discover how much interacting with other characters, handling props, and immersing yourself in stage business has shaped your experience. Acting in a solo show is a unique and challenging experience which requires a distinct set of skills and techniques.

In a solo show, the entire performance rests on one actor's shoulders—yours. We like to call this "solo responsibility." This means having a deep understanding of pacing and timing and the ability to manage transitions. It's a different kind of acting experience because you are in full control of the narrative. With that in mind, here are some performance skills that require a shift in focus when moving from traditional ensemble plays to solo work:

Developing a relationship with the audience. In a solo show, the relationship between the performer and the audience is markedly more intimate and direct than in a traditional ensemble play. In many solo shows, the actor breaks the fourth wall and addresses the audience directly, making them feel part of the story. Additionally, you'll need to decide whether your play is one where, as the solo performer, you will comment on the audience reactions or stay in the scene and in character. A solo artist also needs to develop the emotional intelligence to read and respond to the audience's energy and adjust in real time.

Pace management. As a solo performer, you are solely responsible for managing the timing and rhythm of the entire show. Without other actors to rely on, you must be hyper-aware of the show's tempo, sensing when to speed up or slow down, and use pauses effectively. Understanding the specific pacing of your play will help you make strong choices and maintain the audience's interest.

Arlene was very challenged by managing the pace during the run of one of her shows. The first fifteen minutes were so quick and rushed that she felt the audience couldn't settle into the story, which, in hindsight, hindered her ability to connect with them. Although the director had set the tempo, Arlene was never comfortable with it. Watching the closing show on video weeks later confirmed it—it took her too long to settle into the show. (But there's always the next performance.)

Navigating transitions. Solo artists often need to manage time jumps and multiple locations, move from narration to scenes, and switch characters. These transitions may involve a physical adjustment, a vocal shift, or a simple change in focus within the storytelling. Theatrical elements such as lighting and sound can help with this as well. Transitions must be clear and intentional to maintain the continuity and clarity of a story.

Emotional proficiency. In a traditional play, characters interact with each other in real time, reacting to their fellow actors' choices and behavior. In contrast, the solo artist needs to create the illusion of interaction by performing multiple characters or speaking to unseen characters. This requires the ability to tap into emotions quickly, sometimes within the same scene, to convey different characters' perspectives. This emotional shapeshifting is something we all get better at with practice, moving from joy to sorrow or anger to fear in an instant, without the aid of other actors to prompt these changes.

Managing tells and tics. The body's habitual patterns often disappear when we're playing characters and inhabiting someone else, but they can creep back in when we're narrating as ourselves and breaking the fourth wall. Everyone has specific quirks and fidgets that arise when we're nervous or under stress. Perhaps you tend to speak too quickly or shift your weight back and forth on your feet. Julie's voice tends to rise and get a little "pinched" when she's tense. Go on a fact-finding mission and watch some video of yourself, paying attention to your body's habitual movements. Listen to a recording of yourself talking. What do you notice about your vocal patterns? Don't berate yourself for anything! Just stay curious and make note of repetitive patterns that you may want to adjust.

Taking up space. When audiences come to a solo play, they know that they will be watching one performer in a playing space. They expect a performer who is at home in their skin. It doesn't matter if the performer is large or small, young or mature, beautiful or average-looking. We've seen every imaginable type of body perform great solo shows, so, however you look, get used to owning that—not an ideal version of yourself, but the physical presence you are right now. That's the vehicle you have to convey your experience. And it's enough.

Developing a visual vocabulary. Solo performers often need to imply the presence of objects, other characters, or environments through precise space work and imaginative staging. If you can cultivate the ability to "see" and "interact" with imaginary characters, objects, or environments as if they were real, you'll make them real for the audience. "Visual vocabulary" is what Arlene calls the aspect of American Sign Language where signers use their faces and bodies to paint vivid, cinematic pictures. A solo actor can employ similar techniques. For example, if a performer is describing mountains in the distance, they can use their hands to outline the shape of the hills in front of them and simultaneously convey through their facial expressions the emotion they're feeling as they look at those mountains. Visual vocabulary gives us more information than words alone and extends to pantomiming actions such as slowly opening a door or peeking into a dark, scary cellar, rather than simply telling us about the moment.

Caring for your instrument. Solo performers must intentionally care for themselves emotionally and physically. Doing a solo show can be emotionally challenging, especially without fellow cast members to help you process the experience. Whether it's a bad performance, an amazing one, no audience at all, a chaotic tech night, or any of the countless unpredictable moments that come with theater, it's important to be mindful of the emotional toll taken by performing solo, even if you are lucky enough to have a production team. We encourage you to gather a strong trusted network for support along the way. Be exquisitely kind to your body and voice during the period of rehearsal and performance. Eat well, get plenty of rest, and do all the things your mom, best friend, and doctor have always urged you to do.

TRY THIS!

Whatever you are doing with your body—stretching, vacuuming, taking out the trash—practice bringing a conscious sense of energy and aliveness to what you are doing. Imagine your entire body, head to fingertips to toes, energized, potent, and alive. This is how we practice taking up space. When you're standing in line at the post office or waiting for your coffee order, try planting yourself, grounding your body, and completely inhabiting that square foot of space right where you are.

EXPERT ADVICE

As a director, what is one piece of advice you would give to a solo actor as they take their play from the page to the stage?

SHOW rather than TELL. Build your world through miming objects or scenery if you don't have a set or props. You can build the world with your eyes as well. If you really see the world that you're describing, the audience will see it too. For instance, if you're talking about the rain clouds overhead, and you look up, the audience will follow you as you build the imaginary world. The picture of rain clouds overhead will be painted in the audience's minds by simply following your eyes as you direct them up. Also, inhabit characters and speak as characters in dialogue. Take on their vocal mannerisms and physicality and go too far with it if you need to. Explore and make it big! You can always bring it down later if you need.

Charles Askenaizer

Director, Artistic Director, Invictus Theatre

EXPERT ADVICE

I was inspired by Hal Holbrook's excellent "Mark Twain Tonight!" television special, which aired in January of 1967, back when I was in college. I spent many hours in the campus library searching out Mark Twain stories that Holbrook hadn't already used, and there was a wealth of material, which I started to edit and memorize. I first performed at parties, then dorms, then local high schools and church basements. My chemistry and psychology grades suffered, but I still have that original folder of pieces to which I've added many more pieces of text.

When adapting text to spoken word, prune those long sentences that can slow you down. Keep a brisk pace during descriptive passages, lifting each phrase as you go and making it clear when you've reached the end. Enunciate and project. If you allow your sentences to fall off at the end, your audience will lose your thread and their interest. Lift the last word in every sentence; keep the energy until the end.

Richard Henzel
Actor, Playwright, Audiobook Publisher

Bringing Characters to Life

This is where it gets fun, chickadees!

One of the most exciting facets of the solo show is the challenge of creating and portraying various characters onstage. Unlike traditional plays where the story is woven through the dialogue of an entire cast, in a solo show, the entire world of the play is controlled by one person—you. It requires you to be not only creative in developing distinct, multidimensional characters in your text but also versatile in your performance in order to bring them to life. Part of the fun of solo work is learning how to shift seamlessly between personas, each with their unique voice, physicality, and point of view.

Right about now, many of our students begin to feel trepidation and wonder, "Wait, how am I going to be all these different people?" Inevitably, we get people in our classes who furrow their brows, stare at us defiantly, and huff, "I absolutely do not do characters." We ask, "Why not?" The truth dribbles out: "I can't." We say, "Heck yeah, you can. Let's just play around a little."

How, specifically, do we embody or portray characters? Generally, a performer does this through their voice and body. It doesn't need to be intimidating. You can choose to portray your characters with a simple representational gesture, a small vocal change, or a straightforward directional shift of the body, head, or gaze. Alternatively, you can go big, fully embodying a character in posture, voice, and actions. You get to decide what best serves your vision, your play, and you as the actor.

For instance, you might choose to portray a fourth-grade teacher using only the volume of your voice. You might use a small physical gesture like crossing your arms in an overbearing stance or oscillating your head as if surveying the classroom. Another option is to deliver the teacher's lines with droll sarcasm. Whether you use one of these techniques or all of them, the choice will depend on what best serves the character and the moment. Don't be afraid to mix and match different approaches until you find what resonates most with your performance and the story you're telling.

We recognize that solo artists come from a variety of backgrounds and have varied levels of acting experience. Solo work requires a complex blend of storytelling, character development, and direct audience engagement, but there are many ways to do it. Of course, we can't cover all nuances of acting here, but we will cover some concepts that are unique to the art of solo performance. It's worth noting that if you do not come to the solo work with an acting background, it would serve you well to take a class to get some tools for your solo toolbox.

What Type of Solo Show Have You Written?

The type of show you have written will determine the style of your performance and how completely you'll embody the characters. Are you taking on characters for long periods of time in your show so that you, as the performer, are obscured? Or have you written a first-person narrative show where you're giving us brief, clear glimpses of characters as your protagonist interacts with them, through the protagonist's point of view?

If you've written a dialogue-driven solo play, in which the primary vehicle to tell the story is dialogue between characters, your show will be highly performative. The same can be said of a character-driven solo play, where all (or almost all) of the action is told through various characters directly addressing the audience. Solo plays like this require a performer who can transform themself into different characters to the point that the audience sees each distinct character, and not the actor. The same is often true for a biographical play when the performer is portraying a famous or historical person. The audience wants to be able to "suspend their disbelief" during the show and feel like they are actually watching the character the play is about. This kind of show really does call for some acting chops.

These are the kinds of pieces Anna Deveare Smith creates. Her solo plays (such as *Fires in the Mirror* and *Twilight: Los Angeles, 1992*) are peopled with characters who talk to the audience from their distinct point of view. Anna, as the actor, disappears entirely as she becomes each of the characters. She completely transforms her voice, her body, her affect, and the way she moves. This book cannot teach you the skills you need to be able to pull off performances like hers, but maybe you already have some acting training and you're up to the task.

In a narrative solo play, however, the performer will break the fourth wall and talk directly to the audience. They will use narration and exposition to tell the story in their own voice. While characters may appear, they'll come and go in scenes throughout the play, and the solo performer will slip in and out of different characters for shorter durations. Most importantly, all the characters will be portrayed through the point of view of the main character, you.

What does that mean? Instead of a full-body, dead-on method actor transformation into your Uncle TJ, we'll get your impression of his voice, mannerisms, and the way he shrugs his shoulders. Perhaps you've interspersed bits of dialogue throughout a piece that is primarily narrated. In a play like this, character work can help change up the rhythm and add a dimension that can transcend traditional spoken-word communication.

Arlene's show *Aiming for Sainthood* is a prime example of this type of solo play. Throughout the show, she plays multiple characters, including her sister, Deaf parents, husband, and various odd doctors. She brings these characters to life through slight adjustments in her body and voice. For instance, when she embodies the character of Dr. Lowery, she cocks her head, steeples her hands, and speaks in a quiet, kind voice. Since the character is male, she pitches her voice a little lower. Arlene chose this characterization to create a calm, soothing counterpoint to a loud, chaotic situation. These nuanced shifts allow the audience to instantly recognize the character. Other, lesser characters are portrayed by using only one technique, such as a facial expression.

Character work can be intimidating, especially when you look at John Leguizamo in *Freak* or Patrick Stewart doing forty characters in *A Christmas Carol*. But everyone can add interest, color, and variety to their story on stage by incorporating some kind of character work—something as small as softening a voice, slouching the shoulders, or changing the direction the actor looks.

Vocal Representations

Your voice has lots of little characteristics that make it specifically yours. It has a natural pitch that may be high or low or somewhere in between. You may speak rather quickly or slowly. You may have lots of natural pitch variation in the way you speak, or you may have a more understated monotone.

When you're portraying characters on stage, you're trying to capture some of those particular vocal characteristics. You can manipulate pitch (how low or high one's voice is), pace (how fast or slow one's speech is), volume (how loudly or softly one is speaking), timbre (the tonal quality of one's voice), or cadence (the rhythm, flow, stress, and intonation of a voice, including inflection and the rising and falling of pitch).

Imagine voices that are throaty, aggressively loud, breathy, raspy, nasal, deep, or shaky. Speech that is sing-song-y, has a drawl or vocal fry, uses a dialect, accent, upspeak, unusual pauses, or interstitials like "uh" and "umm." You might also start to notice that voices are placed in different areas—some are nasal, some feel like they are at the front of the mouth, et cetera. Then there is the energy with which a person speaks. All of these factors make a difference. Taking on some of these qualities can help you portray another person's voice. Take, for instance, Meryl Streep's vocal interpretations in the movies *The Devil Wears Prada* versus *Sophie's Choice*. In the former, Streep's lines are delivered in a lower register. Her speech is slow, calm, and undermodulated, emphasizing her power and the contempt she holds for many of those around her. In *Sophie's Choice*, her character speaks in a softer, higher register. Her speech is hesitant, sometimes whispery, and is delivered with an impeccable Polish accent.

Remember, in a narrative solo play, if the audience is going to hear a character through your point of view, just a suggestion will work in many cases. You're not doing a voice; you're suggesting it. Listen to a few audiobooks and notice how professional voice actors interpret different characters with very small vocal differentiations. Subtle changes can be just as effective as exaggerated ones. The best way to capture someone's vocal patterns might be to relax and mimic the most distinctive detail of their speech. Trust that these small adjustments will resonate with your audience and convey the essence of the character without overdoing it.

Gestural Expression and Physicality

Just as a voice has particular qualities, so does a body. Some bodies have a loose and open energy; others are tight and bound. Some move with sustained action; others have a darting, quick pattern of action. Some folks' gestures are light and fluttery, others have deliberate, heavy, or awkward gestures. Notice how different individuals have body language that feels open and welcoming, while others seem to need to protect or cover themselves. Bodies hold tension in different spots, too—the hands, shoulders, lips.

If you are playing a character in a traditional play, you might work for weeks on the physicality of your character, trying to master their particular way of moving through the world and inhabiting them so completely that the audience forgets they are watching an actor. The same is true if your play is character-driven or dialogue-driven. You'll be going deep into transforming yourself into your characters. You can take on the character's facial expressions, body language, eye contact, gait, gestures, movements, and particular mannerisms.

Consider Daniel Kaluuya's physicality in the movie *Get Out.* He uses small, contained gestures that show the tension of restraint. In contrast, his performance in *Judas and the Black Messiah* displays movements that are forceful and aggressive, and he physically commands space. His physical choices reveal a precise embodiment of Fred Hampton, the real-life person he is portraying.

However, if your play is a narrative piece with scenes and characters sprinkled throughout, small physical changes can go a long way. Something as simple as looking up and locking your knees or fidgeting each time you portray your six-year-old daughter will let us know exactly who is talking and might express her youthful essence perfectly.

You are the one who knows your particular six-year-old. But choices like this will allow you to easily slip in and out of narrative around the dialogue you have written.

A character fingerprint is a simple, isolated gesture that serves as a way to delineate a character and add another layer of information. The physical or vocal trait is deliberately chosen to be a shortcut for the audience and also to reveal a character's personality or fundamental nature. A well-chosen character fingerprint can be a powerful signal that communicates a character's background, attitudes, or the social/historical context they inhabit without having to state it explicitly.

For example, a character fingerprint for a fourteen-year-old girl might be a hand flipping back her hair. Each time we encounter this character, she performs this gesture. She might do this gesture in a way that conveys how impossibly annoyed by everything and everyone she is. If her other arm is bent at the elbow and extended as if she has a sizable purse hanging on it, perhaps a purse she is anxious to display, we get an idea of her social class. Understanding this aspect of the character can influence our perception of her actions.

Developing a character fingerprint is also a way to communicate a piece of information about the character's past or internal life. One solo artist in our class had a male character in her show who was small in stature and spoke softly. However, she wanted to portray him in a way that highlighted his strong character and moral compass. Instead of replicating his true physical features and voice, she depicted his stature as taller and more powerful and his voice as louder than it actually was.

Directionality and Physical Location

An actor can move their body in space to indicate conversations between two or more people by subtly altering their position on stage to represent each character. For example, by facing one direction when portraying one character and then shifting to another angle or spot to represent the other, the actor creates a clear distinction between the characters in the conversation. Eye or gaze shifts can also show a verbal exchange, with the actor looking in one direction to address one character and then shifting their gaze to a different point to represent the response. This approach is great for actors who choose not to fully embody characters or do voices.

Another way to use directionality is to employ an up and down focus. Consider a scene between a father and child. An easy way to delineate the characters is for the actor to deliver the father's lines with the head tilted down, as if the character were talking to someone smaller. In response, the actor, as the kid, would look up to speak to their dad.

We've even seen solo artists effectively convey conversations between many people at once. A great example is one of our favorite solo artists, Wendy Hammers, who portrays a family of four characters in a car. She accomplishes this by shifting her weight to show their positions: Dad with hands on the steering wheel, leaning forward and shifting left; Mom staring out the window in the passenger seat, shifting right; and the brother and sister in the back seat, leaning back and to the left and right, respectively. Each character has their own distinctive physical gesture. The scene was choreographed and rehearsed like a dance and was really effective in conveying the dynamics of her family on a long drive to New York City in the summer without air conditioning.

Some of these directionality choices can be driven by the size of the performance venue. While full physical embodiment can be effective in any size venue, when we work with clients who are performing in larger spaces or in front of big groups, we encourage them to develop a broader physicality than a simple eye flicker—up, down, left, or right—to denote conversations between different characters.

If you are working on biographical or autobiographical projects, remember that you have the option of providing accurate depictions—copying mannerisms, physicality, or vocal nuances—or choosing to endow your characters with a fingerprint that communicates something about their personal qualities or nature. Both approaches can be effective depending on the narrative you wish to create.

Experimentation and practice can serve you well when developing characters. We saw a piece by a writer quite new to performance. She had a strong director who helped her make deliberate but subtle physical adjustments for each of the characters in her piece, herself and her three sisters. One sister was portrayed with a gravelly voice and a stance that leaned heavily to the right. That was enough to differentiate her and give a sense of who she was. Another blinked her eyes in a way that was almost, but not quite, a tic. Another had an almost confrontational stance, leading with her chest. Each time these different characters had dialogue, the audience was able to follow who was speaking.

Narrators

Narrators are characters too! There are several ways we can delineate that a narrator is speaking rather than a character in a scene. Some of the methods are quite obvious, such as moving to a certain area of the stage for the narration or choosing a specific point toward which we deliver the narration. A particular light setting, like a warm wash or a spotlight, could signal the narrator is speaking and not in scene. Sound can also be used in this way. In our experience, our clients usually use their natural speaking voice as the narrator. This establishes a baseline for the narrator storytelling voice that is distinct from character voices. Sometimes the audience won't even notice exactly how we are differentiating the narrator because they'll be caught up in the show, which is ideal.

Arlene's method is to use her lower chest voice when she is speaking to the audience as the narrator. She also leans forward toward the audience slightly, three inches or so. In a larger theater, she might take a step toward the audience, as if to suggest, "Let me tell you something . . ." Arlene also allows herself to freely gesticulate when her narrators are speaking and be very much herself, physically. (She's quite a gesticulator.) All of these adjustments are subtle, and it's not important that the audience register them at all, as long as they are understanding the story of the show.

Last, a solo show doesn't always need to involve character work; it can rely on straightforward effective narration. For instance, some of our students have chosen to tell about conversations using phrases like "he said to me" when presenting dialogue. This keeps the focus on the narration rather than taking on a physical or directional technique. They might also choose to communicate the expression or emotion of the dialogue and allow the story to unfold through the narrator's perspective alone.

TRY THIS!

1. Sit in a coffee shop or focus on the people that are sitting around your dinner table. Notice how people walk, hold their head, punctuate their speech with gestures. Notice the breathy voice, the lilting laugh, where they pause or if they put a question mark at the end of every sentence. Then go home and try just one of these on.
2. Pick a character in your play. Choose one physical representation: how they stand, hold their head, move through space, or the expression on their face. This can be a direct imitation or an invented one. Next, choose a voice to give them, considering pitch, pace, volume, cadence, timbre, or dialect. There's no right or wrong here—just experiment. Once you've made these choices, do it again with different options. This process allows you to explore a range of possibilities for your character.

EXPERT ADVICE

Tell us about performing characters in a solo show.

The characters that I do in my solo show are part of my life, and I feel like it gives me some liberty to play with them and stretch them in a way that I don't always feel as free to do in a traditional play. Somehow the characters feel funnier to me and more available. There's something naturally funny about my dad, and when I play him in my show, I just lean into that part of him and stretch it a bit. Now, if I was playing my brother, I don't know that I have a voice for him, so I would maybe do a voice that I can hear my mom doing of him. It's all very intuitive, though. I've taken workshops where somebody put on some music, and a character was just born out of that moment. It felt like magic. It wasn't something I came up with in my head as much as it was in my body. There's something about trusting my body.

Penelope Walker
Actor, Solo Creator, and Performer, Director

Do I Really Need a Director?

We always advise our students to work with a director, though we understand you may balk at the idea. After all, you're the one who wrote your show, so it's natural to feel that you are the one and only person who has a crystal-clear understanding of it. This may be true. But again, we say: get an outside eye. A director can provide another viewpoint and open up possibilities to see the show from different angles. They will have a deep understanding of staging and how to make a play work in front of an audience.

Working with a director on a solo show may be a different experience from working with a director on a traditional play. In a conventional play, the director has creative control over all aspects of the production; they decide on the tone, style, and interpretation of the text, as well as the technical aspects of the show. When it comes to a solo show, especially one you've written, our experience has been that it's often a much more collaborative journey—one in which ideas, suggestions, and negotiations are freely exchanged and explored.

As with a traditional play, the director will work with you on interpreting the text and acting choices and stagecraft. Even if you're limited to a small black box stage and one chair, a director can help the story come alive through staging, lighting, props, multimedia, and sound. They can connect you to designers who can work on technical elements if you have the capacity to hire some. They will also work with you to establish the rehearsal schedule and serve as a support system during your journey from page to stage.

In some cases, a director of a solo show can act as a dramaturg and may work with the development of the script. They can contribute to the material's evolution by providing constructive feedback that shapes the narrative. This could involve suggesting rewrites, cuts, or reworking the script—if you want that sort of collaboration.

If You Are Assigned a Director

You may be paired with a director by a theater company or festival. It's important to have an open dialogue about your ideas, intentions, and artistic vision for the play before you begin any work. Ask if they are open to collaborating with you. If it's a new solo work, it's beneficial to discuss what shape they think the script is in. If they talk about script development, consider whether there is realistically time to work on the text during the outlined rehearsal period, and share your own thoughts.

If You Are Choosing a Director

If you're planning to self-produce or coproduce or are looking for a director to attach to your project, choosing the right individual involves assessing their compatibility with your artistic vision, communication style, process of working, and your budget. Potential directors will need information about your show, and you'll need information about them.

Make a list of a few potential directors to interview. If the word "interview" is too intimidating, substitute "talk to them." You can choose someone who works in town as a director, a trusted friend who is an actor, or someone who has done a solo show themself. Ask around.

Email the people on your list with the full script, an approximate running time, and the particulars of the show. Here are some examples of what to write in your message: "This script is for two performances at the Fillet of Solo Festival. It will be bare bones, black box, limited or no lighting or sound." "This script is for a full production, and we have a lighting and set designer." "I'm self-producing this show in the back of a bar/museum/church basement." (FYI, all of these locations are legitimate—including the gyma-café-torium where Arlene has done some of her best work.)

Outline when you're available to rehearse and share some of your expectations. Here are some examples: "I foresee that this will be a shorter project with a few rehearsals to do some blocking and acting work." "I'm envisioning that this is a full-on directing project with script work for a fully realized production."

Let them know if you are planning to do the show "on book" (using a script onstage) or "off book" (memorized). Clarify whether the text is frozen or if you hope to continue to work on the text as you go along. Sharing your experience level will also be helpful—for example, "I'm a trained actor" or "I've done some storytelling around town" or "I have no acting experience."

Ask them about their rates for this kind of project. There might be people who will work for free to enhance their résumé, while others may charge you a steep price. They may charge by the hour or offer a flat rate for the entire process leading up to opening night. Ask other solo artists or theater people what their experience is. Don't be afraid to discuss money or negotiate.

Ask them how they see the play and what ideas they have. Most importantly, see how you connect. You will be working with this person on a project that you've poured your heart into. It's important that you trust them with your work.

Finding the right director is important to the success of your production, so take the time to assess your options before making a final decision. The right director doesn't just stage your play—they help you see it more clearly. Choose someone who listens well, who respects your voice, and who's willing to go on the ride with you.

EXPERT ADVICE

What advice do you have for a solo artist working with a director?

Asking yourself what you want from a director will be key to the success of this relationship. Do you want reflections on what you have written? Do you have a solid idea of how you want your piece to look? Do you want staging and props, or do you want to be at a music stand with your script in front of you? How comfortable will you be with a director's suggestions? These are all things to think about on your own before you even engage a director. Have frank conversations with one or several directors. This is the way that I work: I believe that you are the writer, and you are the performer, so what you say goes. I like to offer feedback but let you have the final decision. Other directors work differently. I find one of the most helpful things is to ask your director to describe the journey of your story.

Also think about how many rehearsals you need (you will need more than you think). I recommend many run-throughs without stopping followed by note sessions. Yes, you will want rehearsals where you can stop and start and try moments different ways. But there is nothing like running your piece straight through to understand if the journey has a beginning, middle, and end. Does it feel complete? Is the ending earned?

Ann Filmer
Director, Writer, Performer

EXPERT ADVICE

As a director, how do you approach working with a solo artist?

The solo actor/director relationship is built on trust, trust, trust, and trust! As a director, I am there to serve the performer and their text; to make sure the artist's uniqueness and talent are spotlighted; and to make sure the visuals and flow of the show reflect what I call "The Three S's": they must be seamless, stunning, and serve the play.

After talking about the piece, we start with a simple table read. At this point, I get to hear the "voice" of the artist. It's an opportunity for me to have initial flashes of staging inspiration and begin to envision the play. If the actor embraces the fact that I am here to make them and their story shine, we can have so much fun experimenting with world building and characterization. We may try things that may or may not click or make it to the final stage, but it is in the detailed process of discovering movement, staging, lighting, spacing, pacing, and character touches that we can turn a polished or semipolished script into a truly stunning solo!

Stephanie Rogers
Director, Musician, Teaching Artist

How Will You Rehearse?

Julie was thirteen years old the first time she was in a play. Her father taught at a community college in rural Missouri, and her mother had the idea that she should audition for their summer outdoor production of *The Sound of Music*. Julie wasn't at all sure that sounded fun, but she went to the audition and was cast as Louisa, one of the more forgettable von Trapp children. The experience changed everything. By the time she stepped into eighth grade, she was announcing to anyone who would listen, "I'm going to be an actor when I grow up!"

If you've had the good fortune to be in a play, either in a school play or on a professional stage, you know how fun rehearsing can be. Getting to know your fellow cast members, hanging out in the greenroom, running lines with other actors during breaks, falling in love behind the set—it's all part of the process. The type of play and the content of the play make a difference, of course, but the comradery of rehearsals can be, for some of us, an unmatched collaborative experience. If you're lucky enough to be familiar with that kind of rehearsal experience, rehearsing a solo play can take some getting used to. It can be a little . . . well . . . lonely.

Hopefully, you have taken our advice and found yourself a director. You could also have a stage manager or possibly an artistic director sitting in on some of the rehearsals, but it might be only you and the director. Having a structure, a timeline, and norms for working together, just like you would in a play with a larger cast, will be important.

Where Will You Rehearse?

Finding rehearsal space can be tricky. If you're not able to rehearse in the venue where you will be performing (and many of us aren't), you will need to find another place. We know folks who've rented space at a local community center, signed up for a room at the library, used a yoga studio after hours, worked in a church basement, or used their own basement. Even if you need to rehearse in your own living room for a while, as you get closer to production, you'll ideally want a space that feels more neutral, so keep looking and be open to lots of options.

Wherever you rehearse, be sure to use masking tape to mark out the size of the playing space that you'll have for your actual performance. Don't assume! Know where curtains, doors, entrances and exits will be. The more you can recreate the space where you will be performing your show, the more prepared you'll feel when you move onto your stage.

What's the Process?

If your director is experienced, they will most likely already have a process that will inform how your rehearsals will unfold. They'll establish a rehearsal schedule, or you'll decide on it together. Their process may loosely follow the path that traditional play rehearsals generally follow—tablework, running scenes or sections, running the show, tech, and dress rehearsals.

Working with a director on a piece you have written has the potential to be a very collaborative journey—more so than a traditional play. A key difference is that a director will sometimes double as a dramaturg and creative partner, providing constructive feedback that shapes the narrative, such as suggesting rewrites cuts or reworking the script. You get to decide whether that will be part of your director's job. It's also OK to be clear with your director that you welcome all the staging and performance guidance they can offer, but you're not looking for feedback on the text.

As with any new play, your script may continue to change once you are in rehearsal. At the same time, you must solidify the text at some point—early enough that you can be absolutely solid on the lines and blocking. (See our chapter "When Should the Writer Leave the Room?")

How Many Rehearsals Will I Need?

There are no hard and fast rules here, except to say *more than you might think*. Don't be lulled into thinking that because you wrote the piece, memorizing will be a breeze, or that since you only have to worry about yourself, you won't need to rehearse as much. We would suggest no less than twenty-five total hours of rehearsal for a solo play, not including the time needed for memorization if you are planning to memorize. Think about it—if you schedule three-hour rehearsals, that's only eight total rehearsals before opening night.

If you're able to give yourself more rehearsal, perhaps spread out over four weeks, meeting for ten hours or so a week, it will ensure you have the time to know the material "in your bones" before adding technical elements and an audience. More rehearsal time means that you'll have time to explore, to change your mind, and to discover things about your play. We've seen a decent solo script become a really good play through a strong rehearsal process that builds to a great performance. Conversely, we have also seen a really strong script crumble due to an actor who was unprepared.

Memorizing: How in the World Will I Learn All These Lines?

You may have a friend or an acquaintance with a photographic memory. We're happy for them and more than a little jealous. For most of us, however, memorizing takes time—usually more time than you think it will. Memorizing involves repetition and a certain amount of drilling the material over and over. Frankly, even though it's not hard, it's often not fun.

To be clear, it is possible to do a solo show successfully without memorizing it, performing from pages on a music stand or memorizing only portions of the text. Actors who are skilled at engaging with an audience are able to perform from a script so well that the audience actually forgets they have pages in front of them. If memorizing is not a great option for you for whatever reason, you may choose to focus your energy on getting good at performing from a script.

You will still need to be extremely familiar—intimately familiar—with your text, but you won't have to worry about memorizing every word. We've seen a solo actor very effectively use two music stands, one downstage right and one downstage left, with portions of the script set out on them. The soloist chose to memorize the parts of the script that involved scene work and dialogue and deliver other parts of the show from the script on the music stands. Because the actor was adept at connecting with the audience, it worked beautifully.

But most solo performers want to memorize their plays and can, given enough time. If you're a seasoned performer, you probably already have your own process for memorizing text, and that will serve you well. What about those of us who don't?

Memorizing the text of an entire solo show can be very intimidating. Don't let it become so psychologically overwhelming that it trips you up. Break it down into easy bite-sized sections. Set up a realistic weekly schedule and set small goals, such as two pages a day or one scene per sitting or a small section of dialogue during your lunch at work. Whatever you decide, carve out the time. Whether you're a person who memorizes quickly and easily or someone who struggles, you *will* eventually learn the material and get back to really enjoying your show.

There are lots of different techniques to lock text into your brain. Here are few we have tried over the years.

Are you a visual learner? If so, you may have discovered that studying the lines printed on the page works for you. Highlighting specific words or lines can also provide you with mental cues. We know actors who add a kinesthetic component to memorization and swear by writing out their lines longhand on paper in order to learn them. Are you an auditory learner? If you remember things you've heard, record your lines and play them back, speaking along with them.

Call in some favors. Have a friend, partner, or easy target acquaintance be on book for you as you run your show, cueing you and making note of lines you get wrong. Work on your script right before going to bed at night. Sleep is when our brains lock in learning and move short-term memories to longer-term storage. Studies show that even a nap can accelerate memorization. (Julie swears by this.) Rehearse lines in your head in a whisper or full voice while you are walking the dog, driving, or taking a shower.

Some people break a particularly difficult section into mnemonics—a word, short poem, or little song to help you remember. Similarly, you can create an acronym for particularly big sections of text or lists (such as ROYGBIV for the colors of the rainbow—red, orange, yellow, green, blue, indigo, and violet). Arlene uses acronyms quite a bit. Years after a production, she is still able to recall material using this method. Finally, there's a superstition that sleeping with your script under your pillow can help you learn your lines faster. While this may be true, we encourage you to have a backup plan.

Preparation gives you the freedom to feel confident, take creative risks, and stay present with your story. And all of these things require time—time to work, time to process director notes, and time to rest, snack, and reflect. So don't rush things if you can possibly help it. Honor your work. Honor the story you want to give voice to.

EXPERT ADVICE

Two things help me shift from writer to performer: having a director in the room with me and having a deadline. An audience is waiting to see a product, so the goal is always to give myself a month. I think I would be happier with myself if I was able to push that date further back. For my last show, I chose a director who was a physical theater artist because I didn't want to be a talking head onstage. I wanted to become my characters and have their spaces be very differently defined. We had about a month of rehearsals before performing at the Mitambo International Theatre Festival in Harare, Zimbabwe, and I kept making changes to the script during rehearsals based on feedback I had received and trying to further develop the piece. I didn't want to stop. And ultimately, I felt under-rehearsed for my first performance there. I had not had enough rehearsal with the new changes for the show to be solid in my body, so I was square in the center of those characters. The transitions felt rough in my first performance, and that was really frustrating to me.

Jasmin Cardenas
Artivista LLC
Artist + Activist. Storyteller. Theater Practitioner.
Civic + Cultural Worker

EXPERT ADVICE

What tips do you have for memorizing?

I was terrorized by the thought of trying to remember lines and seeing the audience right there in front of me with no script to lean on. But I eventually discovered that being off book and making eye contact with an audience can energize a performance. In the beginning, I would break a story into beats and just try to memorize a beat at a time. And if it's your show, it doesn't have to be word perfect. So I'm trying to let the small things go and not call them mistakes. I want to be like Julia Child, just pick the chicken up off the floor and go on. What rivets a listener is that something is happening live. In the end, I'm trying to communicate something to an audience. I'm trying to give them something, not to have them pay attention to me. I want people to come up afterward and tell me how my work made them think about themselves. When they do, I love that they're not talking about me at all.

Connie Shirakawa
Solo Performer, Storyteller

When Should the Writer Leave the Room?

When you are both the writer and performer of a one-person show, you're juggling two huge responsibilities. There will often be rewrites, cuts, and reworking throughout the rehearsal process. A crucial decision you and your director will have to make is at what point "the writer will leave the room," meaning the script will become frozen text and no longer change. From that point forward, the focus must be strictly on your performance. If this demarcation doesn't happen and script revisions continue until previews or opening night, you may find there is insufficient time to memorize lines and stage business, internalize the play's emotional journey, and feel confident in your performance.

If you're the performer in a solo show and the playwright is someone else, the same principle applies. This negotiation will need to happen. It goes without saying that if you are the playwright and not the performer, be smart about this decision and protect your actor. Even if you come up with a brilliant solution three days before opening night that seems like it would fix every problem in the show, make a note of it and leave it for another time.

We're speaking from experience. Both of us have done a run of at least one of our solo plays that was still undergoing revisions during previews. It was exhausting doing double duty, paying close attention to the writing and performance at the same time, and it didn't allow us to do our best work. We needed to essentially rememorize parts of the script at the last minute and adjust our acting choices based on the material being added, revised, or cut.

For example, several years ago, in the middle of an important scene, poor Arlene found herself performing a section of her play at the wrong time. She had unintentionally reverted to a previous version of the play. This particular scene had a very specific description of a medicine cabinet filled with "pretty little yellow pills, rainbow capsules, and ones resembling tiny hotdogs." It had been rewritten and moved a few times. She inadvertently delivered half a page of dialogue twice. She managed to recover, but she's convinced the audience definitely noticed.

TRY THIS!

Take out your calendar and mark opening night. Now walk it back at least four weeks—that's your target "freeze date," the moment your writer-self agrees to step aside so your actor-self can step in. Discuss it with your director and negotiate a mutually clear deadline for locking the script. Be sure you also account for things like tech week and line memorization, and make sure the number of rehearsals before that date feels sufficient. Circle it. Highlight it and decorate it with glitter if you need to.

Performing Your Show (Hallelujah! Finally Doin' It!)

The day will finally come when you'll step onto a stage or playing space and perform your show. Don't be surprised if it feels like it has taken forever to arrive. Don't be surprised if the time has flown by and you cannot believe you are here so quickly. That's how life is, right? Here are some thoughts on actually doing your show. After all your hard work, you deserve to *enjoy it.*

Turn Your Nerves into Excitement

Have you ever noticed that stress and excitement can show up similarly in the body? Try overriding nerves and anxiety by assuring yourself that the sensations you are experiencing are a very normal physical reaction to doing something new and could also be interpreted as excitement. Employ all your other personal strategies to combat feeling anxious, of course—your deep breathing and positive affirmations and lucky socks. But do not underestimate the power of telling yourself "I'm excited!" rather than "I'm so dang nervous." Remember that audiences *want* you to do well. Understanding and believing that they are on your side will also help you step onto the stage with confidence.

Address the Practicalities

Paying attention to some details ahead of time will help you feel more secure as you take the stage. One common physical response to stress (or excitement!) is a dry mouth. This is especially unhelpful when we are about to be onstage talking for a good amount of time, so make sure you have water easily accessible. Some performers set a glass on a side table in full view of the audience, while others hide a water bottle behind a chair. Build moments into the transitions of your show for a sip of water, whether you actually feel thirsty in the moment or not, to ensure you don't dry out in the middle of your next scene. Proactively hydrate the day of your show, before you even get to your venue. One more tip for dry mouth in the moment: bite the tip of your tongue, which will release saliva.

Might you need a tissue to address a sweaty brow or moist orifice in the course of your performance? Stash a Kleenex immediately offstage or in your pocket. Do you have dry lips to the point that they can distract you? Lip balm, friend. Powder the nose pads of your glasses so they don't slide down. Set a reminder to silence or turn off your phone before heading on stage so that's one less thing to worry about.

Many people like a pre-show ritual to help settle them into the right headspace. Some folks enjoy chatting and fooling around in the dressing room, while others like to have a quieter environment. Some wear headphones to listen to music or block out distractions. We worked with two women who used the time doing their own hair and makeup in front of the mirror as a way of centering. Some actors we know situate themselves away from all people and distractions and do a gentle meditation backstage that focuses on breathing and quieting the mind. Others spend time reviewing their script or running lines to themselves. Arlene does an intricate little pre-show ritual before going out into the house to connect and greet audiences before taking the stage. Then there are all the little superstitions and customs that people adhere to, such as surrounding themselves with personal photos, lucky totems, and inspirational sayings. Do whatever will make you feel safe and in control and put you in a positive frame of mind.

Trust Your Work

Regardless of how prepared or unprepared you feel on opening night, you are now a solo performer. Directors and actors almost always feel that they would ideally like a few more previews or even another week of rehearsal to get a show to a more solid place. "If we just had two more run-throughs . . ." There are always more tweaks, fixes, improvements we could make. But that's not how it works. Our job as professionals is to get the product to be as polished as it can be by opening night. The very best thing you can do for yourself and your show at this point is to put aside second-guessing.

Your performance will grow and improve as you get shows under your belt. A confident performance can obscure a host of little imperfections in the script or minor line flubs. You've made a best-faith effort to bring a quality product to the stage, and you must trust that the forces of the universe are on your side. You've worked very hard, and you are *brave*. You have done something a small fraction of folks has the guts to do. Let that fortify you.

Every Night Will Be Different

Audiences vary from night to night. One night, you'll get very big laughs and lots of reactions from the audience. The next night, the audience will feel more contemplative and quieter. Resist the temptation to assign value judgments to these responses or assume that an audience isn't enjoying a show because they're not as vocal as a previous night.

If you feel like an audience is unresponsive, check in with yourself. Are you rushing? An audience won't laugh if they don't feel they have the space to do so or feel like laughing will cause them to miss your next line. Are you pushing, or are you really present in the moment, allowing yourself to connect with the folks in front of you? Sometimes, an audience is just quiet, and it's not a reflection on you or your performance.

If a performance feels really good—if the audience is rolling in the aisles during the funny bits and there is rapt silence during the serious moments—it can be tempting to try, the next night, to recreate that experience. Take it from us (and every other seasoned actor)—it doesn't work. We need to do our best to keep things fresh and connect with the audience that shows up each night.

Another thought about comparisons. We've seen clients who have had a stellar show, the best show, a peak, mountain-top performance. They felt like they were one with themselves, the audience, and the material. They talk about feeling high or lifted by a force greater than themselves. When this happens, it feels miraculous.

However, a performance like this can become dangerous if it becomes the benchmark by which all subsequent performances are judged and measured. Everything else then feels like a letdown. Arlene still remembers the sweetness of a performance she had a decade ago and works hard to remind herself not to compare that pinnacle performance to every other one. Be grateful for those magical performances, put them in the pocket of your heart, and recognize them for what they are.

You will need to consider how to stay sharp between performances and during time off. Think about what would be most helpful and budget time for it, whether it's a line-through, speed-through, walk-through, or running tricky or troublesome scenes. We've found that even a partial run-through can help retain your muscle memory. Some people like to do vocal or physical warm-ups between performances, and we say, "Have at it."

Focus on the Show

This might feel obvious, but we want to remind you that during the run of your show, your priority is *you* and *your play.* Folks will, with the best of intentions, try to deter you. Relatives will want to spend time with you and take you to dinner beforehand. If that works for you, great! If a full meal before a performance doesn't sound like a good idea for your body, tell people you can grab a drink with them afterward. Your cousin will want to know if you can get them comps and arrange for special seating. Your mother will want to take pictures. Your babysitter will want to videotape the funny bits with her phone—is that OK?

All of these requests will come out of genuine excitement around your show, but don't let anyone sap your energy right now. Ask your partner or BFF to handle this stuff for you. You can make it up to them later.

When Julie was about to open one of her shows for a limited short run, her parents and sisters had plans to come into town, stay with her, and see the show. It felt like a lot. She considered asking her family to stay in a hotel during this particular visit but was loath to miss out on any potential time with them. In the end, she let them know she was thrilled to have them stay with her but set clear expectations that she would not be able to entertain or cook in the ways she usually did. For the first time, she hired a cleaning service to get her house spic and span before their arrival.

Be attuned to your body and support it as much as you can. This may sound obvious, but we encourage you to eat well and to sleep. Adrenaline and mental focus draw a great deal of energy. There are different mental and physical challenges whether you do a show every weekend, eight times a week, or for just one night only. We both know how hard it is to work a day job and do a show at night. It can be exhausting, so pay attention and honor your instrument.

TRY THIS!

Wherever you are in your process, start a list right now of things you can put in place to support a good performance experience. Keep this list on your phone or in your journal, adding to it as new ideas come to you. Create a five-minute warm-up ritual designed to anchor you. This can include a vocal warm-up, a bit of breath work, a moment of stillness, or a short visualization where you imagine your show landing beautifully with the audience. Practice it until it feels like muscle memory, so that when nerves show up, your body already knows what to do. Also, plan for pickup rehearsals, run-throughs, and speed-throughs if necessary.

EXPERT ADVICE

I can absolutely get lost in wanting it to be perfect or just right. And that means swallowing a pill of humility, because sometimes the result is that you're going to put work out there that maybe isn't quite as strong as you want, and there is no more time for rehearsal and there's no more time for rewrites and there's no more time to do anything but get on that stage and do the best with what you've got. I have to remember that I am a professional. I'm not going to apologize. I'm just going to offer what I have and then receive whatever comes back from the audience. Most of the time, the audience is very gracious, open, and excited about the new work and they're with me. And if I just trust that relationship, if I show up as my most authentic self without the excuses but having done the work, my audience is capable of receiving me and catching me. And it surprises me every time.

Jasmin Cardenas
Artivista
Artist + Activist. Storyteller. Theater Practitioner.
Civic + Cultural Worker

Reviews

Reviews are great publicity. Getting a newspaper, website, or blog to review your show can help you find an audience that will really appreciate your play. This is especially true if the review is good—even if it's only partly good. We've certainly had the experience of buying a ticket for a play or movie we've read a middling review of simply because we're interested in the artist or the subject of the work.

A good review feels *wonderful*. It can provide you with a nice boost of confidence. You've put so much work into your show, and here's some well-deserved praise from a person you don't even know! An impartial expert! However, you might work equally hard on a project and the reviews are *not* glowing, they're mixed, or they're downright mean. If you've invited press to see your show and are lucky enough for them to attend, it will be important to prepare yourself for public feedback. Putting this feedback in perspective is crucial.

Reviews are written by normal individuals with likes and dislikes and a history, just like everybody else. Professional critics are part of the theater ecosystem and are (supposed to be) on the side of art. It's not their job to exalt or trash shows, but to honestly point out the strengths and weaknesses of that show within its genre and help the folks who will appreciate it most to find it. Some critics don't love musicals. If they're good critics, they won't trash every musical they see. They'll know what makes a strong musical and shine a light on that in their review, while not ignoring any glaring weaknesses. However, reviewers also have good days and cranky days. They're not always going to be right.

It's not our job to try to outsmart reviewers and make them like us. It's our job to create the best work we can and let the chips fall where they may. We can't control what a reviewer is going to write about our show, but we can decide how we will let that review affect us. Will you read reviews of your show in the midst of your run or wait and read them after your show has closed? Will you never read them?

Let's consider the difference between reading reviews as the playwright of your solo play versus the actor performing your solo play. For a playwright, reviews can provide an objective outside view from someone who doesn't know anything about the play's development. A review might offer insight into why a moment lands or doesn't. Reviewers for reputable outlets see hundreds of shows a year and generally approach their work with deep knowledge. They know something.

You will have asked for and received feedback within your personal and professional circles before solidifying your script and getting onstage. Feedback from a review can be valuable in a different way, especially if you're open to doing rewrites on your show before seeking additional productions. You won't be able to use that information until the current run is over. Please don't try to rewrite anything in the middle of a run! But you may find it useful later.

For an actor, reading reviews is trickier. It can be hard for even a very experienced actor to not take a review personally. A negative review read during the run of a play can be discouraging and can make it harder to deliver confident performances going forward. It can suck all of the joy out of a previously triumphant experience. Even if the criticism of a play is centered on the writing, a performer still has to get onstage and deliver their lines with commitment night after night until the show closes. Even a positive review of a performance can be detrimental.

Years ago, writing about Julie's performance in a Chicago production, a reviewer raved about how astonishing a specific emotional moment was. From then on, the moment was never the same. Julie found it hard not to be a little self-conscious at that moment of the play each night Was it still good? Was she doing it as well as on opening night? Was her performance living up to the reviewer's effusiveness?

Only you can decide what works best for you. A solo show that you've written and performed is personal, whether it's autobiographical or not. You could have a friend "curate" your reviews and only pass along the positive ones until the run is over. You may decide to forgo reading reviews until you feel really solid in your performance and ready to tackle whatever they might say.

You may find it harder to avoid reviews than you expect, however. Theaters tend to take excerpts from positive reviews and immediately post them online or outside the theater, which, admittedly, can feel awfully nice. If you decide not to read your reviews, be prepared for your friends and acquaintances to excitedly accost you with "Congratulations! I saw your review in the *Tribune*." You'll have to gently interrupt them with "Oh, I'm not reading any of the reviews right now, so please don't say more." If the reviews are less than glowing, you may notice the opposite: a hush, as no mention is made of anything by anyone.

If you're confident in your ability to handle reviews no matter what, you might decide to read each review as it comes out. Be sure to remind yourself that reviews are *the opinion of one person*. Don't let them define you as a writer or actor. Even Meryl Streep, who has been nominated for more Oscars than anyone, has had some rotten write-ups.

When you receive a review, look for any positive words or phrases you can pull out to feature in your marketing, website, and social media. We talked to a big-shot LA manager about this topic. He said that, in every review, there are one or two positive phrases that can be lifted and quoted for his clients' PR materials. Sometimes, it's literally three words. Reviews are an important part of the publicity engine of your work.

The vast majority of playwrights and actors have received a poor review at one point or another. We certainly have. We're happy to say that we survived and have even forgotten the details of most of them. Julie now makes it a rule not to read reviews until a show has closed. Arlene, on the other hand, reads every review because of an early experience that left a lasting impression. In a play where she appeared for only one scene, a reviewer declared that her performance undermined the entire theatrical production. Understandably, she was beside herself with grief and took to her bed, convinced that she would "never work in this town again." However, the very next day, another review came out in a publication of much higher repute that lauded her performance as a triumph! The same performance, seen on the same night, resulted in two very different outcomes and taught her a valuable lesson.

(That said, she still remembers the name of the reviewer, which she will not share publicly in this book but will gladly besmirch in a one-on-one conversation.)

TRY THIS!

Find time to read several reviews of past theater productions you have seen. Notice where you agree and disagree with the reviewers. Do this with all the shows you see over the next few months, making note of great "pull-out quotes" that could be used for marketing the show. You'll see that even shows with imperfect press find ways to use reviews to market their production.

Sellin' Yourself

Finding a Venue

One of the advantages of coproducing or self-producing a solo show is that you will be empowered to create the show you envision. You'll retain more autonomy, flexibility, and decision-making power than you would if a theater were producing your show. One of those decisions will be the venue. There are plenty of them out there, both traditional and nontraditional, that can fit your budget and your vision.

We've seen successful solo shows done in large, well-established theaters; small storefronts; gallery spaces that held twelve broken-ish chairs; and a dreamy outdoor amphitheater in the backyard of a Malibu mansion, complete with twinkle lights and terminally hip people. FYI, the amenities were great in Malibu, but the parking and the play were much better at the storefront.

Budget

Budgets make most people fret. Don't. Think about your goals. Would you be happy to do the show and break even, or do you need to make money? After making a list of all the theaters and venues you know, search online for rental theaters as well as performing arts and special events spaces in your town. You'll be able to find pricing information online, but we encourage you to call and have a discussion to explore all the options. A multiweekend run will be priced differently than a Monday through Wednesday run or performing on an existing set on off-nights.

Collaborating with other artists can stretch your budget. Depending on the length of your solo show, consider collaborating with other artists for double-header performances or staging your shows in rep. You can distribute the producing responsibilities among a few people and increase the chances of attracting a bigger audience.

For example, Arlene and three other solo artists rented a two-hundred-seat theater with a blooming courtyard that surrounded a beautiful fountain. Wine and light snacks were served. They used this opportunity not only to get on a stage and perform but to invite LA producers, agents, and artistic directors to get "seen" by the industry for future work. They were satisfied with breaking even. The rental price was high, so they opted for a limited run during the week, advertised as "a special encore performance, two nights only." Everyone hustled, many comps were provided, and the houses were sold out. Each performer did thirty-minute excerpts from their show, and it was a beautiful experience to share the stage with other talented solo artists.

Size

Size matters. We always say that a large percentage of your audiences will come from your own contact list and their connections. How many people do you realistically think will come from that group? Many performers prefer to choose a smaller venue for a longer run. However, we know of a solo artist who rented a 250-seat venue for an initial three-performance run. She told us that she made much more money doing fewer performances in a bigger arena, allowing her to have several subsequent runs in smaller theaters over the next two years.

Amenities

Is having a dressing room or a lobby with a bar for post-show mingling important to you? Does brand-spanking new and clean matter to you, or is older with charm acceptable? Some rentals or venues take care of the ticketing or box office for you or handle a limited amount of advertising, which can take a load off your to-do list. Otherwise, you will need to use an online ticketing service and work the door. Consider the type of support you'll need for your show, such as lighting, sound, multimedia requirements, and stage setup. Does the theater provide the technical crew, or do you need to arrange that separately? If you have a set, will you be able to store it there? Be sure you have a clear understanding of all the financial aspects before moving forward. This includes insurance. Some theaters require you to purchase your own insurance, while others will cover you on their policy.

Certain seasons and holidays may also impact your show, but not always negatively. For instance, a solo artist we know produced a show featuring several storytellers every Christmas Eve at a large comedy club. The performance was tailored for a Jewish audience, many of whom did not celebrate the holiday. She called it "Chop Shtick." It was always a hit.

Location

Consider what might be important for your particular target audience. Does your venue need to be close to public transportation, or is the priority to have decent parking? Would your audiences be open to driving a distance? Consider the surroundings. A location in a row of dark warehouses next to a viaduct could be unsettling for some but just fine for others.

Comfort

Poking your head into a theater is not enough. This may seem obvious, but it's a good idea to sit in the seats to make sure they're reasonably comfortable. If they're not, your show will feel really long. We cannot tell you how many janky seats we've encountered. Walk the stage and look at the common spaces. If there is something that concerns you, like a dirty lobby or a pile of boxes in the bathroom, ask about it. Remember, they are trying to rent the space. You can negotiate. We personally put a priority on the audience's comfort over the perfect stage space.

Accessibility

Your venue should be wheelchair-accessible and comply with the requirements of the Americans with Disabilities Act (ADA). Some small theaters lack truly accessible facilities. Issues might include a small step up into the theater, no designated space for a person using a wheelchair that isn't in a fire lane, or bathrooms that are not accessible. If you're going to host an ASL performance, make sure you've figured out the appropriate lighting for the area where the interpreters will be standing.

Some theaters are now offering "relaxed performances" specifically tailored for individuals on the neurodivergent spectrum. The purpose is to allow audience members to experience the show and react in any way that is comfortable for them without judgment. With this kind of approach, adjustments are made to lighting and sound to accommodate audiences that might be more sensitive to lights and loud noises. The dimmed house lights are often kept on, onstage sounds can be toned down, and audience members are free to make noise, move around, come and go as they wish. Earplugs and a quiet space outside the theater itself are often provided as well.

The COVID-19 pandemic changed the way we did theater for a while. Safety for immunocompromised people can also be considered an accessibility issue. If that is a factor for your particular audience, you might consider ventilation and spacing in your venue, or even mask requirements for selected performances.

Genre and Themes

The nature of your play can influence the choice of venue. If your play explores themes or subject matter tied to a specific type of location, consider what would be a good fit. For example, a play about nature might work well in an outdoor setting. Think about the mood of your play. A play with a minimal set may work well in a simple black box, while a play with bigger sets or lots of multimedia needs may require a more traditional theater. An experimental, immersive, or site-specific piece might be perfect in a nontraditional venue like a historic house or the altar of a church. We have played on both. (At the church we wondered when God was going to strike us down but it was just religious guilt nibbling at our talent.)

What About Nontraditional Venues?

When it comes to your one-person show, nontraditional spaces can offer lots of unexpected advantages, so don't be afraid to think outside the box. Some of these off-beat spaces will help you stick to your budget, while others might bring an interesting element that can complement the material of your solo show.

For instance, Arlene has been offered the May Chapel in the beautiful Rosehill Cemetery in Chicago. She is waiting for the right material, theme, or opportunity to organize a show. Perhaps a Halloween show? Or maybe a show entitled "Losing My Religion"? If anyone has suggestions, reach out!

We've brainstormed all of the places we've seen plays and solo shows, and here are some ideas:

- art galleries, museums or cultural centers
- warehouses or lofts
- libraries
- private rooms in bars or restaurants
- the lobbies of theaters
- the ballroom of a hotel
- outdoor spaces like parks, gardens, rooftops, and courtyards
- art studios or other creative spaces
- private homes
- park rec and community centers
- bookstores
- churches
- dance studios
- historic mansions or buildings
- the ever-popular venue for those of us who tour, the gyma-cafe-torium

Solo or fringe festivals usually find exciting and innovative spaces to hold performances. If your city has hosted one, look at its website to see where past performances have been held. The most nontraditional venue we've ever come across was a site-specific solo show held in an "allegedly" abandoned building, which matched the edgy tone of the play. The production generated a lot of buzz but was shut down before opening due to a rodent problem and a ceiling leaking black sludge. Another theater company saved the day by offering their space on off-nights. Ironically, there the set was not dark or moody, but a black box theater painted entirely white.

Finding the perfect venue for your play is about so much more than just stages or bricks and mortar. In the end, one person telling a good story to a group of people can transcend any venue. Go find yours!

In Solo, You Are Your Own Brand

We're here to tell you that artists, no matter their medium, need to be able to market themselves and craft a public image. This chapter has some ideas for building an online presence that will highlight your solo work and you as an artist. Building a solo brand means translating your real-world personality into the online world and showcasing who you are as a solo artist. It's about curating how you want to be perceived and making it easy for people to find you and your accomplishments without having to peck around.

We Googled the name of a noted arts leader from a theater in Chicago. This person is a known playwright, with productions in fancy venues across the country and teaching experience at prestigious institutions. To our surprise, the first two hits resulted in tiny bios. The next search results were for a photographer and a football player who had the same name she did. After that, we found a few reviews of her plays from years ago, followed by a bio of a teacher who enjoys fencing and coffee. Because she opted not to have a social media platform that she controlled, we had to really dig to find even a small glimpse of this playwright who has a deep résumé.

Who Are You and What's Your Work About?

Some folks prefer having their own website to promote their work, while others focus their online presence on social media. One advantage of a website is that it can serve as a curated warehouse for all the information you want people to know about you and your show. When people search for you online, your website will come up first, and it's the place where you get to control what the public sees. Whatever platform you choose to highlight your solo work, it should allow you to craft a narrative that includes your training, experience, and projects.

Julie's website reflects her experience as an actor, writer, teaching artist, and solo performer. When you Google her name, it's the first hit that comes up. Each section has a beautiful slideshow of pictures. However, what sets her website apart from others is the section entitled "My Teaching Philosophy," which really captures her personality. Her site is clean and easy to read and navigate.

Arlene uses her website to showcase similar categories of experience but relies less on visuals and leans more toward text. Another difference is that her site features an updates page where she shares good news, upcoming classes, and performances, along with her blog. Her site is as busy and chatty as she is.

We've both decided not to include personal details or photos of our private lives on our websites. However, a Chicago director we know takes a different approach by dedicating her blog page to her family adventures, complete with pictures. Another Chicago actor uses her website to showcase both her work as a podcaster and actor and her business as a consultant. These are personal choices that share the person you want the public to see.

What Are Your Goals?

Figure out what you want your platforms to accomplish. Do you want to let people know what you are doing creatively, personally, or both? Are you trying to build a following and increase your visibility?

Are you appealing to industry professionals? Or trying to hook a special interest group related to your solo show? These considerations will guide the type of website and social media branding you choose.

If you are new to solo work or performance, don't feel that you must misrepresent yourself or make yourself look more experienced than you are. You can simply highlight some of your other life accomplishments through a linked résumé or a snappy story explaining how you got here. For example, we worked with a solo artist who was returning to the acting and performing part of her life after many years away. She was embarrassed that she didn't have a good résumé or credits to speak of. A year before she was ready to get the show on its feet, she made a simple website. We had to fight her on this, but she finally acquiesced because we can be as persistent as a kid who wants a candy bar in the supermarket.

On her site's home page, she had a headshot, an announcement that her solo show was coming, and another page called About Me with two paragraphs about why she was writing the solo show and what was important about the topic. She also added a contact page. That's it. Easy peasy. When this solo artist had an informal reading of the play, she had some pictures taken during the feedback session and added them to the site with accompanying text.

Gradually, the website expanded. She put together a graphic and included a synopsis of her play. When she performed her show at a solo festival in Chicago, she had already established a presence, and someone in the audience contacted her about bringing the show to their school. Boom. A paying gig.

Where to Start

Here are some suggestions about what to include, whether you're creating a website or you're building your artistic or solo presence through social media posts. We think you'll be surprised at how much content you already have, and you can pick up lots of ideas by doing a little snooping around on other people's websites. Steal ideas that appeal to you. Personalize them for yourself.

1. Who You Are

- Introduce yourself. Let us know who you are as an artist, even if you are a new one. Your information could take the form of a résumé or bio.
- Include a contact page or your contact information.
- Explain your artwork. Why do you make the art that you do?
- Let us know your accomplishments, awards, publications, fellowships, and any notable achievements.
- Explain personal experiences that have influenced your writing, performing, storytelling, or artistic journey, even if it's been a short journey. If you've been inspired by a mentor or a solo show you've seen, explain how that has impacted your work. Tell us why you're writing a solo show.
- List education or training you have in writing or the performing arts.
- Give us reviews and testimonials from any parts of your performing, directing, storytelling, or creative life.
- Include links to social media where you are showcased, such as other people's podcasts, blogs, or storytelling websites.
- Photos and images? Always.

2. About Your Solo Show

- Write a brief synopsis of your solo show and say what you hope your audience will take away.
- Drop some teaser videos or photos of performances, rehearsals, or behind the scenes. People love to see the machinations of theater.
- You may choose to include written excerpts from your solo show script.
- Have you talked about your show as a guest on a podcast? Has your show been the subject of a story in print media? Include it.
- What have you learned in the process of writing and performing your show?
- Post countdowns leading up to your performance.

- Create videos or interviews with your director, designer, or the artistic director of the theater or festival.
- Share quotes, testimonials, and reviews if you have them.
- Create a travelogue connected to your solo show. Photos or videos of marquees, the theater, programs, audiences—anything and everything that will make someone look twice while they are scrolling.

3. Other Odds and Ends

- Create a calendar or post about upcoming projects, events, and good news so that people can see the breadth of what you're doing.
- Post pictures of yourself onstage, teaching, or attending a reading, play, or storytelling event.
- Include throwback photos. Nothing delights us more than seeing your third-grade performance of *Death of a Salesman*.
- Give us links to your other social media, podcasts, interviews, and articles.
- Be sure to use the "signature" section of your email to your advantage to share good news and upcoming events.

Remember, the internet never forgets. We recommend regularly searching your name online and reviewing your digital presence. What does the web reveal about you? This means looking at posts, tagged photos, mentions in public documents, websites, and organizations you're connected to. Ask yourself if this is how you want the world to see you. If not, take steps.

TRY THIS!

1. We like to use the 3×3×3 exercise. Ask three people to give you three words that describe you personally, professionally, and creatively. Tell them to consider your skills, strengths, and personal style. Once they respond, ask yourself if this is the way you want people to perceive you. How can you highlight the most meaningful traits on your artistic platforms?
2. Explore other artists' websites and social media profiles across all their platforms. What are they highlighting? What do you dislike, and what feels right to you? Take note.

Creating Marketing Materials

You've worked hard to develop a solid script to put out into the world. Yay! Congratulations and well done. Now let's create a marketing game plan and make sure people come see your show.

Many of our students and clients feel the most overwhelmed by marketing. The goal is to present a well-planned and unified marketing campaign to support your vision. You get to decide how much time, money, and energy you want to put into it based on your goals and resources.

The first thing that will drive your approach is determining how your show is getting out into the world. Are you self-producing? Coproducing with an organization, theater, or festival? Is a theater company producing your show? Is your solo show part of their full season, which means the full support of their PR machine, or is your solo show part of an off night or late-night series, which may receive fewer resources?

No matter how your solo show is getting produced, you will need to mount some type of advertising campaign of your own. On the DIY end, your campaign may involve doing nothing but texting your parents and posting on social media, or you may hire an outside PR firm.

Headshots? Heck, Yeah

At the very least, every performer needs a headshot—your visual business card and the foundation of your online presence, regardless of which platforms you use. You'll need one for the theater where you'll do your show, and also for programs, interviews, podcasts, and any other publicity tied to your play.

If you have a professional headshot, great. Make sure it looks like you and reflects the feel of your solo show. It shouldn't be a headshot that you had taken for the staff directory at your job. If you don't have a good headshot for your artistic life, Google "actor headshot photographer" and take a look around to find one that you like. Prices vary widely, so keep that in mind.

Though we never would have suggested this five years ago, it's possible to take a headshot on your own. Phone cameras are getting better, and content developers and filmmakers use them to great effect. Go online and get some ideas from professional headshot photographer sites.

Here are some things to keep in mind for DIY headshots:

- Find a friend willing to help you. Frame the shot from the chest up and look directly at the camera.
- Decide how you want to be perceived—friendly, serious, humorous, quirky, sexy. Pick one that aligns with the tone of your solo show.
- Take advantage of natural light. It's really flattering. Choose a simple background that won't distract from your image. Good options include fences, concrete, stucco, or brick walls. Blank walls with great colors can also work. And no bed sheets. Ever.
- Professional photographers take hundreds of shots to get a handful of good ones. Do the same. Vary colors, sleeve lengths, collars, and necklines of your outfits. You never know what will pop.

Pics and Graphics for Your Show

A headshot or an action shot might be sufficient to market your show, but you might also want to create a compelling graphic. Start paying attention to the graphics for movies, TV, and plays and see what appeals to you. Consider the tone of your solo show, your personal style, and your target audience.

For example, one of our clients, Victoria Montalbano, who is an actor, comedian, and improviser, created an award-winning solo show called *The Princess Strikes Back: One Woman's Search for the Space Cowboy of Her Dreams.* While the show is hilarious, it also addresses more serious themes, such as the portrayal of women in popular media and how those depictions can reinforce limiting stereotypes and expectations.

For her marketing campaign, Victoria used an image of herself mimicking Princess Leia's iconic pose in the gold bikini outfit. She even incorporated this costume, with her own unique twist, into her performance. She wrote witty copy that reflected the tone of the show and used her iPhone and a free photo editing app that offered a wide range of templates.

Postcards and Posters

Tried and true, postcards and posters are still an effective way to publicize a show. Some folks like small postcards the size of business cards, easily slipped into a wallet. Larger 4x6 postcards are relatively inexpensive to make, and they provide plenty of room for pictures and text. Include a blurb or short synopsis, a bio, and snappy review quotes if you've got them. Include location, performance dates and times, ticket prices, and how to purchase, including a QR code. If you don't include the dates/times/ticket info and leave a bit of blank space instead, you'll be able to use the same postcards for more than one run of your show by creating sticker labels with that variable information for each run.

Images tell the most engaging story, so make sure your postcards have eye-catching visuals and use the same design on your posters. Theater posters are ubiquitous in Chicago, especially in coffeehouses. No one needs proof of the Venn diagram overlap between theatergoers and coffee shop patrons. You can start asking your favorite establishments if they'll hang one in the window four to six weeks before your show opens.

Writing a Synopsis

A synopsis is a summary or general overview of your solo show, akin to a trailer for a movie. You should include a synopsis as part of your press kit and marketing materials. A synopsis should accompany your play when you send it to theaters, organizations, festivals, or play competitions. Applications for fellowships, residencies, and grants require a synopsis, as do potential publishers and theatrical literary agents.

Synopses seem deceptively simple but are notoriously difficult to write. A synopsis outlines the bones of your story, including the main characters, major plot points, and conflicts. It includes the essential question and the play's themes and reflects the style and tone of the show. Limit yourself to one page or less, though coming up with a version that's shorter, around 250–300 words, will also be helpful, particularly for marketing. For a press release, four lines or so is ideal. Typically, a synopsis is written in the third person and in the present tense. For example:

> In this opera adaptation of *The Wonderful Wizard of Oz*, Dorothy, a girl from Kansas, lives a simple life on a farm with her Uncle Henry and Aunt Em. One day, a tornado strikes, carrying her and her farmhouse to the Land of Oz, a magical world inhabited by strange creatures. In her quest to find her way back home, Dorothy encounters foes like flying monkeys, a field of poisonous poppies, and the Wicked Witch of the West. On her journey, she makes friends with the Scarecrow, Tin Man, and Cowardly Lion, who help her find her way back and realize that "there's no place like home."

Using Performances to Create Materials

You can utilize your show's development process to generate marketing materials. For example, we worked with an innovative client, LeeAnn Marie Webster, who rented a small theater for a two-day run for friends and invited guests in order to create an advertising press kit.

LeeAnn's approach included a catchy title, great graphic designs, and a fancy program. She hired a videographer to record the show and testimonials from the audience and turned them into two sizzle reels: a short clip that was three minutes and a longer one lasting seven. Action stills and additional images were taken of the packed theater. LeeAnn also arranged to have a filmed conversation with a colleague to discuss her goals for the show.

Another way to create material for your advertising strategy is to host an informal reading. It could take place in your living room, a common area, a rec room, or the back of a bar. You can invite an audience and get shots of their reactions, or you can stage yourself as if you were performing to get some good shots.

A Unified Strategy

We asked a brand and marketing consultant for one piece of advice when developing a social media strategy, and she emphasized the importance of consistency in both tone and appearance across all web, digital, and print graphics.

A great example of this is Kayla Boye, an artist who has traveled throughout the US and Europe with *Call Me Elizabeth.* Her show is a biographical piece, set in the 1960s, about the movie star Elizabeth Taylor, to whom, incidentally, she bears an uncanny likeness.

Kayla maintains a uniform aesthetic online by posting across all of her platforms pictures of herself when she's onstage, in costume, getting ready for a show, connecting with audience members, and in front of theater marquees, as well as photos of programs. She has a beautifully filmed and edited version of her solo show on Broadway on Demand for a small fee. Her IMDb profile, a casting network, and her agent's website all have similar photos. Even in her personal posts, Kayla portrays a glamorous style reminiscent of the 1960s. She also posts reviews, podcasts, and interviews she's done. She has deliberately chosen to use her social media to support her career, so she does not post food, animal videos, or political views.

TRY THIS!

Consider getting some help crafting the first draft of your synopsis: Sit down with a friend or family member and try to summarize your show for them. Afterward, inquire about what information felt like too much detail and what more they needed to know to understand the story. Do this with a few folks, and you'll start to figure out what's most crucial and interesting.

Press Releases and Media Kits

When Arlene did her first solo show, she thought it would have a nice little run, and that would be that. Even though her theater company was producing it, she worked hard to bring in audiences. The show ran on an existing set on Tuesday and Wednesday nights when the theater was otherwise dark. It received lovely reviews, sold out on some nights, and she thought, "Maybe I'll submit to a festival or have another run one day."

Unexpectedly, inquiries came from Deaf, CODA, and interpreting organizations for one-off performances. The news had spread simply by word of mouth. The problem? Arlene didn't have a proper media kit. She had no detailed information about her show, no website, and nothing that provided contact information. She wasn't ready for the opportunities that came her way, and it was a slapdash rush to put everything together for potential paying gigs. The lesson? Be ready. A solid media kit can make a big difference and might give your one-person show a longer and much bigger life. Additionally, having this material is important if you plan on doing fringe or solo festivals.

The Press Release

The most important component of your media kit is a press release. A press release is a short announcement to inform the public and the media about your upcoming solo show. Sending one out will give you the chance to talk about your show and generate interest and media attention. A press release tells the who, what, when, where, and why of your play and is one of the tools you can use to get your work listed in print and online theater calendars and, if you're lucky, reviewed.

An effective press release isn't a dry, bullet-pointed list of information. It should tell a good story, and you, as the artist, are the best person to write it. You understand better than anyone else what makes your play unique and interesting. Maybe it's the plot, or maybe there's a specific mission or theme that is important. Perhaps the spark that inspired you to write the play in the first place will draw attention. The press release should reflect you, as well as the tone and spirit of the show.

Many theater folks we talked to said that there is some flexibility with writing a press release. Some send out detailed press releases that are several pages long, while others use only 350–500 words. When writing the press release, state the information clearly, so that, when someone scans it, they have a good and quick understanding of what you're selling. We've crafted a basic template that you can customize.

[Logo or your visual graphic for the show]

[Date]

FOR IMMEDIATE RELEASE
[Contact Name]
[Company, Theater (if applicable)]
[Email]
[Phone]
[Press Kit Info]

[Catchy, compelling, and interesting headline]

[Name of your play]

[City, State]—[Date]—[Your Company] is happy to announce the upcoming production of *"[Play Title]"*, a [genre] solo show. This production is set to take the stage at [Venue] from [Start Date] to [End Date].

[A short, exciting paragraph about the play.]

[Provide a brief synopsis of the play. Include bios of the actor/performer, director, or creative team. If you are inclined, you can include some quotes from the actor/performer or the team.]

[Include snippets of good reviews or testimonials. Think in the widest terms.]

[Detail the venue information, including the name and address of the theater.]

[Performance Dates and Times]

For more info or tickets, please visit [Website URL] or contact [Ticketing Information].

[Name of Theater Company (if applicable)]

[Provide a brief description of your theater company, including its mission, notable achievements, and any relevant background.]

For media inquiries, please contact:
[Your Name]
[Title]
[Email Address]
[Phone Number]
[Press-Kit Info]
[Social Media Platforms]

The Media Kit

A media kit, also known as a press kit, is a set of promotional materials that provides information about your play, capturing the spirit of the performance and the person behind it. It can help generate interest and get butts in the seats. It can be as simple as a one-sheet with basic details about the show's run, a bio, and a photo. Or it can be a one-stop outlet mall with many options, such as headshots, creative action shots, bios of all the collaborators, reviews, updates and news, video clips, blog posts about the show, information about touring, and more—like handing someone your solo show wrapped in a beautiful gift box complete with a bow. Who doesn't like getting a present?

A media kit might include any or all of these elements:

1. **A well-crafted bio written in the third person.** What credentials do you have? What is important for your audiences to know about you? If you've got the time and inclination, we advise creating a 25-word, 50-word, and 75-word bio.
2. **A compelling synopsis of the show.** Distill the play's plot and themes. The narrative should be clear and leave the reader wanting more.
3. **A press release.** The official announcement of your show provides essential information, such as the date, venue, and how to buy tickets.
4. **Photos.** Include a headshot and some action shots from the play. Include high-resolution and low-resolution and horizontal and vertical photos in the press kit. You can stage these photos or have them taken during a performance. We have done both. Don't be afraid to use pictures that may not be your most beautiful self but are dynamic. Julie has a terrific action shot for her media kit. She has an animated expression; her body is in motion, and the photo feels alive. Is it her prettiest look? No, but it catches attention.
5. **Reviews and quotes.** Include feedback from critics, collaborators, and audience members.
6. **Promotional materials.** Include the posters or images that you've created. Make sure that they're eye-catching and reflect the show's aesthetics.

7. **Contact information.** Include info for bookings and hyperlinks to your website or social media platforms.
8. **Multimedia formats.** Offer your press kit in both digital and print formats. Your press kit should live somewhere online. Some of our students have a special category or tab on their personal websites, while others create a dedicated website for their solo show (e.g., Squirrelface.com).

Where to Send Your Media Kit

Theater makers we've talked to have mixed feelings about when and where to send a media kit. But everybody's in agreement that a *press release* is nonnegotiable. Some of our experts say, "Just shoot out a press release with a link to your digital media kit in the body of the document." Others swear by sending the whole darn media kit along with the press release. Take your pick!

Include your media kit when you are pitching your show to theaters, performing arts venues, festivals, conferences, or organizations that may be a good match for your play.

When you are planning a marketing campaign for an upcoming run, send your press release and media kit to theater journalists and critics in your area; the features section in your area's free papers; online media including bloggers, influencers, and local reviewers; hyperlocal neighborhood newsletters; and organizations and groups that may be interested in the subject matter of your solo show.

EXPERT ADVICE

What advice do you have about media kits?

All of the information about a play should be in the press kit. Don't make the press release too long. Keep it concise and focused on the key details. While it's good to highlight a play's strengths, don't overhype it by using hyperbole. Most publications will allow you to input your show into the calendar page of upcoming events. I like to do a combination of electronic and physical press kit. I send it as both PDF and Word so press folks can just lift from it. The press kit is there to make their job easier. I've also seen some innovative ways to get the information across, like using a QR code or a jump drive. Another important resource would be the online reviewers who see every play, love getting comped, and get the review out before everyone else does. They're local people who love theater. Many have developed followings and are as important as reviewers from traditional media outlets.

Ann Filmer
Director, Writer, Performer

Getting Butts into Seats

Making a solo show is a very personal act. Feeling nervous about putting it out into the world is perfectly normal. What will people think? What if nobody comes to see it? The business of selling a solo show requires a completely different skill set than the one required to create the show, but there's help available. You can do it.

Even if you're being produced by a theater company that will be publicizing your play, it's important to get a PR strategy together. For those of us who are self-producing, it's absolutely essential. For theaters, solo shows are easier to produce than a play with a cast of ten, but filling a house can present more of a challenge because, instead of ten actors drawing their fan base to the theater, there's just one performer, you. A certain number of tickets need to be purchased to fill your houses, and you can find that number by multiplying the number of seats in the theater by the number of performances. That number may look daunting. This isn't a cause for panic, just a plan.

Direct Marketing

Whether you have a theater helping you or you're self-producing with very little support, you can take steps to publicize your show. We understand that you might be uncomfortable publicizing your own work. Don't be. Learn to live with the discomfort. Strategize all the methods you want to utilize in your campaign in advance. Plan it out. Set goals. Alert your army.

You can start publicizing your show the moment you know that it's getting produced, and you can make announcements every step of the way. Research tells us that, on average, in order for someone to buy a ticket for an event, they need to come into contact with promo material between three and seven times.

You can begin getting the word out with simple messaging conveyed through email, text, word of mouth, or social media:

- It's happening! My solo show *Breakfast for Dinner* is coming this spring.
- Just secured the venue for my show at Chicago Dramatists Theatre. *Breakfast for Dinner* will be running May 15–June 29. Deets later.
- My first rehearsal for *Breakfast for Dinner* [include a fun fifteen-second clip] May 15–June 29. Tickets here.

The artists we know who've been most successful in selling tickets in advance are those who begin advertising at least six weeks before they open. If you can, offer an early-bird discount to create a sense of urgency.

Mine and Organize Your Personal Resources

While most people tend to use their social media platforms rather than their personal contact list to advertise their upcoming shows, we advise otherwise. Use social media, for sure! But people hop on and off platforms all the time, and they scroll past posts quickly without really paying attention. You may not have a lot of active followers. Also, the algorithms of social media change frequently, and platforms are not as reliable as your personal emails and phone numbers.

Create three contact lists. First, make a list of folks you have a personal connection with or those who have indicated that they are interested in you or your work. Take time to update and organize these names, email addresses, and phone numbers. These people will be the most significant part of your audience. This list should consist of family, coworkers, friends, and people from church or your fantasy football league—everyone in your acquaintance circle. Yes, we're including those people you've only met twice at a cocktail party thrown by your cousin, as well as your book club, pickleball group, and neighbors. If you have kids, include the other parents, teachers, and coaches. This compilation of people you know or have met needs to be shameless.

The second list consists of those in your inner circle that you think might help you in recruiting audiences. We call this your circle of influence. These are the people you can rely on to be a publicity machine for you—everyone from your best friend, significant other or current date mate, family members, and your fans, to people who owe you a favor (finally, a payoff for helping your friends move). The function of the inner circle is to send out emails and social media posts on your behalf. Think of it this way: if your mother sends a note to her Pilates friends, you are bound to get some of those folks in.

The third list consists of community groups, businesses, and relevant organizations that may have an interest in the topic of your solo show. They can help promote your play to their people or offer special deals to their members. For instance, one of our students had a play that dealt with dementia. She reached out to Alzheimer's groups and offered to host a fundraising performance. The organizations brought audiences, and she gave them 20 percent of the box office. She got a full house, and they got a nice donation.

Once you have these lists, start reaching out. The frequency of this kind of direct contact is up to you. It's common to blast an email once a week when you're six, five, and four week out, and then step it up to twice weekly two to three weeks before opening. Depending on how tickets are selling, you can contact more frequently as the run progresses. Mark the time to create urgency: "One more week for early-bird tickets!" or "Your last chance to see this show." You know enough not to bombard folks, but understand that people are busy and sometimes need a loving nudge or reminder. Make it as easy as you can for folks by always providing a link or a QR code for a digital ticket. Always.

Texting and phone calls are very effective, though many of our private clients absolutely cringe when we suggest it. Some text their networks individually, which can be time-consuming, but this does result in the highest number of returns.

In the 1990s, every ensemble theater company in LA had a "phone tree," a numbered list in which the first person called the second person, the second person called the third person, and so on. The message was usually simple: "We have a small house this weekend. If you haven't already seen the show, this is the time to do it. Bring your friends." This personal invitation always brought people in. These days, this same concept can be used with texting. Go to your contact list and create a group of recipients. Text those folks and ask them to pass your message along to their circle of friends and family. Recently, we got a text from one of our friends letting us know she was stepping into a role that she had been understudying at a big theater. She provided the link, we bought two tickets right away, and we forwarded the link to a few of our friends asking them to join us. It does work, so don't squirm.

Send Your Press Release

Even if you haven't created a full media kit, you'll want to have a press release. (You'll find detailed instructions for creating one in the previous chapter.) Ideally, aim to send your press release four to six weeks before the show's opening night. This gives media outlets and journalists sufficient time to cover your event. Always check the specific requirements and deadlines of each media outlet or platform you plan to approach.

Where to send it? If you don't know what media sources and critics are out there, go online and search for theater, arts, and culture contributors in your local area. Then, Google reviews for a play that had a recent run in your town and see what comes up. The search results should provide a list that's wider in reach, including online reviewers, bloggers, podcasters, and influencers.

Contact local newspapers, magazines, radio stations, and TV stations in your city. Look for arts and entertainment sections or theater critics. You can send the press release to their editorial departments directly, or to the individual journalists who cover arts and entertainment or theater. To be included on their calendar page, many news outlets allow you to send information and materials through their submission portal. Reach out to influential bloggers or social media people who cover theater or culture-related topics. Share your press release with online forums, social media groups, or websites frequented by theater enthusiasts. You can send them a press release, or even just a pitch email about your show. Many local arts and culture organizations have email lists for sending out information about upcoming events. Contact them to see if they would be interested in adding your show to their list. Publish your press release on your official website or blog and promote it through your social media platforms.

Be Creative and Fearless

Ask people you know and trust if they would host an evening at your show. Arlene loves this strategy. She asks people with whom she has a good relationship if they would be willing to "host" an evening by contacting a few of their friends and saying something like, "Hey, I'm going to see this show on Friday night. I'm getting a group together. Here's the link to the tickets. We could meet afterward and have a drink." Arlene typically asks more than a dozen people to host—friends, students, other instructors, family members, or work pals. She's had people bring one or two friends, while other overachievers brought eight or nine. She always tells her husband, who works in the corporate sector, that he's responsible for organizing an evening and filling at least one house with his people, and she doesn't care how he does it. He has also made the event a fundraiser for his company's local charity, organized post-show cocktails next door to the theater, and made the show a family reunion. Writing a solo show is a big deal and a lot of work, and the people closest to you know that. They want to celebrate that accomplishment with you. The key to this strategy is to reach out and ask the hosts personally. It's hard for people to say no when you reach out individually.

Consider cross-promoting your play at related events. Ask other artists, storytelling groups, or theaters if they would be willing to trade their contact list or if they would be willing to advertise on your behalf. We've had one student actually purchase a mailing list. When Julie is doing a solo show, she will often book herself in storytelling lineups that will get her face and name in front of people, making sure that the host announces the 411 on her solo show.

Tell everyone about your show and invite people. This might sound obvious. You may not be in the habit of talking about yourself all the time, but, right now, make it about you. When people ask, "How are you?" or "What are you doing?," you need to include a tidbit about your show in all your conversations, including with your physical therapists and acquaintances you run into at the grocery store. Julie was finding it hard to talk about her most recent show until she sat down and crafted a succinct two-line description. Suddenly, it was no big deal. Write an elevator pitch and be sure you can describe your show in two short, engaging sentences that reflect how interesting and exciting your play really is.

Now is the time to distribute postcards and posters! Get postcards into the hands of everyone you cross paths with. Ask if you can leave a stack or hang a poster at your favorite establishments. Pay attention to where folks are hanging posters and use that map as a starting place. Provide materials to all the people involved with your show, including tech people, designers, and the theater itself. Ask them to distribute as they go about their days—they're all part of your team. This kind of PR brings people to your show and also cements your presence as a working artist in the community.

If your theater allows it, offer promotional discounts like early-bird and student prices, discounts for teachers, veterans, and senior citizens. "Pay what you can" evenings can attract those who may not typically be able to attend. Offer an industry night where ticket prices are cheaper for actors, writers, and people in the arts. Don't be afraid to offer a free performance as a gesture of goodwill.

Arlene once dropped postcards into the mailboxes of everyone in her neighborhood with a little label that said, "Hey, I'm your neighbor at (your address here), and I have a solo show that I'd love you to come to." She got ten people within a four-block radius of her home. In a 40-seat theater, that's 25 percent of the house.

We know a solo artist who has been traveling with her show across the country for many years. Her show, a "different kind of immigrant story," is about how she left her small town in Jamaica and came to the US. On tour, whether she has a two-night gig or a longer run, when she arrives in a town to do a show, she always makes sure to hit up all of the Jamaican businesses, restaurants, clothing shops, and hair salons. She chats up the people; leaves posters, cards, and discount codes; and always credits the business for attracting audiences.

Get some pre-show press. Find your hook and promote your show through interviews on local television, radio shows, or podcasts. Find the features or lifestyle editor and pitch a story with an interesting POV. We've had students connect with the press for Pride month celebrations, holidays, domestic violence awareness week, and breast cancer or mental health awareness days, as well as birthdays or anniversaries honoring famous figures.

One of our students called a suburban affiliate of a major newspaper in Chicago and pitched a humorous article around themes from his solo show. The paper, which served the suburb where his parents lived, told him to write the article and they would consider it. He pulled material straight from his play and made it funny and endearing, just like his show. The paper loved it. They tweaked the copy and sent a photographer over, and he had a half-page color spread days before his show opened.

Get on any public media outlets that you can, including local radio, TV, news outlets, or cable. It isn't as hard or intimidating as it sounds. Don't be afraid to reach out—they're always looking for content. Just ask or send a media kit. Look for media outlets that have arts-related programming or programs thematically connected to your play. An author friend of ours doesn't mind doing the 7:00 A.M. morning show, even though it may be sparsely viewed, because she uses the clips later on her social media platforms.

Arlene likes to meet every single person as they file into the theater before her show. She introduces herself, thanks them for being there, connects with the people she knows, introduces herself to the people she doesn't know, and sometimes introduces strangers to each other. It makes people feel welcome and promotes great word-of-mouth advertising. Have we mentioned that word of mouth is still the most powerful marketing tool?

Create special events and add-ons. Host Q&A sessions or panel discussions that are connected to the topic of your show, however tangentially. Comp the panel members; some might bring friends. Throw a killer opening night party or a post-show Valentine soiree to celebrate your show. Offer food and make booze available, maybe a Groundhog Day celebration or winter solstice gathering. In other words, find interesting ways to capture people's attention and direct it toward your work.

Give away or sell merch. We've had students create fun merchandise for their shows, especially when they were at fringe or solo festivals. We've seen tattoos, finger puppets, t-shirts, pins, and totes (especially if the title is fun or catchy). Arlene received a beautiful gift from a woman in her writing group—five hundred pens with the name of her show emblazoned on them. She left them outside the theater for people to grab. It was a beautiful gesture. Everybody loves a little swag.

Offer group discounts. Reach out to special groups that will be a good match for your show and invite them. For example, one of our students wrote a show about running a marathon, and he promoted it through the local running clubs. Chicago has at least twenty running clubs, ranging from the social groups who run and then drink to the more serious ones who are training for races. He joined the clubs' Facebook and social media groups, offering discount codes to his play, and even featured a panel discussion afterward with members from some of the running organizations. We've seen solo artists who've reached out to college professors (early) to let them know about a show that had content related to their discipline. Instructors can organize a field trip for their class or offer attendance at your show as extra credit.

Paper a house. It can be difficult to play to a theater of four people, though we've both done it. If your ticket sales are low for a particular show, sometimes it's great to give away a few tickets. Post on your social media that you have a few comps available and ask folks to contact you. That said, don't be dismayed if only four people are in the house. Though they don't happen often and they're not a situation we'd choose, we've found those shows can end up surprising us in all sorts of ways. They're intimate. Cozy. Unexpectedly rewarding.

Encourage audience members to leave good reviews and positive comments on social media platforms after they see your show. This can be listed in the program or posted at the theater. One of our students had her friend interview audience members as they came out of the theater after opening night. Recording on an iPhone, she asked one question: What did you like about the show? With a few permissions, all of that went on social media to create buzz.

Connect with influencers or bloggers who can amplify your show to their followers. For example, Arlene has asked people she knew if she could be on their podcasts or featured on their blogs. If they said maybe, she sent them a media kit. One podcast was about caring for older parents who had dementia, another about mental health issues, and still another about being a solo artist and a creative. In each interview, she was able to talk about her upcoming solo show, and she then had a few podcasts to post online as interesting content and for credibility. Double whammy win. Invite influencers for opening night and ask them to review your play. You'll be surprised how many people you know who fall into the TikTok/Podcast/YouTube/blogger category.

Support your fellow creatives and friends. Go to their plays, their kids' basketball games, storytelling gigs, poetry readings, and birthday parties. When you go to the theater, reach out afterward to those people whose work you admired. It can be as simple as a congrats on social media or in a text. We prize these little nuggets when we receive them. Oh, and don't be a lurker on social media. Click, like, and comment to support other people and make yourself known.

Using PR Firms

If you have the luxury, a PR firm can help. These firms offer a range of marketing plans, each with its own price point. They can do a comprehensive soup-to-nuts plan or a modified plan that suits your needs and budget. If you use one, it's important to choose a PR firm that specializes in the arts community and has established connections with print, media, and digital platforms.

PR firms create compelling content, pitch stories, and generate opportunities for engagement. They can get you interviews on radio stations, local TV channels, online platforms, and other outlets to promote your name and show. Additionally, they collaborate with digital content creators to make sure that you have high-quality photos, graphics, and sizzle reels.

For example, one solo artist who was produced by a Chicago theater company was not messing around. In addition to the theater's promotional campaign, she hired a small PR firm that created a comprehensive media kit for her, which included a press release, photos, videos, and digital graphics. They successfully placed feature articles in a Chicago newspaper and suburban papers and arranged interviews on local morning shows and radio programs.

The show was about body image, so the PR firm targeted women and identified organizations that would be interested in this topic. The firm collaborated with other digital content creators to expand the show's reach, maintained an active social media presence, sent press releases, and provided comp tickets to reviewers from both Chicago and the suburbs. The artist even agreed to engage with Zoom book clubs, demonstrating a willingness to embrace any opportunity.

Yes, PR firms can be pricey. Another option is to adopt a hybrid approach by combining some DIY strategies with help from outside sources. There are college students and other creatives who do freelance publicity as a side hustle, so do some investigating.

For many of us, publicizing and marketing our performances is one of the most taxing and personal parts of the work. We often do it with little or no theater or organizational support. We hope you'll take some of these ideas and put them into action. Your show deserves audiences.

EXPERT ADVICE

I invited two other solo performers from my class to do half-hour excerpts from their solo works before my full-length show. I chose them because the themes of our plays were loosely related, and it gave me a way to talk about the whole evening. Another thing I did was ask someone in my solo class to create fliers, graphics, and everything else I needed so we looked professional. I also went old-school and made little quarter-sheet fliers and carried them everywhere I went. I put a listing in the free section of my local paper, and they thought it would be interesting to do a story about me the week my show opened. It was a big feature with a picture that talked about the themes of my show and why I thought the solo show was important. And here's another thing: I was so confident about my writing and the time I put into rehearsing that it made me authentically want to share it with people. And I really believed in the other people performing beside me as well. That was the foundation before I did any promotion.

Molly Surowitz
Solo Performer, Actor

EXPERT ADVICE

Don't think you're too good for any opportunity to promote yourself. You never know what connections you might make and where it could lead. Have fun and have no shame. Be yourself. You are what people are coming to see. When you feel disheartened, remember: No promotion is lost. If people don't come to this production, perhaps they'll come to another one in the future. At the very least, someone else is aware of you and your show, and you're learning what works and what doesn't in promoting yourself. Look at the many different forms your solo show could take. Could it be a movie? A radio-show recording? A children's book? I am considering all of these things for my show. I wrote an ensemble version of my show, and now it's been published. It's also on NPX, New Play Exchange, and it's been produced several times throughout the country.

Laura Force Scruggs
Solo Performer, Playwright, Fairy

Fundraising for Your Show

You might be surprised how many opportunities exist for individual artists to get funding from outside sources for producing, touring, and marketing their solo shows. We've had clients apply for and receive money to develop their marketing materials, cover travel expenses, reimburse application fees, help create a website, and hire ASL sign language interpreters. Folks have also received funding to pay for a director, designers, or space rental.

Grants

Many cities and states offer individual artist fellowships or grants, so explore your local arts council. Additionally, there are many arts and culture grants that cater to nonprofit organizations; if you are a member of a theater company or other nonprofit, you can often apply under their umbrella. GrantWatch is a great resource for creatives looking for funding opportunities.

You don't need to have experience writing grants to create an effective application, though you may be asked to provide lots of details about your work and your plans. That's OK! We've found that really thinking through these details is helpful, even if they end up changing later. Most importantly, do your best to convey your passion for your project through the application.

Crowdfunding Campaigns

Many of our people have successfully used crowdfunding to help get their show onto a stage. There are several great platforms for crowdfunding campaigns, allowing artists to raise money for their creative endeavors. Each platform operates differently, so be sure to look at the hidden costs like setup fees and the percentage these organizations take from each donation. Usually, a good crowdfunding company will provide strategies around what works best for their particular community, and we advise you to pay attention to such tips. We've seen students be successful on all of the platforms.

The most important consideration when you are developing your crowdfunding campaign is to create a connection between you and your audiences. Putting together a good campaign starts with explaining what your project is, what inspired this work, and why it is important. It's helpful to write a personal story stating why you want to take part in your project. It will be the foundation for all of your crowdfunding. Include videos, photos, or interviews.

We worked with one solo artist who decided to share the story behind the solo show she had created. She made a four-minute video in which she told the story of being adopted from another country. She included photos and film from her childhood. She also included twenty seconds of video from her show taken during a rehearsal. The segment reflected her personality and her self-deprecating sense of humor. It was not strictly scripted and had a casual off-the-cuff feel. She didn't correct little flubs, giving the piece a personal touch as opposed to a slick production. Everything was DIY, recorded on an iPhone and edited in iMovie in one evening. The final product was a charming way to help her audience feel more connected to her. She made her modest $600 goal. Later, she raised funds to make a short film based on the same story which won prizes at several film festivals. Most recently, she fictionalized the events in her show and made a full-length feature film.

Be creative, but also be transparent with your supporters about where their money is going. One particularly effective campaign included goals for each dollar amount achieved. The solo artist stated that $200 would allow her to pay the entry fee for a particular festival.

If she reached the goal of $500, it would enable her to enter the festival and also work with a director for two sessions, develop a lighting design, and purchase a prop for the show. Reaching the goal of $750 would allow her to have all of the above, as well as money to travel and to make postcards. This technique is appealing because it assures your donors that you have a budget and are serious about it.

You can establish incentives to encourage donations, such as including the names of sponsors in the programs or on your website, offering free tickets to your next show, and personalized texts and videos sent from backstage or on your travels. We also worked with a singer who offered an incentive for a voicemail message sung to the tune of "Happy Birthday." Be creative—make people smile.

Finally, it's important to keep updating a crowdfunding campaign. Share news and announcements. The more you feed and water a campaign, the better the results. When goals are met, add extra videos thanking people. Crowdfunding also has the added benefit of creating buy-in and making people feel personally invested in your success.

Fundraising Shows

Home shows are the most underutilized fundraising tool and often the easiest to execute. Ask a friend, work buddy, or relative if they would be willing to host a gathering in their home. Send out invitations to their circle and set up chairs in their living room, finished basement, backyard, or condo rec room. You get to perform in a really loving and intimate setting, and afterward, guests can contribute to your fund. Many times, the host will be bringing in an audience that normally would not be part of your email list or social media followers.

Home shows are one of Arlene's favorite ways of supporting her clients. She provides drinks, a nosh, and a sign-in. One of her folks even brought an actual hat to collect donations, but a card with your Venmo contact or a QR code also allows people to donate right away when they are still in the afterglow of your performance. You'll find civilians love talking to creative types, and everyone has an interesting night out.

Enlist your friends. One artist gathered five fellow solo artists who were willing to donate their time to perform an excerpt of their show to raise funds to send her to the Hollywood Solo Festival.

Zoom opens up opportunities and allows for remote participation. This type of home fundraising can also be done with a live reading or recording of the play and a talkback with the artist. In this way, friends or family out of town can attend or host their own circle of friends.

Many artists feel hesitant or uncomfortable asking for money for their projects, but don't shy away from fundraising. Let your supporters contribute to your success. We've both happily supported many fellow creatives who were trying to reach an artistic goal. Everyone wants to be a part of something special.

Festivals, Fringe, and Touring

Fringe and solo festivals are a rich and coolio part of the solo show ecosystem, and they're a great way to get your work out into the world. The first fringe festival happened in 1947 when eight theater companies showed up to the Edinburgh International Festival uninvited and decided to perform on the "outer fringe" of the event. By their nature, fringe festivals are grassroots, renegade, subversive, and DIY. They're typically a performing arts smorgasbord that includes theater, dance, puppetry, spoken word, visual arts, and other offerings that might be so odd and interesting that they cannot be categorized into a genre. Fringe or solo festivals are often held in unconventional spaces like bars, movie theaters, storefronts, loft spaces, and galleries, as well as traditional theaters. The audiences who attend are open and ready to see a variety of work, including yours.

There are dozens and dozens of fringe festivals year-round all over the world, including an entire circuit of festivals dedicated solely to solo shows. Many of our solo students have done them. You will find lists of festival directories online that cover details such as dates, locations, and submission deadlines by using search terms like "solo show festivals," "fringe festival directory," or "international fringe festivals." There are also social media groups and forums you can join.

In a juried festival, performances are selected by a panel, resulting in a curated lineup. Nonjuried fringe festivals, on the other hand, use a lottery or first-come, first-served approach, allowing for a wider range of performances and greater inclusivity. We have both participated in festivals over many years, and the thing we love most is the unbridled enthusiasm and camaraderie among the performers. We've seen some amazing work and have always left feeling like part of an artistic community that honors creativity. There are many financial models used at fringe and solo show festivals. Here are the ones we've seen most often:

- **Pay-to-play.** You'll pay a fee upfront, which covers the venue and other costs. This model is great if you want to focus on performing without stressing over ticket sales.
- **Box office split.** There are no fees up front. You and the festival will share the ticket revenue. They take a cut to cover expenses, and you get the rest.
- **Flat fee.** You'll pay one fixed fee that covers everything, and then you'll keep all the ticket sales from your show.
- **Guaranteed performance honorarium.** You'll get paid a flat fee for performing, and the festival will keep the box office earnings.
- **Free fringe model.** No upfront fees here. Instead, you'll rely on donations from the audience at the end of the performance.

Billeting

Some festivals offer artists the opportunity to "billet," which means nice people from the community, usually connected with the festival, will offer accommodations. Some of our more adventurous soloists couldn't do a festival any other way. They've stayed on air mattresses in living rooms, were provided with their own room, or were offered an apartment or guest house. Once, Arlene and her director were given free rein of a beautiful mansion with a swimming pool and an orange grove. But that was just once.

Billeting can be a great way for people to get free or low-cost accommodations. It fosters a sense of community and local support, but it may raise concerns about privacy and comfort, requiring clear communication with hosts. Consider your budget, your comfort level, and your safety. We've had soloists leave with new friends and artists that they are still connected to years later.

Odds and Ends

Each show is stacked back-to-back into a venue with a time slot. Make sure your show fits into the allotted time, usually fifty minutes to one hour. If you go over time, some festivals turn the lights off. Yes! As the artist, you should always respect the performers who come after you. Julie had a terrible experience when the performer before her ran over time and only allowed her ten minutes to set up as the audience was filing in. While she is not a grudge collector, she should be.

Depending on the location your show is assigned, you may get the option of some lighting and sound. If this is the case, most festivals will provide you with one tech rehearsal, usually only sixty to ninety minutes. Make your tech as simple as you can. Be sure to bring a script in a binder for your tech person. A larger font is always a courtesy. Make sure that you've already done your homework and have marked up a few simple lighting or sound cues in your script as a starting place. Be flexible enough to adapt to your circumstances. The less complicated your cues and tech are, the more time you will have with the tech person to rehearse transitions.

Festival tech employees are generally overworked, underpaid, and exhausted during festivals. They're working with dozens of shows, usually with only one rehearsal. When they're perfect at their job, no one notices. When they make a mistake, everyone complains. It's a difficult and thankless job. Be nice to them. Bring them treats. Give them thanks, and if something screws up . . . oh well, that's the way of the festival.

Only use props you're willing to lug around. Some venues will allow you to store them backstage, but don't count on that. If you can stow your belongings, always label your stuff with your name, the title of the show, and a kind note for others to keep their mitts off. Most venues will have a few pieces of furniture for general use, like a chair, stool, or side table. Ask in advance. Nothing is guaranteed.

You're in charge of your own stuff. For touring of any kind, Arlene always has an extra copy of her script tucked away into a separate suitcase or carry-on and a copy of her electronic press kit and script in the cloud. She uses a backpack with wheels for her costume, makeup, phone charger, a small flashlight, lint roller, script, highlighters, pens, a little tin of meds, a scrunchie, snacks, and water. The bag is self-contained and travels easily. She has straight-up learned this the hard way from years of touring.

Make catchy, fun, interesting postcards or business cards to pass out at festivals. You may think this sounds old-fashioned, but they're not viewed that way at festivals, where they serve several functions. Arlene likes to leave one side blank so she can write dates, times, and venues. Include your contact info or a QR code.

Touring Your Work (for $$)

There is a plethora of organizations, theaters, colleges, schools, libraries, performing arts centers, churches, and bookstores that are just waiting for you to get on their stage. The trick is finding a good match for your show.

Arlene's first solo show, *What Does the Sun Sound Like*, played really well with CODA organizations, interpreters for the Deaf, Deaf clubs, and colleges with ASL programs. She did the first few gigs for small honorariums to build her résumé and get letters of recommendation and blurbs. After that, much of the marketing work became word-of-mouth and being brave enough to ask people to reach out to their colleagues. Arlene has worked on great stages and also in gymnasiums, cafeterias, and the ballroom of a Hyatt. In each case, glamorous or not, the connection with the audience made up for any shortcomings, including people finishing dessert as she performed.

Some of these performances are "one-offs," meaning one or two, not a run. They can make substantial money. Don't be afraid to ask other solo artists what their going rate is for one-offs, so you can be in the right ballpark. Many artists have one rate for corporate gigs and another for nonprofits. You can either allow the organizers to arrange your travel and accommodations or negotiate a flat rate and arrange them yourself. The great thing about the latter is that you can decide how much money you want to save or spend.

Another way to get produced is to take a look at theater companies in your town, state, or region that do work aligned with your solo show. For example, there are theaters that champion women-driven material or showcase pieces from Black or LGBTQ+ perspectives, or those that specialize in producing new or solo works. We know a solo artist whose solo play is about his first year of being a substitute teacher in Los Angeles; he has been able to book his shows with local teachers' organizations and school districts for in-service days and teacher conferences. When we talk about these opportunities, many people say, "Yeah, but I don't have a 'mission-based' show. My show doesn't deal with cancer or death or disability or sexual abuse." We say no worries—if you're willing to do the hustle, you can find opportunities. We recently had a student pitch her show to libraries and get a very nice paycheck for talking about her chaotic dating life. Another solo colleague, Wendy Hammers, pitches her shows to Jewish organizations. While her show is not about Judaism or being Jewish, she self-identifies as Jewish and talks about her family. (She also has one of the funniest lines ever: "Jewish girl eats bacon, finds God.")

Arlene also offers customizations and ways for her plays to be adapted for the specific theater or organization that is booking her. She ensures organizers are aware that the show has a duration of seventy-five minutes and includes sound and lights, if technology permits. She also offers a condensed fifty-five-minute version of each of her shows. This is particularly valuable for schools or colleges with time constraints due to class periods. She offers to facilitate talkbacks or panel discussions centered around the themes explored in the play.

She also provides the option of conducting master classes in solo performing or *Telling Your Story* workshops with community members. High school or college drama classes often appreciate a visiting professional. Furthermore, Arlene always has strong referral letters and contacts available upon request. If she's working out of town, she'll reach out to other colleges, organizations, or schools in the area, as well as asking the organizers if they have any suggestions.

Finally, for touring to large performance arts centers, there are conferences which offer showcase opportunities, such as the Association of Performing Arts Professionals. Costs associated with participating are steep, but the potential returns are high. Does all this this sound like a lot of work? It can be, especially at first. But it's also very rewarding. It's a way to generate income and be part of an adventure that can teach you so much about your show and yourself as an artist. There really are audiences out there who are hungry for your show.

EXPERT ADVICE

When you're looking at an application for Fillet of Solo, what are some things that make a strong submission?

I love a story that is personal and focused. Specifics, details, small moments that have meaning make good stories. And a story that makes discoveries in front of us, rather than just telling us about a thing that happened.

More technically, I'm drawn to shows that aren't cluttered with a bunch of props/sound cues/projections. Tell your story without those trimmings. In a festival format with limited tech time for each show, make it easier for yourself and the venue: figure out how to make it simple. Put the show entirely in your own control.

I also appreciate adherence to the submission guidelines. If the maximum time slot is forty-five minutes, submitting a ninety-minute show flashes a "not ready" sign. We'll suggest you work on it and resubmit for next year, with a reminder that it's a requirement to have a director attached. It's important to get outside eyes on a piece.

Curating the festival is joyful work. Bringing performers into a single place to see each other's work and find new fans, partnering with establishments in our neighborhood that are excited to have business in the dark of January—that's the fully joyful part of it.

Dorothy Milne
Director, Storyteller, Fillet of Solo Co-Curator

EXPERT ADVICE

Every Fringe has a marketing person—make them your best friend leading up to the festival. Make sure you get a PR list from them and send out press releases. Ask how many postcards and posters they recommend you have. Printed materials should have a QR code to your ticketing page at that specific festival, and make sure your show dates and times are also listed.

The way to get butts into seats is to be boots on the ground, hustling every day. Do the Fringe preview night, where you get 1–3 minutes to talk up your show. Make sure you have a great pitch, wear your memorable costume/hat/T-shirt, bring a prop, and make sure you're getting a postcard into the hands of every person there. Artists too. A lot of Fringes have a "Fringe Central" where you can hang out with audiences and artists. This is actually the most fun part! Pick the shows you want to see, ask the box office which shows are selling the best, and hand out postcards to folks waiting in line.

I'm not making money yet, but I am sustaining a tour, my bills are paid with my day jobs, and I feel the best I've ever felt in my twenty-year career.

Victoria Montalbano
Actor, Comedian, Solo Artist

EXPERT ADVICE

I try to adopt a mindset of very simple, practical expectations. Will I make a lot of money? Probably not. Will I have packed houses? It could happen, but I don't expect it. Will I meet the love of my life? Hasn't happened yet.

Here's what I tell myself:

1. You're going to another city/state/country to perform your piece for audiences of total strangers. These strangers are not your friends, and they owe you nothing. You will get objective, unbiased feedback and reviews.
2. You're not going to worry about not making enough money because, in the months before leaving town, you'll do some fundraising performances and hit up a few sponsor types so that anything you make out of town is gravy on the taters or frosting on the cookie.
3. You'll do your best at promotion, but you'll make sure you take advantage of seeing as many fringe shows as you can! There are so many great shows and a few terrible ones, and you can learn from both!
4. You'll meet amazing artists to connect with and become part of a new artistic community, and these people might become your fans and help build audiences. Some lovely people might become your friends.
5. And through it all, you will keep reminding yourself that you're a brave little badass who got off the block and went on tour!

Thinking like this helped me so much when I opened a show to forty empty seats. I thought, "Well, at least I didn't lose any money and now the tech crew can leave early." It also helped when, in another city, my show was referred to as the "sleeper hit" and had fantastic audiences and great press! Plus money!

A humble approach leads to a healthy experience.

David Boyle
Solo Artist, Musician

Protecting Your Work

To be clear, neither of us is the type to look for trouble, incite worry, stir a pot, poke a bear, kick a hornet's nest, rock a boat, or deliberately try to create drama, except onstage. But we'll offer a few words on this subject, in the interest of covering our bases. (Enough with the idioms? Agreed.)

Most solo artists and storytellers make their work public through performing it, and may never end up publishing their texts. And most of them don't end up having their work stolen. But if it will calm your nerves, making sure your work is officially protected enough to stand up in a court of law isn't all that complicated.

An idea cannot be copyrighted, only written work can. However, the moment that work is in a fixed or physical form, it's technically protected by copyright laws, which are intended to give the author of both published and unpublished literary works the sole legal right to copy and distribute the work. Dating your work and saving it to your hard drive (fixed form) provide a certain amount of protection. Some writers print the material and have it notarized or send it to themselves through the mail, so it receives a dated postmark.

However, these measures won't officially do enough for you if you're involved in an actual lawsuit. They will help build your case and provide evidence, but they won't be enough to earn you damages. Some writers register with the US Copyright Office because it ensures that they are entitled to legal fees if they win a lawsuit involving their work. It also makes the facts of the copyright public record, and they receive a certificate of registration. Copyrighting is fairly inexpensive and easy to do on the US Copyright website. After this step, an individual can use the © symbol whenever they put their work online or print it out.

Only you can decide if you're concerned about lawsuits and want that layer of protection. If you've written a first-person narrative, the chances that someone else will steal your words and pass them off as their own is probably low. That doesn't mean someone won't take an idea from your piece, but there's really no way to protect against that anyway.

Several of our students who've written screenplays based on their solo shows or are frequently submitting their manuscripts to theater companies or competitions have chosen to register their work with the Writers Guild of America. The WGA is a union that represents writers in TV, film, radio, and digital media. By registering your work, you protect it as intellectual property and create proof of material alongside a timeline. If an infringement happens, the WGA will provide backup to your claim and legal assistance. Registering is an easy process that can be done online, and the fees are nominal, even if you are not a member of WGA. You'll receive a registration certificate, which must be renewed every ten years.

Our advice? Later, if and when you are developing your solo show into a screenplay, we strongly recommend registering your work, simply because screenplays are so widely disseminated in the consideration process. They're passed around and end up in many hands. For your solo piece right now, it's up to you. If you're likely to spend time and energy worrying about theft, register your work. If not, be sure to always date and save to a hard drive. Publish your work whenever you can. Not necessarily to protect it, but because it's a wonderful thing to do!

The Ghost Light

The theater has big aspirations. It's life-affirming, unpredictable, and occasionally tragic. So, it's no surprise that it's full of superstitions. Saying the word "Macbeth" in a theater curses the show and can only be reversed by the ritual of running around the theater three times, spitting, and quoting a line from another Shakespeare play. It's a jinx to whistle backstage. And, of course, you should never wish an actor "good luck" or some misfortune will befall them—instead, tell them to "break a leg."

But the superstition that has intrigued and delighted us the most is the ghost light: a single bulb on a stick standing in the middle of an otherwise dark stage, left burning whenever the theater is empty. The ghost light is the last thing placed on the stage at night and the first thing to be removed in the morning.

Rational minds attribute this practice to safety when the theater is dark. That may be true—but we say bollocks to that. We love the mystical lore of the theater and believe, like many, that leaving a ghost light on gives the spirits that haunt the theater a spotlight to dance in. Not providing a light onstage might incur their wrath, causing them to make mischief or disrupt a performance when the humans return. To others, the ghost light is a demonstration of respect and reverence, not just for the theater space, but for the art itself—symbolizing that the theater is never truly closed.

We find beauty in these superstitions because they connect us to the generations of theater artists who came before us. As you work on your solo show, no matter how long it takes, remember that you are part of a great tradition that goes back to ancient Greece.

Let the ghost light inspire you in moments when you falter in your faith. Let it serve as a symbol on your creative journey, allowing the spirits to come out even when the theater is dark.

We are your fans,

Arlene & Julie

Acknowledgments

Thank you to our editor, Megan Stielstra, who supported our vision and believed in us from day one, as well as Maia Rigas, Mike Levine, and everyone else at Northwestern University Press who made this book possible.

Thank you to our experts for their wisdom: Charles Askenaizer, David Boyle, Jasmin Cardenas, John Michael Colgin, Amanda Delheimer, Ilesa Duncan, Melissa DuPrey, Ann Filmer, Khanisha Foster, Elizabeth J. Gerard, Richard Henzel, Tekki Lomnicki, Dorothy Milne, Victoria Montalbano, Kurt Naebig, R.C. Riley, Stephanie Rogers, Laura Force Scruggs, Connie Shirakawa, Janna Sobel, Molly Surowitz, Willa Taylor, Penelope Walker, and Ric Walker. How humdrum this book would be without you. And thank you to every solo artist out there who is working on a large or small stage to push our genre forward.

Thank you to our student and professional contributors, who generously allowed us to use their work as examples: Ada Cheng, Julie Danis, Tim Gillis, Wendy Hammers, Joyce Hicks, Lynnette Li, Jackie Maruschak, Errol McLendon, Stephanie Medlock, Melisha Mitchell, Paul Pasulka, Victoria Podesta, and Francesca Sobrer.

Arlene's Acknowledgments

To the glorious Julie Ganey, it has been an honor to write this book with you. I am grateful to my extraordinary writing group—Michele Weldon, Veronica Chapa, Teresa Puente and Pam Todd—your wisdom and generosity have left an indelible mark on my work. I am forever grateful for the brilliant directors, dramaturges and artists who have shepherded my work: Ann Filmer, Wendy Hammers, Carson Becker, Mark Travis, Kerry Haynie, Carrie Sandahl, Will Rogers, Lisa Portes, and Russ Tutterow—your care has been a compass. To Nobuko Miyamoto who not only put me on a stage but taught me that mission-based art can heal the world. Thank you to every solo artist, theater collaborator, teacher, mentor and student that I've had in my life, you've taught me how to be a better citizen of the world.

To my Lifelongs—Ken Ehlen, Thom Smith, Karen Roth, Tim and Bette Ecklund and my CODA sibs, Francine Stern, John Arce, and Billy Collins, thank you for being my joyful constants. I am profoundly grateful to my beautiful parents, whose dazzling Deaf hands spun yarn into gossamer gold. Your strength, resilience, and grace are the foundation upon which I stand. A special "heart touch" to the Deaf and CODA communities who raised me—you were my most important storytelling teachers.

And finally, to Dan Clark, my favorite person—you have put up the scaffolding around my life that allows me to be an artist. Thank you for your unwavering support, patience, joy and love. You are my heart.

Julie's Acknowledgments

Thank you to Arlene Malinowski. I cannot imagine a more fun and joyful collaborator. I'm grateful to 2nd Story, especially to CP Chang, LaTanya Lane, Deb Lewis, Andrew Reilly, Ric Walker, and the inimitable Amanda Delheimer. Megan Shuchman and Mike Przygoda, you are my forever collaborators. Willa Taylor, thank you for creating the GeNarrations program at the Goodman Theatre. I am indebted to my students there, who have taught me so much about writing, performance, and how to live a good life in this imperfect world. I also owe a debt to Ann Filmer, Dorothy Milne, Russ Tutterow, Rives Collins, The Theatre School at DePaul University, and Thomas Ganey, my first example of a writer/teacher/storyteller. I'm not sure how to thank my mother, who is with me every day. My siblings, Christopher, Rosemary and Emily are the very best. And most importantly, I'm grateful to Brad and Dorothy Harbaugh. Regardless of what I am up to, I can always count on your boundless love and enthusiasm, and I find it absolutely essential.